Mastering the Craft of Making Sausage

Warren R. Anderson

 **BURFORD BOOKS**

Printed in the United States of America.

10   9   8   7   6   5   4   3   2   1

Library of Congress Cataloging-in-Publication Data
Anderson, Warren R., 1939–
     Mastering the craft of making sausage / Warren R. Anderson.
          p.   cm.
     ISBN 978-1-58080-155-3
     1. Sausages.   2. Cookery (Sausages)   I. Title.

TX749.A688 2010
641.3'6—dc22   2010010724

Contents

CHAPTER 1

Introduction

A Brief History of Sausage

The word *sausage* has a dignified and long pedigree. It originated with the Latin word *salsus*, which means "seasoned with salt." From Latin, the word successively went into Late Latin, Old French, Middle English, and finally Modern English. At each step, the pronunciation and meaning changed a little until it became *sausage*, the word we use now.

When humans began applying salt to meat, the foundation for the evolution of sausage was established. At first, salt was applied to meat because it not only helped preserve it, but also made it taste better. And, because meat was precious, even the scraps were salted. Scraps of salted meat were put in whatever containers were available; eventually it was discovered that offal, such as cleaned intestines, bladders, and stomachs of the slaughtered animals made ideal containers.

It is believed that the Sumerians, living in the area that is now called Iraq, were making sausage as early as 3000 BCE. In approximately the 13th century BCE, the ancestors of the modern Chinese began using salt to preserve food. In Chinese literature dated 589 BCE, a sausage made of goat and lamb meat was mentioned. Sausages are also depicted in paintings of Chinese kitchens dated around 500 BCE. In ancient Greece, the famous poet Homer mentioned a kind of sausage made of blood in *The Odyssey*, and around 500 BCE, a Greek play was written entitled *The Sausage*. Sausage eating became so popular at Roman festivals that the conservative church banned it. Sausage has existed in the diets of cultures around the world for a very long time.

As time went on, sausage making evolved in most of the world's cultures, particularly in those that raised domesticated animals to eat. Meat from pigs, cattle, sheep, and goats was used most often to make sausage. Native Americans, however, used wild game to make a sausage-like product called *pemmican*. The seasoning used in the various sausages was determined by availability and tradition.

Climate, too, had an influence on the kinds of sausage that evolved. In the hot Mediterranean region, dry-cured sausage requiring no refrigeration appeared. In the cooler climate of Germany, the semidry-cured sausage had a sufficiently long storage life.

The most profound changes in the taste of European sausage came with the gradual influx of exotic spices and herbs brought from the Spice Islands and other parts of Indonesia.

The pilgrims who settled in America brought with them the knowledge of sausage-making that existed in England, their mother country. Soon, they were able to get breeding stock from England, and could make sausage using pork and beef, as well as wild game. Most of the seasoning and other ingredients used in the sausage were those that were locally available, and uniquely American sausages appeared.

As America developed and expanded westward, various immigrant groups such as Germans, Italians, and Poles came to the United States to share the American dream. Most of these groups brought with them the love of sausage and, more importantly, many of them brought sausage-making skills.

Industry was rapidly developing in the large cities, and employment opportunities concentrated the immigrants there. The skilled sausage makers among them opened sausage shops, and they flourished. Some of these shops eventually grew into sausage-making companies.

With the opening of slaughterhouses and sausage shops in the large cities, sausage making was becoming more of an industrial activity than a farming activity. As such, more efficient production methods were needed. In the early 19th century, lever-operated sausage stuffers were invented. Meat choppers (grinders) were also invented; the first ones were made of hardwood, with steel blades. A hardwood box housed three hardwood gears, and the steel blades were attached to two rotating hardwood cylinders. Hunks of solid meat were put into one end of the grinder, and chopped meat came out the other end. These and other technical advances, such as refrigeration, helped mark the beginning of the sausage-making industry and the decline of sausage making at home or on the farm.

The United States sausage industry currently produces about 200 kinds of sausage, and makes more sausage than any other country in the world. In Germany, however, there are over 1,000 kinds of sausage on the retail market and the per capita consumption of sausage is much higher than the United States. If the population of Germany were the same as the United States, it would be the world's major producer.

Homemade Sausage Today

In the history of sausage making, there has been no better time than the present to make sausage at home.

High quality fresh pork, beef, lamb, and various specialty meats used to make many of the world's sausage varieties are easily purchased at local grocery stores. It is no longer necessary to wait for cool weather to butcher the animals and gather the scraps of meat for sausage. We can buy large primal cuts, such as a whole pork shoulder butt, and make sausage any time of the year.

When we buy our fresh, chilled meat at the grocery store, we take it home and safely store it in our refrigerator, or we can even freeze the meat if we can't get around to making the sausage soon. The refrigerator and freezer also keep wild game fresh until it is made into sausage. When meat is being processed into sausage, the refrigerator is used repeatedly to keep the raw materials cold. Nowadays, we take the refrigerator for granted, but the availability of refrigeration in our home means that we can make the sausage more leisurely. We need not worry so much about the spoilage that was so common in the old days.

In this age, there are almost no restrictions on spices and seasonings. We are not limited to items that are produced locally. Most of the flavorings we need are available at our local grocery store. Obtaining seasoning for an exotic sausage might require searching for it in ethnic grocery stores or on the Internet—but a few minutes search on the Internet will locate almost anything. In short, we can find the seasoning ingredients needed to make almost all the sausages of the world.

We no longer have to mince the meat on a chopping block with a cleaver in each hand—the inexpensive hand-cranked meat grinder does a better and faster job. With a little more money, we can even buy an electric-powered one to make grinding even easier and faster.

One of the most tedious jobs in the old days was stuffing the casings by using a special handheld funnel and poking the sausage paste into the casing with a wooden dowel. The invention of several configurations of stuffers has now made sausage stuffing a task that many find pleasurable, and certainly not tedious.

With the Internet, sausage-making supplies and equipment are literally at our fingertips. No matter where we live in the world, our Internet order will be put on our doorstep—if a delivery truck can reach our house.

YES, there has been no better time than now to make sausage at home.

About This Book

A book about sausage making is actually a kind of a manual—at least it should be. If a manual is well designed, it will be fast and easy to find needed information. This manual has been organized into chapters, each of which present information on one broad subject. For example, sausages recipes have been grouped into chapters according to type. Hence, recipes for common uncured fresh sausages are in the same chapter. Cooking techniques are in a chapter dedicated to that subject, equipment requirements are in a single chapter—and so on. The table of Contents will get you to the correct chapter quickly. When you know the chapter that you want to find, flex the right side of the book downward and spin the pages with your right thumb. The chapter numbers and titles on the top of the right hand pages will flash before your eyes.

For specific sausages or specific topics, the index will get you to the exact page you are looking for quickly.

Why This Book Was Written

I moved to southern Japan with my family in 1980 to teach English as a second language. After living in Japan for five years, I longed for some good breakfast sausage, smoked salmon, pastrami, bratwurst, and the like. Some of these things might be available in Tokyo in special stores dealing in imported foods, but they were not available in southern Japan where I lived. I decided to try to make these things myself, and I had my brother send me every book he could find on food smoking and sausage making.

Very few books were available on these subjects, and the books that did exist did not provide adequate information. I persisted, nevertheless, and by trial and error, I was able to learn how to make the products I had been longing for.

After smoking food and making sausage for over twenty years, I felt that I knew enough about the crafts to write a book or two that would be helpful to others and contribute to the accumulated knowledge on these subjects. The first book I wrote was on food smoking: *Mastering the Craft of Smoking Food*. It contained a chapter on sausage making, but the present book is entirely dedicated to that subject. I hope you find this book useful and helpful.

CHAPTER 2

Equipment

Many varieties of sausage can be made without special equipment, or with very little special equipment. Some special equipment is not essential, but it makes the job easier. Equipment useful for sausage making at home is listed below. Appendix 5 may assist you in locating hard-to-find items.

If the equipment described is measuring equipment (for measuring volume, thickness, weight, etc.), the desirable measurement ranges are first given in the measuring system used in the United States, and then they are given in the metric system (in parentheses). In cases when a precise metric equivalent is not critical, it may be rounded off. The practice of indicating both systems of measurement is used throughout this book.

The list of equipment, below, is in alphabetical order, not in order of importance.

Casing Perforator (Sausage Pricker)

Casing perforator (sausage pricker).

When sausage is stuffed into casings, invariably there will be air pockets visible just under the casing membrane. If these air pockets are not eliminated, unsightly fat and gelatin will accumulate there.

Getting rid of these air pockets is very easy; just perforate them with a sharp needle or a tool called a *casing perforator* or *sausage pricker*. When the sausage is being cooked, these tiny holes will be sealed by coagulated protein, preventing the escape of juices.

This tool is available by mail order from sausage equipment suppliers, and it costs about $7. It has three needles embedded in a plastic handle. However, a large, sharp needle, such as a large sewing needle, works equally well. I use a homemade casing perforator—a sharpened stainless steel rod embedded in a wooden handle.

Cutting Board

It is difficult and awkward to prepare meat for making sausage without a cutting board. If you don't have one, you might consider buying the modern plastic type. Wooden cutting boards are porous and difficult to clean, so they are good breeding grounds for germs and bacteria. A big board is better than a small one. A stiff scrub brush, used with dish detergent and hot water, is very effective for cleaning your cutting board. Use a bleach-and-water solution to remove most stains and to sterilize the board.

Food Processor

A food processor is required if the emulsified sausages in Chapter 10 will be made. A food processor for home use will do the job, but it must be a powerful machine. If emulsification is attempted with a small, underpowered processor, it might destroy the motor. A large and powerful Cuisinart brand food processor, or the equivalent, is up to the task. With a 7-cup (680 ml) Cuisinart, I am able to process 1¼ pounds (570 g) at a time. The Cuisinart model I use is equipped with a 560-watt motor.

Hog-Ring Pliers and Hog Rings

Special hog rings and hog-ring pliers are made for use with large sausage casings, such as fibrous casings. (They are not the same as the hog rings used for things such as furniture upholstery.) These special hog rings for sausage making may be used to close both the bottom and the top of fibrous casings, but they are most often used to close the top. They are a little easier and faster to use than twine, and they look professional.

The spring-loaded hog-ring pliers are easier to use than the common type because they hold hog rings in the jaws of the pliers, allowing two hands free to twist the casing closed. However, the spring-loaded type cost about five times more than the common manual type.

For 2½-inch (6.4 cm) diameter casings, use the ⅜-inch (10 mm) hog rings. The 3-inch (7.6 cm) diameter casings require ½-inch (12.7 mm) hog rings. Please see the last section in Chapter 5, *Stuffing fibrous casings,* for photographs and additional information. (If you wish to purchase these special hog rings and hog-ring pliers, please see Appendix 5.)

Knives

Trimming and cutting meat is a major part of making sausage, but only two or three kinds of knives are required. They should be of the proper shape and length to do the job at hand. If they are always kept sharp and used properly, your work will proceed efficiently and safely. They need not be expensive; almost all of my knives were bought very cheaply at garage sales or Salvation Army-type stores. These used knives were of high quality and in good condition. They had been discarded simply because they were dull.

Knives with plain edges are better than knives with serrated cutting edges. Serrated edges tend to saw food, rather than cut it cleanly. Furthermore, serrated blades are difficult or impossible to sharpen.

Knives should never be washed in a dishwasher, especially knives that have wooden handles. The very hot water used for washing in a dishwasher, and the high heat used for drying, will gradually damage the wood by removing its natural oils. The loss of natural oils and the resultant cracking of the wood will cause the handle rivets to loosen.

If you are going to buy a knife, you may wish to consider the various materials described below that are used to make a knife blade.

KNIFE BLADE MATERIAL

Carbon steel is the choice of many because it holds its edge fairly well and it is easy to sharpen. One disadvantage is that the blade will rust and tarnish—but, if you use it often, it will not get a chance to rust, and most of the tarnish can be removed with steel wool. Another minor negative point is that a carbon steel blade may impart a metallic taste and odor to acidic foods such as tomatoes, onions, and citrus fruits.

Stainless steel used to make high quality knives is not the same kind of stainless steel used to make your mixing bowls or your rustproof mailbox. Stainless steel is a general term for many different alloys. Your mixing bowls are probably made with 18 percent chromium and 8 percent nickel. An alloy used to make high quality stainless steel knives might contain small amounts of molybdenum, vanadium, manganese, and carbon in addition to the chromium and nickel. In other words, *stainless steel* is not an exact term, but a high quality stainless steel knife will be made of an alloy that will hold its edge for a long time. This is good, of course. The other side of the coin is that a knife that holds its edge well, such as a high quality stainless steel knife, will be difficult to sharpen once the edge is dull.

High carbon stainless steel knives are among the most expensive knives. The steel used in these knives has the rust- and stain-resistant properties of ordinary stainless steel knives, but they sharpen as easily as the carbon steel knives. Of course, because they are easy to sharpen, they do not hold their edge as well as the common stainless steel knives.

BONING KNIFE

The term "boning knife" may be a slight misnomer. With its slender blade and blade length of 6 inches (15 cm) or less, it is a very handy knife for boning meat, but it is more often used to trim meat. For example, the first step in making sausage is to trim the meat before cutting it into cubes for grinding. Cutting out the gristle, tendon, sinew, and blood clots is not a difficult job if a boning knife is used. The boning knife is one of the essential knives for making sausage.

GENERAL PURPOSE KNIFE

A knife with a blade about 8 inches (20 cm) to 10 inches (25 cm) long is an essential knife to have for general use and for cutting meat into cubes that will fit in the grinder. A chef's knife, or some other kind of knife with a stepped blade, is the best choice. (A knife with a stepped blade is a knife that has the cutting edge considerably lower than the handle.) The stepped blade keeps your knuckles from banging on the cutting board or counter top.

SLICING KNIFE

It is easy to slice large-diameter sausages if you use a straight knife with a blade at least 12 inches (30 cm) long—longer is better. If, however, you do not intend to make large sausages, there will be little need for a slicing knife.

Meat Grinders (Meat Choppers or Meat Mincers)

Meat grinders are also called meat choppers or meat mincers. All these terms refer to the same kind of hand-operated or electrically powered machine. The terms will be used interchangeably in this book.

Freshly ground meats bought at a food market can be used to make sausage. Eventually, however, you will need a meat grinder in order to process meats to suit your taste; for example, ground pork sold in grocery stores usually contains too much fat to make quality sausage. Also, some ethnic sausages should be made with coarsely ground meat, which is difficult to buy at a common grocery store.

HAND OPERATED AND ELECTRIC GRINDERS

An old-fashioned (hand-operated) meat grinder made of tin-dipped cast iron will do the job very well. Either the size #8 or the slightly larger size #10 is adequate for home use. These meat choppers clamp on a table, a countertop, or

A cast iron #8 meat grinder—Model 6249—made by Grizzly Industrial.
Photo courtesy Grizzly Industrial, Inc.

on the breadboard built into most kitchen cabinets. If you buy a meat chopper that attaches to the countertop by suction cups, you will be disappointed; suction cups are inadequate to hold the machine in place.

An electric meat grinder does the job faster and with much less effort, but it is not necessary unless you intend to make large quantities of sausage frequently. It should be mentioned, however, that cleanup is much easier for the electric meat grinder because you need only wash the relatively small and lightweight parts in the front of the electric grinder that come in contact with the meat. If a manual grinder is used, the entire grinder comes in contact with the meat and must be washed, and because the grinder is made of cast iron, the heavy weight makes it cumbersome to clean.

If you decide on an electric grinder, buy a powerful one. The VillaWare® Elite ProGrinder™ model V5267 (or the equivalent) is a good choice. It has a 550 watt, ¾ horsepower motor and a handy reverse switch. It will cost about

An electric meat grinder for home use. This is the VillaWare® Elite ProGrinder™, Model V5267. *Photo courtesy Jarden Consumer Solutions.*

A KitchenAid standing mixer with a grinder attachment. *Photo courtesy KitchenAid Corporation.*

$165. If you happen to have a heavy-duty KitchenAid standing mixer, you might want to consider a grinder attachment; these grinder attachments work very well and they cost only about $65.

GRINDER OPERATION

All meat choppers operate in the same way: Pieces of meat are put into the hopper, and an auger (worm shaft) forces the meat into the holes in the plate. A four-bladed knife lies flat against the back of the plate, and it rotates to cut off the meat that has been forced into the holes by the rotating auger. If the grinder is not chopping the meat properly, or if it is chopping the meat too slowly, it may be because the plate collar is not screwed down tightly, or it may be due to something preventing the knife from lying flat against the plate (gristle, sinew, etc.).

The size of the holes in each plate determines the coarseness of the chopped meat. You should have three plates with some combination of the following four hole sizes: ⅛ inch (4.2 mm), 3⁄16 inch (4.8 mm), ¼ inch (6.4 mm), and ⅜ inch (9.5 mm). Additional plates with holes smaller or larger than the holes mentioned above are sometimes useful, but they are not required.

CARE OF MEAT-GRINDING EQUIPMENT
No matter what kind of grinding equipment you are using, it should be washed in hot, soapy water as soon as the grinding work is finished. If the particles of meat remaining on the equipment become dry, they are very difficult to remove. If the equipment cannot be washed immediately, spray it with water or soak it in water in order to keep the meat particles moist.

After the various parts have been washed and rinsed, they may be air dried unless they are made of unprotected cast iron or steel. Unprotected parts should be dried with an absorbent cotton cloth to prevent rust formation.

Take particular care of the plates and the knife. If they are made of carbon steel, they can become corroded and pitted if left in contact with the sausage paste for an extended period. In addition, these carbon steel parts should be dried immediately after washing, and then wrapped individually in heavy, oiled paper such as brown paper from a paper bag—or, paper towels may be used. Put salad oil or mineral oil on the paper, plates, and knife; do not use petroleum-based oils. Salad oil will become gummy and sticky when it oxidizes, so make sure that the parts are separated with the paper; otherwise, they will stick together. These parts, wrapped in oiled paper, are conveniently stored in a small plastic food container or in a wide-mouthed jar.

If a grinder knife becomes dull, professional sharpening is strongly recommended; special sharpening equipment is required. Some grinder knives cannot be sharpened, particularly those used in electric grinders, and buying a new knife is the only recourse.

Mortar and Pestle, Electric Spice Mill
Chemists, primarily, use the mortar and pestle. A pharmacist might use them occasionally, but not as much as he or she would have used them in the old days.

The mortar and pestle are also useful for a person who makes sausage or smokes food. Use them to powder spices that season sausage or smoked foods. Powdering a spice will cause more flavor to be released. Powdered spices are good for making sausage because they are less visible and are more uniformly distributed.

Mortar and pestle.

The mortar and pestle can be obtained from a laboratory supply company or a chemical supply company. A pharmacist may be able to order a set for you. Because they are popular with gourmet cooks, they are also often available at a large culinary supply store.

Nowadays, the electric spice mill is gaining in popularity because it is much faster and easier to use than the mortar and pestle.

Refrigerator Thermometer

The internal temperature of a refrigerator is *very* important; the proper temperature retards spoilage and helps to prevent food poisoning. The refrigeration compartment should be kept within a range of 36° to 40° F (2.2° to 4.4° C).

There is a temperature adjustment dial in your refrigerator. The easiest way to measure the temperature is to use an inexpensive refrigerator thermometer. Leave this thermometer in the refrigerator so the temperature is easy to monitor.

A refrigerator thermometer is specially designed so that the reading will not change the moment the door is opened and warm air rushes in. It will take fifteen seconds, or so, before it begins to change. During that time, the thermometer will show the temperature *before* the door was opened. You can find these thermometers in any hardware or culinary store.

Rubber Gloves

A pair of rubber gloves will be useful to protect your hands from salt when mixing sausage. In addition, when ground meat is taken out of a 38° F (3° C) refrigerator to be mixed with seasoning, the hands may be in contact with the cold meat for several minutes. The pain caused by bare hands touching cold meat for an extended time is considerable. Rubber gloves will insulate the hands from the cold very well, even if the rubber is thin. Additionally, it is obviously far more sanitary to mix meat while wearing rubber gloves than it is to use bare hands.

Disposable latex or nitrile gloves made especially for food handling are excellent, and a box of 100 of them can be obtained at a wholesale grocer or restaurant supply store.

Rubber gloves of the type used to wash dishes and do light household cleaning are also effective, easy to use, inexpensive, re-usable, and obtainable almost anywhere. Of course, these gloves should be reserved exclusively for making sausage.

Food Mixers

It is not at all difficult to mix up to five pounds of sausage by hand. If you intend to make more than that, or if you have some kind of physical limitation, you might want to consider a standing mixer with a paddle attachment. KitchenAid makes good, heavy-duty mixers for home use. They also offer a meat grinding attachment that works well. The sausage stuffing attachment is not recommended (see *Sausage stuffing tubes and sausage stuffers*, below).

Sausage Molds

In Chapter 5, please see the section *Making sausage patties* for information about sausage molds.

A KitchenAid Artisan standing mixer. *Photo courtesy KitchenAid Corporation.*

Sausage Stuffing Tubes and Sausage Stuffers

OLD FASHIONED STUFFING FUNNELS

Before the early 1800s, when levered and gear-powered sausage stuffers were invented, sausage casings were stuffed by hand using a special kind of funnel designed for that purpose. These funnels were known by several names: *stuffing funnels, cones,* or *horns.* They are increasingly difficult to buy, but you might be able to find one on the Internet.

MODERN STUFFING TUBES

The various words that were used for the handheld stuffing funnels are now used for the modern sausage stuffing tubes that are mounted on a mechanical or an electric stuffer. Consequently, in addition to *tubes*, they are called *funnels*, *stuffing cones*, or *horns*. The words nozzles and spouts, too, are sometimes used.

A mechanical or an electric stuffer is usually supplied with three stuffing tubes. The exact diameter of each tube varies with the manufacturer, but ⅝ inch (16 mm), ¾ inch (19 mm), and 1 inch (25 mm) are common. The tube with the smallest diameter is used for sheep casings, the medium one for hog casings, and the large-diameter tube is used for large casings, such as fibrous casings. The tube used for collagen casings depends on the size of the casings.

STUFFER ATTACHMENT ON A MEAT GRINDER

Some stuffing tubes are designed to be attached to a meat grinder. Most electric meat grinders, and some hand-operated meat grinders, come with one or more sizes of stuffing tubes. Stuffing sausage with a meat grinder will do the job, but when stuffing tubes are used with a grinder, two people are required to stuff the casings. One person must keep the hopper full of the sausage mixture and try to keep it packed firmly to reduce the number of air pockets; the other person tends the casing as it is being stuffed. Because two people are required, and because air pockets in the sausages are more likely to be created with this method, using a stuffing tube that attaches to a meat grinder is not recommended.

However, if a grinder is used as a stuffer, make sure that a *spacer plate* is used in place of the knife and grinding plate; this prevents the sausage from being ground again as it is being stuffed.

LEVER POWERED SAUSAGE STUFFERS

Three-pound/1,360 g (or five-pound/2,270 g) cast-iron or stainless steel lever-powered sausage stuffers are popular. (They are also called *push stuffers*.) They are called three-pound stuffers because the manufacturers claim that they will hold three pounds of ground meat—they won't, but that does not cause an insurmountable problem. (In fact, if a three-pound stuffer is loaded with more than about 1½ pounds/680 g of sausage paste, it is very difficult to push the lever handle down: If the stuffer is more than half-full of sausage paste, the leverage decreases significantly.) These lever-powered stuffers will do the job; they are very durable, are reasonably priced, and can be operated by one person. They will allow the stuffing of any size of sausage casing.

The feet of these sausage stuffers have notches so that the stuffer can be mounted on a platform with bolts. If it is not mounted on a platform, it is

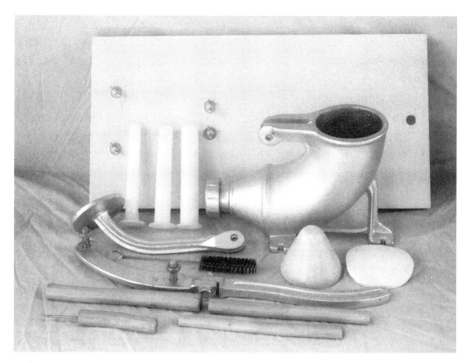

A disassembled sausage stuffer (lever-powered) with components and accessories:
• Left front: A homemade sausage pricker.
• Front: Three homemade tube plungers (for pushing meat out of the tube at the
  end of a sausage stuffing session).
• Handle for the sausage stuffer.
• Small bottlebrush (for cleaning the stuffer tubes).
• A homemade cone made of water putty. This is used for pushing out the meat that
  will remain in the tapered front section of the stuffer when the stuffing session is
  nearing completion.
• A homemade disk-shaped gasket made of dense, white foam rubber. This helps to
  prevent "backflow" around the pressure plate.
• Three diameters of sausage stuffing tubes.
• Stuffer mounting platform. The feet of the stuffer can be attached to the front of
  this board with four bolts.

certain to slide on the countertop and even tip over when the casing is being
stuffed. Mounting on a board, or directly on a tabletop, is imperative.

The diameter of the pressure plate is a little less than the internal diameter
of the elbow-macaroni-shaped ground-meat hopper. The smaller diameter is
necessary so that the pressure plate can pass through the curved hopper cavity
without binding. This smaller diameter of the pressure plate creates a minor

problem, however: When the lever is pushed down, most of the sausage will flow out of the tube and into the casing as it should, but some of the sausage will flow back around the edges of the pressure plate. This problem is called *backflow*.

This backflow problem can be minimized or eliminated if a homemade gasket is used. Cut a circular gasket from dense foam rubber; the diameter should be a little larger than the internal diameter of the hopper cavity. Wrap this gasket in plastic food wrap (to keep it clean), and place it between the sausage paste and the pressure plate. The gasket will prevent almost all of the backflow.

Another way to reduce backflow is to tear off about one foot of aluminum foil and fold it twice, making a square with four layers of foil. Place this between the sausage paste and the pressure plate. The foil functions as a gasket and reduces the backflow.

Another minor problem with these stuffers is that the pressure plate will not push out all of the sausage. This is because the pressure plate will stop near the front of the stuffer at the point where the nose of the stuffer begins to taper down toward the stuffing tube. About ⅓ pound (150 g) of sausage will remain in this conical-shaped cavity. Most of this sausage can be pushed into the stuffing tube by using the following method:

Crumple two sheets of newspaper into a ball, and place it in a plastic bag. Seal the bag with a bread-bag twist tie and place it just under the pressure plate. Most of the sausage paste remaining in the stuffer will be forced into the stuffing tube by this crumpled newspaper in the plastic bag.

Another option is to use a molding compound called *water putty* to mold a cone that will push out the remaining sausage paste into the stuffing tube. (Such a homemade cone is pictured in the photograph of the lever-powered sausage stuffer.) Water putty is available at all hardware stores, and instructions for use as a molding compound are on the container. For sanitary reasons, the cone should be wrapped in plastic food wrap before each use.

Appendix 5 offers suggestions about where to purchase these stuffers.

GEAR-DRIVEN STUFFERS

The most popular gear driven stuffer is the five-pound capacity upright style (also called *vertical stuffer*), and this style will be discussed below. Except for the different orientation, the horizontal style that lies on its side will operate in about the same way as the upright style.

A gear-driven, 5-pound stuffer—vertical type. Manufactured by Grizzly Industrial—Model H6252. *Photo courtesy Grizzly Industrial, Inc.*

Compared to the lever-powered cast-iron stuffer, the gear-driven stuffer has a couple of negative points—but many positive points.

The negative points are:

- The price of the gear-driven stuffer is several times that of the lever-operated, cast-iron model.
- The gear-driven stuffer will not tolerate as much abuse as the nearly indestructible cast-iron stuffer. The gear-driven stuffer has some plastic and synthetic rubber parts, and the most fragile of these parts are the plastic gears and plastic push-rod threads. If gorilla-like force is used

when the piston reaches the bottom of the cylinder, the threads might be stripped, or the gear teeth might be broken. If reasonable care is exercised, however, it should last for many years. When the piston reaches the bottom of the cylinder, STOP—don't try to force out another thimble-full of sausage paste!

The positive points of the gear-driven stuffer are as follows:

- The crank on the geared stuffer extrudes the sausage paste more easily than the lever on the cast-iron model; much less force is required for the crank.
- The gasket ring that attaches to the circumference of the piston prevents the backflow problem that is common with the cast-iron lever stuffers.
- The weight of the geared stuffer is much less than the weight of the cast-iron one.
- A mounting board is not required for the geared stuffer; two "C" clamps will prevent the stuffer from moving on the counter.
- Cleanup is easier for the geared model because the stuffer is lighter and because only the parts that are exposed to the sausage paste need be washed.
- The five-pound (2,270 g) geared model will hold five pounds of sausage paste. However, the lever-powered stuffer is almost impossible to use if more than half the rated capacity is loaded; this is because a load of over half of the rated capacity rapidly reduces the leverage.

Appendix 5 offers suggestions about where to purchase these stuffers.

WATER-POWERED SAUSAGE STUFFERS

Water-powered sausage stuffers with a horizontal orientation allow hands-free operation. Both hands can be used to manage the business of stuffing the sausage paste in the casing. The disadvantage is that two garden hoses must be attached to the stuffer. One hose connects to a faucet with threads suitable to screw on a garden hose, and the other hose goes to a floor drain or a catch bucket.

CARE OF STUFFING EQUIPMENT

No matter what kind of stuffing equipment you are using, it should be washed in hot, soapy water as soon as the stuffing work is finished. If the particles of meat remaining on the equipment become dry, they are very difficult to remove.

"C" clamps prevent movement of the stuffer on the countertop.

If the equipment cannot be washed immediately, spray it with water or soak it in water in order to keep the meat particles moist.

After the various parts have been washed and rinsed, they may be air dried, unless they are made of unprotected cast iron or steel. Such parts might rust if they are allowed to air dry, so they should be dried by hand right away.

Thermometers for Cooking

Thermometers are desirable for cooking all sausages that have been stuffed in casings. The method of cooking determines the best kind of thermometer for the job; sometimes two thermometers, used simultaneously, make the cooking easier. The thermometers described below will meet all of our needs adequately, and all of them are affordable.

We should not expect these inexpensive thermometers to be perfectly accurate throughout the measurement range. Presumably, they were calibrated at the factory, or they met the tolerance standards of the manufacturer. For a home-use thermometer, the manufacture's tolerance is usually about plus or minus two degrees. Nevertheless, it is a good idea to check the thermometers for accuracy. I bought a digital thermometer with a cable probe recently, and I tested it using the method described below. I discovered that my thermometer read 192° F (89° C) instead of 212° F (100° C)—an error of 20 degrees! I telephoned the manufacturer, described how I tested it, and they sent me a replacement immediately.

To test the thermometers, fill a saucepan with water and bring the water to a boil. Next, measure the temperature of the boiling water. We know that the temperature of boiling water is 212° F (100° C). When the thermometer is read, the accuracy will be obvious. Of course, water boils at a lower temperature than 212° F (100° C) if it is significantly above sea level. Consequently, if you live somewhere like Denver, Colorado, compensation must be made for the high altitude.

If your thermometer does not read correctly, check the instructions to see if it can be calibrated. If it cannot be calibrated, compensation should be made for the error whenever it is used, or the manufacturer should be contacted for a replacement. The most important range for a sausage thermometer is 155° F (68° C) to 165° F (74° C), but it is difficult to check the thermometer for accuracy in that range. We are forced to assume the error in this range is the same as the error we observed when measuring the temperature of boiling water.

DIAL AND BABY-DIAL THERMOMETERS

The baby-dial thermometer is very useful to check the internal temperature of cooked sausage. When it is used in this way, you might say that it is a kind of miniature meat thermometer. It has a temperature dial about the size of the face of a men's round wristwatch. The stem of the baby-dial thermometer will withstand very high temperatures, but the dial itself is delicate, and it cannot withstand the hot temperatures present inside a kitchen oven, for example. *Using this thermometer in such a hot environment will likely destroy or damage it.*

The baby-dial thermometer is also very useful for poaching sausages. This thermometer can be used to check the water temperature, as well as the internal temperature of the sausages. It can also be used to check the internal temperature of sausages being cooked in a hot smoker; however, the sausage is usually removed from the smoker before using the thermometer. Because it is an instant-read thermometer, the dial will show the internal temperature about 15 to 20 seconds after it is inserted.

The calibration of the baby-dial thermometer is from about 0° F (-18° C) to 220° F (104° C). You should be able to obtain one from a mail-order es-

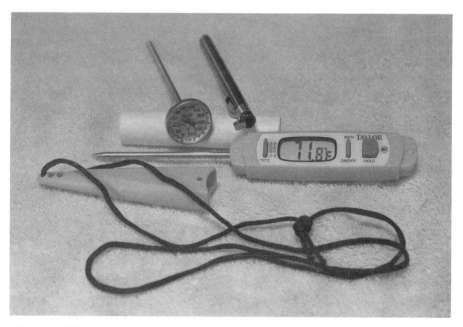

A baby-dial thermometer and a digital stem thermometer.

tablishment that deals in sausage-making equipment and supplies, a hardware store, or from a retailer that sells culinary items.

A larger type of dial thermometer is calibrated in the same way as the baby-dial thermometer, and can be used in its place for most applications. It has a longer and thicker stem, and it will probably cost over twice as much as a baby-dial. The dial of this thermometer is just as delicate as the dial of the baby-dial thermometer; it cannot be used inside an oven or in a hot smoke chamber.

These dial thermometers have the temperature sensors near the point—not at the point—so they must be inserted about 2 to 2½ inches (5 to 6.5 cm) into the meat to get a representative sample of the internal heat.

DIGITAL STEM THERMOMETERS

Improving technology has made it possible to manufacture digital stem thermometers and sell them at a price that is competitive with dial thermometers. The cost is more than for the dial thermometers, and they require a battery, but many people do not hesitate to spend a little more money for high-tech equipment.

DIGITAL THERMOMETERS WITH CABLE PROBES

Digital cooking thermometers with a cable and a probe are used to monitor the internal temperature of meat, and they are very useful for cooking sausage. The

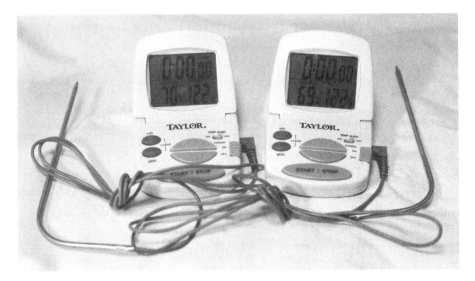

Digital thermometers with cable probes.

internal temperature of the sausage can be checked at glance, so the chance of overcooking is minimized. They can be found wherever kitchen equipment is sold.

An additional advantage of using these electronic thermometers for smoking sausage is that the smoke chamber need not be opened to check the internal temperature of the meat. Heat is lost every time the chamber is opened, so the total cooking time will increase with every peek.

The probe is inserted into the sausage that is cooking in the smoker, the steamer, or is being poached in hot water. The cable connected to that probe plugs into a digital display unit that is placed on the kitchen counter or on the outside of the smoker.

If you try this kind of thermometer just once, you will probably conclude that you do not want to be without it. In fact, you may discover that you want two of these instruments when the sausage is being poached, steamed, or smoked—one to constantly measure the internal temperature of the sausage, and one to monitor the temperature of the hot water, the inside of the steamer, or the inside of the smoker.

Volume Measuring Equipment

You will need a set of American standard (or metric standard) measuring cups and spoons. Fluid ounce units are never used in this book.

All volume measurements are intended to be *level measurements. One teaspoon of salt*, for example, means *one level teaspoon of salt*. (However, fluffy spices such as coriander and rubbed sage should be packed in the measuring spoon so that the amount will be consistent from batch to batch.)

Weight Scales

To the extent possible, measurements have been specified in terms of volume rather than weight. That is, whenever possible, the amount of an ingredient is indicated in American teaspoons, tablespoons, or cups (together with the metric equivalent). There are significant differences between the British and the American system of measurement, even though the same words may be used; the British system is not supported in this book.

Obviously, the quantity of meats must be expressed in units of weight, and you will need a scale to weigh the meats. An inexpensive kitchen scale that will weigh up to about five pounds (about 2 or 3 kg) will do the job. If you intend

A kitchen scale for ounce or gram weight measurements.

to make large batches of sausage, a kitchen scale that weighs up to 11 pounds (5 kg) would be better. Such scales have sufficient accuracy if used properly.

Whetstone and Butcher's Steel

You will need a whetstone to keep your knives sharp. A Carborundum whetstone is inexpensive, and it is easily found at a culinary supply store or at a hardware store. It is suggested that you buy one that is at least 8 inches (20 cm) long and 2 inches (5 cm) wide. A laminated stone that is coarse on one side and fine on the other is convenient. If a thin stream of water is allowed to fall on the stone while knives are being sharpened, the stone's surface will not become clogged with metallic dust. The kitchen sink is the best place to sharpen knives. Use a dishpan turned upside down as a platform for the stone.

A butcher's steel (also called *knife steel* or *sharpening steel*) looks something like a long rattail file. Most sharpening steels will not remove metal from the knife blade, but they will straighten the edge curl that develops when a knife is used. The butcher's steel is not essential equipment, but frequent use of one will prolong the sharpness of the blade. The longer the butcher's steel, the easier it is to use—especially for knives with long blades. Ceramic rod is also used to make this knife-honing tool. Ceramic works equally well.

CHAPTER 3

Supplies

You will need a number of consumable items. Your exact needs will depend on the kinds of sausage you are going to make and the seasonings, herbs, and spices you wish to use.

The following list of supplies is in alphabetical order, not in order of importance.

Breadcrumbs

Sausages made in the United Kingdom usually contain breadcrumbs. Traditionally, a kind of breadcrumb called *rusk* is used. Some of the commercially produced sausages in the UK contain rusk, and others contain common breadcrumbs. Amateur sausage makers in the UK tend to use common breadcrumbs because rusk is difficult to buy in small quantities. Any kind of dry, unseasoned breadcrumbs can be substituted for rusk, but coarse breadcrumbs are best. The best substitution, in my opinion, is the Japanese style breadcrumbs known as *panko*. Because panko has become popular with United States culinary buffs, it is now made in the United States. Small boxes of Kikkoman-brand panko can be bought in well-stocked grocery stores. Larger, more economical packages can be bought in Asian grocery stores.

Casings

Many kinds of sausages, particularly the uncured, fresh sausage varieties, do not require a casing. These varieties are often made into patties or crumbled and used as a seasoning in cooking. However, for many other sausages, tradition requires that they be stuffed in a casing.

Most certainly, not all the casings listed below will be needed. In fact, it is recommended that only two or three kinds of casings be purchased in the beginning. When a casing is required for any sausage in this book, one of the following two casings will do:

- 29 to 32 mm (about 1⅛ to 1¼ inch) diameter small hog casing
- 2½ or 2⅜ inch (about 63.5 to 61 mm) diameter fibrous casing

There is a third kind of casing to consider: 24 to 26 mm (1 inch to 1¹⁄₁₆ inch) sheep casing. This casing is splendid for stuffing breakfast links, or any sausages such as frankfurters, that are best when stuffed in a small-diameter, tender casing. They are highly recommended for some sausages, but hog casings can be used in their place.

There are six categories of sausage casings: natural, synthetic (fibrous), collagen, muslin, cellulose, and plastic.

NATURAL CASING

The most commonly used natural casings are hog, sheep, and beef casings made from the carefully cleaned small intestines of these animals.

The inside lining and the outside muscle tissue are removed, and the remaining thin, tubular membrane is used as the casing. The casings are sized, dredged in salt, and then tied into a bundle called a *hank*. (In the case of hog casings, a hank is 100 yards long—about 91 meters.)

There are several advantages to using natural casings, especially hog and sheep casings made from the small intestines. Natural casings are fairly easy to obtain; they can be purchased in small quantities (one hank); they are easy to twist into links; and, when making dried or semi-dried sausage, the casings shrink as the meat shrinks.

You may find ready-to-use casings that are packed in a special clear solution rather than dry salt. These casings must be used within one month, so they are not recommended unless you make a lot of sausage and use them quickly. It is best to buy casings packed in salt. (Some producers pack the casing in *saturated brine*—brine with a lot of undissolved salt in it. Packing in saturated brine is equal to packing in salt.)

In addition to the small intestine, other parts of pork and beef innards are traditionally used to stuff special varieties of sausage. In this book, the synthetic fibrous casing (described below) will be substituted.

HOG CASING

Hog casings made from the small intestine are normally sold in four sizes (1 inch is equal to 25.4 mm):

- 29 to 32 mm
- 32 to 35 mm
- 35 to 38 mm
- 38 to 42 mm

They are, of course, edible. One hank of the smallest size will stuff 90 to 100 pounds, and a hank of the largest diameter will stuff up to 135 pounds. In this book, the smallest size is used for many sausages; it varies from about 1⅛ inch to 1¼ inches (29 to 32 mm). As mentioned above, for home use it is best to purchase casings that have been packed in salt or saturated brine; such casings can be preserved for years under refrigeration.

Hog casings made from innards other than the small intestine are available: hog middles, hog bungs, and hog stomachs. Certain large sausages are traditionally made with one of these special casings, but fibrous casings are easier to use, are more economical, and do not have an offensive odor.

SHEEP CASING

Natural sheep casings are smaller and tenderer than hog casings, but they are more expensive. Depending on the vendor, as many as four sizes are available (25.4 mm equals 1 inch):

- 20 to 22 mm
- 22 to 24 mm
- 24 to 26 mm
- 26 to 28 mm

Sheep casings packed in either salt or a special preservative solution are available, and they are used in the same way as hog casings. If they are packed in salt (or saturated brine) and stored in the refrigerator, they will keep for many years.

BEEF CASING

Beef middles, beef rounds, beef bungs, and beef bladders can be obtained without much difficulty if it is necessary to stuff a certain sausage in its traditional casing. However, large hog casings and fibrous casings can be substituted for less money. Beef casing, by the way, is too tough to be considered edible.

COLLAGEN CASING

Collagen is a protein that is extracted from the bones, connective tissues, and hides of cattle. This special protein is used to manufacture *collagen casings*. (It is also used to manufacture gelatin.) These casings are made in various sizes. The wall thickness varies with the intended use of the casing. For example, casings used for smoked sausage links need to be strong if they will be hung in a smoker, so they will have thicker walls. Casings used for fresh sausage are thin and tender, but they may split when stuffed. Some of these casings require refrigeration while being stored, but others do not.

Because collagen casings are uniform, and because their use requires less labor than natural casings, they are widely used by commercial processors even though they are a little more expensive than natural casings. People who do not want to eat sausage that has been stuffed in animal "guts" use them. Collagen casings are also useful for making kosher sausage.

The various types of collagen casings are explained below.

ROUND COLLAGEN CASING (SLEEVES)

Round collagen casing is manufactured as a long, smooth tube, and then compressed into a much shorter tube of accordion-like pleats. The resulting *sleeve* is slid on the metal or plastic stuffing tube in much the same way that a shirtsleeve is slid onto an arm. When a sausage is stuffed, the pleats are pulled off the end of the tube a few at a time. (These sleeves are also called *strand collagen casings*.)

Some stuffing tubes are shorter than the collagen sleeve, and some stuffing tubes are tapered (the overall diameter of the tube may be greater near the stuffer). In these cases, the collagen sleeve may need to be cut in half in order to expose the end of the stuffing tube when the sleeve is slid on the tube.

As indicated above, there are two kinds of collagen casing sleeves. One type has thin walls, and it is used mainly for fresh sausages. If this casing is used for smoked sausage, the links must be laid on a smoking rack because the casing will tear if the links are hung in coils. The type of collagen casing with thicker walls is used for smoked sausages that will be hung in coils on a support rod. The thicker casing is strong enough to support the weight of the sausage coil without tearing. Both types must be stored in an airtight plastic bag in the refrigerator to prevent them from becoming dry and brittle. Both types are stuffed dry; they must *not* be soaked in water before using.

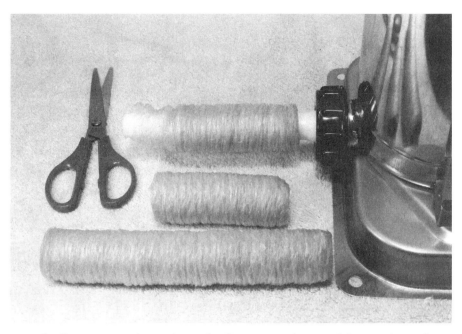

Round collagen casing sleeves (strand collagen casing). One of the two sleeves has been cut in half because it was longer than the stuffing tube.

Both the thick wall casings and the thin wall casings are more difficult to stuff than natural casings because they are not elastic. Because natural casings will stretch, they are more forgiving if the sausage is slightly overstuffed or insufficiently stuffed. In addition, if collagen casings are twisted into links, they will unwind. Consequently, it is best to divide the sausage rope into links with butcher's twine rather than twisting it into links.

The casing with a thin wall is very tender and is a pleasure to eat. The type with a thick wall is technically edible, but few people eat the casing because it is very tough.

In my opinion, the bottom line for collagen casing sleeves (strand collagen casing) is this:

- For the home sausage maker, the thick wall type has no redeeming merits at all, unless natural casings cannot be used for personal reasons.
- The thin wall type might be considered if the negative points can be tolerated. The cost and the tenderness of this casing are comparable to sheep casing. It can be used for smoked sausage if the links are laid on a smoking rack instead of hung on rods.

FLAT COLLAGEN CASING

Flat collagen casings look similar to synthetic fibrous casings, and they, too, are used to stuff salami-size sausage and luncheon meat. They are not edible, even though they are made of collagen, and they must be soaked in salted water before use. If casing made of natural material is an important factor to the sausage maker, this casing may be of interest. However, flat collagen casings are not as strong as synthetic fibrous casings, and they must be stuffed more gently. If you intend to use these casings, please read the recommendations in the next paragraph regarding casing diameter and length. These size recommendations apply to flat collagen casings as well as to synthetic fibrous casings.

SYNTHETIC FIBROUS CASING

Synthetic fibrous casings are very useful for large-diameter snack sausages or lunchmeat sausages. These casings are not edible, but they are very strong, and they will not tear while they are being stuffed. Fibrous casings are available in diameters ranging from 1½ inches (38 mm) to over 4¾ inches (120 mm). If fibrous casings are used, it is best for the beginner to use casings of no more than about 2½ inches (63 mm) in diameter, and no more than 12 inches (30 cm) long. This size is easier to process, and the cooking time will be faster than it is for casings with larger diameters. In this book, this size is usually recommended for the sausages that are stuffed in fibrous casings. To make them supple, synthetic fibrous casings are soaked in warm water before stuffing. Follow the manufacturer's instructions. If the instructions are not available, soak them in warm water for 20 or 30 minutes before use. Be sure to flood the inside with water.

Depending on the vendor, sometimes the fibrous casings are not closed on the bottom, or sometimes they are sold in 24-inch (60 cm) lengths only, and need to be cut in half. If the casings are not closed on the bottom, or if they need to be cut, common twine may be used to close them. However, a great deal of pressure is put on the bottom closure when the sausage is being stuffed. Consequently, if it is tied with twine, the very strong *butterfly tie* (also called *butterfly knot*) should be used. The top portion of the photograph demonstrates how to close the end of a synthetic fibrous casing with the butterfly tie:

- Cut a length of twine—about 5 inches (13 cm) long.
- Fold the end of the casing in zigzag-like pleats. (It is best to use something like a clothespin or a paper clamp to hold the pleats in the folded position.)

The butterfly knot is tied in three steps at the top of the photo. At the bottom left, the end of the synthetic casing has been tied by the manufacturer. At the bottom right, a casing clip has been used to close the end of the casing.

- Tie the end of the casing with a common square knot about ¾ inch (2 cm) from the end.
- Bring the ends of the twine around the bottom of the casing, and tie another square knot in such a way that the ends of the casing flare ("butterfly") to the left and right.

Another way to close a casing on the bottom is to use an aluminum casing clip. Please see the *Casing clips* section of this chapter (below).

Fibrous casings are sold in two colors: clear and mahogany. The "clear" casings are actually translucent and resemble very strong wax paper. They acquire a beautiful reddish-brown color when they are smoked. However, if the sausage is not smoked, the clear casing looks pale and anemic. The mahogany-colored casing, on the other hand, looks good no matter how the sausage is processed.

Fibrous casings do have one small negative point: They are not waterproof, although they are water resistant and remain strong when wet. Instructions on cooking sausage in Chapter 6 describe how this minor negative point can be addressed.

MUSLIN CASING

Finally, you may make casings of muslin. Such casings may sometimes be used in place of synthetic fibrous casings, and they are traditionally used for German liver sausages such as Braunschweiger, liverwurst, and some salami-like sausages. Because the muslin absorbs moisture readily, it is best that they not be used for steamed or poached sausage. Hot smoked sausages are the best use for muslin casings.

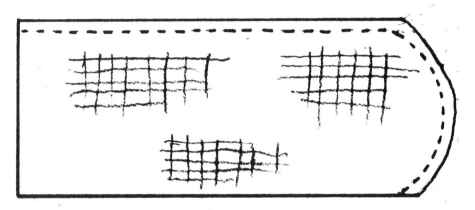

A sausage casing made of muslin.

Tear—do not cut—a strip of muslin 8 inches (20 cm) wide and about 12 inches (30 cm) long. (To the extent possible, the material should be torn rather than cut; tearing reduces the amount of cloth fibers that will get into the sausage.) Fold the strip in half lengthwise. The folded cloth will now measure about 4 inches (10 cm) wide. Sew it along the side and around one end; this will produce a round casing with a diameter of about 2¼ inches (5.7 cm). If the cloth material is new, it is best to launder it before it is used. Laundering will remove the fabric conditioners that are present in new material. Turn this closed-end tube inside out, wet it with vinegar, and stuff it with sausage. The vinegar prevents the cloth from bonding to the sausage.

CELLULOSE CASING

Cellulose casings are not edible, and they must be removed before the sausage is eaten. They are used for skinless sausages, such as breakfast links, hot dogs, and Mexican chorizo. When sausage links are cooked, the protein in the meat just under the casings coagulates and makes a natural "skin" that holds the sausage together when the cellulose casing is removed. Skinless frankfurters are made in this way. (If you look closely at a commercially made skinless frankfurter, you will be able to see a faint slit mark where a sharp blade has cut through the cellulose casing to facilitate its removal.) Home sausage makers rarely use cellulose casings, and they are not suggested for use in this book. However, if you want to try them, contact Allied Kenco Sales (please see Appendix 5).

PLASTIC CASING

The price of plastic casing is about the same as fibrous casing. Because it is waterproof (if care is taken to seal the ends properly), plastic casing is useful for large sausages that will be steamed or poached. The use of a waterproof plastic casing for steaming or poaching ensures that the sausage will not be harmed by water entering the casing. However, smoke will not penetrate plastic, so they should not be used for sausage that will be smoked.

The use of plastic food wrap when steaming or poaching fibrous casings helps to provide water-resistant properties similar to those of plastic casings. Please see Chapter 6 for details.

Plastic casings are more difficult to obtain than fibrous casings, but one source is PS Seasoning & Spices, a company that sells sausage-making equipment and supplies. PS Seasoning & Spices offers two sizes: 2½-inch (6.35 cm) diameter and 4-inch (9.8 cm) diameter, and both are orange. Please see Appendix 5 for contact information.

GROUND MEAT BAGS

Ground meat bags resemble plastic casings. They may be used for breakfast sausage; the raw breakfast sausage is stuffed in the bag, chilled, and then sliced into round, patty-like disks and fried. They are not suggested for use in this book, but most mail-order suppliers can supply them. (See Appendix 5.)

Casing Clips

An aluminum cap-like device called a *casing clip* can be used to close the end of a synthetic fibrous casing. (Some retailers may still use the original name, *Clark clamp*.) First, the end of the casing is folded several times until it is small enough to fit inside the casing clip. Next, this folded end of the casing is inserted into the clip, and the clip is secured by squeezing it with pliers. They are easy to apply, and they provide a dependable closure for the end of the casing.

There is a photo of a casing clip in the *Synthetic fibrous casing* section earlier in this chapter. Casing clips can be purchased wherever sausage-making supplies are sold; please see Appendix 5.

Curing Powder

The following is a bit technical, but a basic understanding of curing powders is necessary for those who make sausage.

Curing powder is also known as *Cure #1, Cure #2, pink salt, pink powder*, or *cure*. It normally contains either sodium nitr<u>ite</u> ($NaNO_2$) or a combination of sodium nitr<u>ite</u> and sodium nitr<u>ate</u> ($NaNO_3$). These preparations are widely used by commercial meat processors, amateur smokers, and sausage makers. Many sausage formulas presented in this book require a curing powder.

These nitrites or nitrates in the curing powders are largely responsible for the pink color of some types of sausages. Nitrites or nitrates also cause the pink color of ham, bacon, and luncheon meats. The red color of corned beef, and the reddish color of most commercially produced jerky, are more examples of the effect of nitrites and nitrates. Without these chemicals, all the fully cooked meats mentioned above would be brownish or grayish, like ordinary cooked meat. The lean part of bacon, for example, would turn brown while cooking, and luncheon meats and frankfurters would not be pink—they would be brownish.

Meats cured with nitrites or nitrates (including sausage) also have a distinctive flavor that many people like; the flavor difference can be readily understood by comparing the taste of cured ham with the taste of roasted pork. Furthermore, rancidity is inhibited, shelf life is extended, and positive protection against botulism is provided with the proper use of these additives.

In spite of all the benefits provided by these curing chemicals, they are harmful if used in *large* quantities. Fortunately, it takes only a very small amount to obtain the desired result, and the amount of these chemicals specified in this book is considered safe. Nevertheless, if you never eat commercially processed meats because of the additives they contain, you may not want to use a curing powder in your sausage. However, if you make that decision, then you should forgo making *smoked* sausage because *smoked* sausage without the addition of nitrites or nitrates presents a considerable risk of botulism poisoning. It could prove fatal.

It was mentioned above that nitrites and nitrates are used in very small amounts. In fact, the amount required to cure 2½ pounds (1.135 kg) of ground meat is so small (approximately $\frac{1}{32}$ teaspoon), it can only be weighed accurately with scales found in a scientific laboratory or in a pharmacy. This is obviously impractical for both the amateur smoker and a small commercial processor, and it is not possible to measure such a small amount accurately with a measuring spoon.

To overcome this obstacle, several companies have mixed salt with sodium nitrite ($NaNO_2$) to make a product containing 6.25 percent sodium nitrite. Such a blend that uses salt as a carrier can be measured with reasonable accuracy by using measuring spoons commonly found in the household kitchen. Only $\frac{1}{2}$ teaspoon (2.5 ml) of this curing powder blend will cure 2½ pounds (1.135 kg) of ground meat. *Prague Powder #1*, *Modern Cure*, and *Insta Cure #1* are three brands of curing powder that contain 6.25 percent sodium nitrite. These curing powders have pink food coloring added so that they will not be confused with salt. Consequently, curing powder is sometimes called *pink salt* or *pink powder*.

When curing powders are commercially produced, a special process is used to bond the proper ratio of salt and sodium nitrite into each crystal so that the blend will always remain uniform. Homemade curing powders can be blended, but homemade curing powders will not be uniform, and the salt can separate from the sodium nitrite. This is why the commercially prepared curing powders are recommended. A uniform curing powder helps to insure that the correct amount of nitrite is added to the product.

Whenever *Cure #1* is specified in this book, you may use any brand of curing powder that contains 6.25 percent sodium nitrite. These commercial curing powders are readily available by mail order from establishments that offer sausage-making or smoking equipment (see Appendix 5). Butcher supply firms often sell curing powder; check out *butcher supplies* in the yellow pages. You may also be able to obtain it from sausage-making establishments. You will not find these products in a common grocery store.

There are some curing products available in grocery stores that contain a very low percentage of sodium nitrite (about 0.5 percent) in the salt carrier. However, such products are not recommended because (if used as directed by the manufacturer) they allow very little control of the salt content in your products. Your products will probably be too salty.

Prague Powder #2 and *Insta Cure #2* contain sodium nitrate in addition to sodium nitrite. These special curing powders are mainly used for fermented sausages. Fermented sausages are not covered in this book, so these curing powders will not be used. However, a class of sausages called *fermented-style sausages* is covered in this book, but these fermented-style sausages require the common *Cure #1*, which does not contain sodium nitrate. (For additional information, please see *Nitrites and nitrates* in Chapter 6.)

Fermento

Fermento is a manufactured seasoning made entirely from dairy products. It contains lactic acid—the same acid produced by bacteria when fermented, dry-cured sausage is made. It is the lactic acid in the dry-cured sausage that gives it its fermented flavor and characteristic tang. Fermento imparts this fermented flavor without fermentation of the sausage. The use of Fermento allows us to make products like pepperoni, summer sausage, and Thuringer without the lengthy and difficult dry-curing process. Please see Appendix 5 for sources of this product if you wish to make the fermented style sausages described in Chapter 11.

Liquid Smoke

Liquid smoke is something you may want to add to your list of supplies. The use of liquid smoke will enable you to make smoke-flavored sausages, even if you do not own a smoker.

If your smoker is a water smoker, you may want to try liquid smoke. Water smokers do not impart as much smoke flavor as a regular smoker, so you may want to use a little of the liquid smoke to boost the smoky aroma of water-smoked sausage. This is especially true if the smoking time is short.

Most large grocery stores offer Wright's Liquid Smoke, but liquid smoke other than this hickory aroma (mesquite, for example) can be obtained from some companies that offer sausage-making supplies.

Use liquid smoke sparingly. If it is used in excess, the sausage will have an unpleasant taste. Try ½ teaspoon (2.5 ml) for a 2½ pound (1,150 g) batch. Reduce or increase the amount of liquid smoke in the next batch of sausage.

Meat

No matter what kind of meat is being used for sausage, it should be fresh. If the meat was frozen while it was still fresh and is then properly thawed, it is equivalent to fresh meat. Ground meat will spoil faster than solid meat, so it is best to start with fresh solid meat in order to ensure a wholesome product.

Traditionally, sausage experts consider the perfect fat-to-lean ratio to be about 25 percent fat and 75 percent lean. However, the USDA Food Safety and Inspection Service permits up to 50 percent fat in fresh pork sausages, breakfast sausages, and whole hog sausages. Considering this, 25 percent fat does not seem to be excessive, but many people who make their own sausage prefer a healthier, leaner sausage.

Pork is the most commonly used meat for making sausage, and an economical cut variously called Boston butt, shoulder butt, pork shoulder, or pork butt is most often used. Besides being inexpensive, it is a very convenient cut to use because it contains about the perfect ratio of lean to fat. Any cut of pork can be used, so use the most economical. In this book, the expression *pork butt* will be used; however, please understand *pork butt* to mean any cut of pork that contains about 25 percent fat—or the amount of fat you prefer. If you need to add fat, medium-hard pork fat is the best kind of fat to use because it has a high melting point. Use a type of medium-hard fat known as *back fat* or *fatback* whenever available. It is very convenient to have a supply of cubed back fat in the freezer to add to any kind of meat that is too lean.

If beef is used to make sausage, any cut of beef may be used, but the expression *beef chuck* will be used in this book. Beef chuck is economical, and it usually contains about the right amount of fat.

If wild game meat is used, it is best to trim and discard all the fat from the meat; very few people like the taste of wild game fat. To replace that fat, use enough pork fat to bring the percentage of fat to the desired level.

Poultry flesh is increasingly used for making sausage. Sometimes sausages are made entirely of poultry, but it is more commonly added to pork, beef, or a blend of pork and beef. I often substitute turkey or chicken thighs for the more expensive veal.

Often, there will be some pork, beef, or fowl left over after preparing meat to make a batch of sausage. This meat may be frozen for future processing, even though it was previously frozen. Every time meat is frozen, the ice crystals formed in the meat will cause physical changes that allow juices to escape when it is thawed. This will cause no serious deterioration in quality unless it is refrozen many times.

COLD WATER THAWING

Thawing in a refrigerator is safe, and it is commonly recommended. However, cold water thawing is just as safe, and it is much faster.

If cold water thawing is employed, the pieces of raw material must be sealed in plastic bags to prevent absorption of water (*this is important*). It is best to put only one piece of raw material in each plastic bag. Remove as much air as possible. Place the bagged material in a deep container, and fill the container with cold tap water. The meat should be pressed below the surface of the water. Set the container in a sink, and allow a thin stream of cold tap water to run into the container—or change the water in the container from time to time.

A large joint of meat (a whole pork shoulder butt, for example) might require only a few hours to thaw in cold water, but the same joint of meat might require several days to thaw in the refrigerator. This will be true even if the temperature of the water in the container is the same as the temperature of the air in the refrigerator. Why does cold water thaw more effectively? The heat conductivity of water is much greater than that of the air in the refrigerator, so thawing is much faster, even if the thawing temperatures are the same.

Cold water thawing can be used in combination with refrigerator thawing. Even if you began thawing in the refrigerator, you can finish the thawing quickly in cold water. This is especially useful when you have underestimated the refrigerator thawing time and you need to begin your processing schedule.

Plastic Food Wrap

Plastic food wrap, which many people still call *Saran Wrap*, may be one of your most frequently used supplies. If you find that you use a lot of plastic food wrap, you might want to purchase a larger, more economical roll such as those used in restaurants and commercial kitchens. These rolls are about 6 inches (15 cm) in diameter; they are bulky, but the easy-to-use cutter provided with each roll makes wrapping easier than with the home-use roll. These large rolls can be found at restaurant supply grocery stores. The plastic wrap is normally 1 foot (30 cm) wide, and the roll contains 3,000 linear feet (914 meters).

Salt

One of the best kinds of salt to use for all sausage-making purposes is the kind of salt known as *pickling salt* or *canning salt*. This salt is over 99 percent pure, and it contains no iodine or other additives. Another variety of salt that is equally acceptable is known as *non-iodized table salt* or *plain salt*; only a free-flow agent (usually calcium silicate or magnesium carbonate) is added. This salt is also over 99 percent pure, and the taste of the small amount of free-flow agent will not be noticeable. When used for sausage making, curing, and canning, the impurities or additives in salt, depending on the kind and amount, can cause discoloration and bitterness in meats, fish, and vegetables. The free-flow agent will not cause problems for sausage making or meat curing, but the salt with no additives should be used for pickling and canning.

A 5-pound (2.27 kg) box of pickling salt can be obtained in most grocery stores for about $1.50. A 25-pound (11.35 kg) bag of plain table salt (containing the acceptable free-flow agent) can be purchased at a wholesale grocery store for about $3.50. There are few reasons to use anything other than one of these two varieties for making sausage. Iodized salt and sea salt contain minerals that are good for you, but they are not the best salts for making sausage.

Pickling salt and table salt are *fine grain* salts. Fine grain salts are best for sausage making because fine grain crystals dissolve faster than large crystals and because fine grain salt can be measured accurately by volume.

Kosher salt, especially the fast-dissolving flaked kosher salt, is quite acceptable for sausage making because it is a pure salt with no additives. A negative point is that any given volume measurement of kosher salt will weigh less than the same unit of fine grain salt; consequently, one tablespoon of kosher salt will weigh less—and contain less salt—than one tablespoon of fine grain salt. All the sausage-seasoning formulas in this book are based on the use of fine grain salt. If kosher salt is used, the volume measurement of the salt needs to be increased, and the amount of increase will depend on the brand and kind of kosher salt you are using.

Store salt in a tightly sealed plastic bag to protect it from humidity. Pure salt may become lumpy even if it is stored in a plastic bag, but its quality will not be diminished. Storage time does not lessen the quality either; so don't hesitate to by a large quantity if that is most economical.

If the salt becomes lumpy, break the lumps and use it. The best way to deal with lumpy salt, sugar, or spices is to put the seasoning into a strainer or a flour sifter, and then break the lumps. If the seasoning passes through the wire mesh, it is fine enough to use.

Spices and Herbs

For most of us, there is no clear distinction between the word *spice* and the word *herb*, especially when the subject is seasoning for food. Even the experts do not always agree, so let's use the word *spices* to mean both *spices* and *herbs*.

The main reason why one kind of sausage tastes so different from another is because of the different spices and seasonings used in each. Of course, the varieties of meat used in each sausage contribute to the differences in taste, but the spices and seasonings determine their main character. Appendix 1 contains a list of spices and seasonings commonly used in sausage making.

The sausage formulas in this book will suggest certain spices. If you have experience with the suggested spices, and if you can imagine the resulting taste, you should make changes to match your preferences. If you can't imagine the taste of the finished product, but you want to try the suggested seasonings, you should make a small batch of the product. In fact, it is wise to make a small batch anytime you make a sausage for the first time. For a small batch, it is suggested that the meat and all other ingredients be cut in half. The resulting taste will be the same as a full batch.

The spices used should be of good quality. However, as far as quality is concerned, we have little choice but to trust the reputation of the brand. Very few of us are qualified to judge the quality of a spice by peering through the glass or plastic container.

The freshness of dried spices is, to some extent, under our control. There is often an expiration date on the spice container. If you have some spices sitting around the house and the dates have expired, or if you have no idea how old they are, the best thing to do is to throw them out.

The company that processes and packs the spice decides the expiration date. The expertise of specialists in the company is used to determine the shelf life of the particular spice. They assume that the spice will be tightly sealed, struck by an average amount of light, and exposed to room temperature. If the actual storage conditions are worse than expected, the spice will go bad faster. If the actual storage conditions are better than they expected, the particular spice may be usable well past the expiration date.

In summary, the freshness and shelf life of the spices you use can be greatly extended by following these suggestions:

- Buy your spices at retail outlets that have a rapid turnover of goods. Dried spices sold at such stores are likely to be fresher than spices sold at mom-and-pop-type retailers.
- Buy spices in quantities that will be consumed in a reasonable amount of time, so that the length of storage time before consumption is minimized.
- Buy a brand name you trust, or get your spices from a distributor you trust.

- Check for the expiration date; some brands have that date stamped on the container. The expiration dates on the containers sitting on the same shelf of the grocery store may vary considerably, even if it is the same spice with the same brand name. The spices towards the back of the display may be fresher than the spices toward the front. The expiration date is sometimes stamped on the bottom of the container.
- Keep the spice in a container with a tight-fitting lid, preferably a screw-on lid, even if this necessitates transferring the spice to a different container. This will help to protect the spices from humidity, and it will help to retard the evaporation and deterioration of aromatic oils.
- If there is space available, store spices in the refrigerator or freezer. This will help to protect them from the other two enemies of spices: heat and light.

Sweeteners

Some kind of sweetener is used in many varieties of sausages. Sweeteners help to mellow the harsh taste of salt, and some of them act as a binder.

WHITE SUGAR

Whenever the word *sugar* is used in this book, please understand it to refer to the common granulated white sugar made from either sugar cane or sugar beets. In some countries—though not in the United States—non-granulated white sugar is more common than the granulated type. If the non-granulated type is used, and if you measure by volume, pack it in the measuring cup or measuring spoon. Use about 10 percent more to achieve the same degree of sweetness.

BROWN SUGAR

Dark brown sugar has a stronger taste than light brown sugar because of a thicker film of molasses on the surface of the crystals. Using brown sugar to flavor sausage is not common, but each one of these sugars can impart a slightly different nuance of flavor to your sausage. Brown sugar is usually not granulated. The common ungranulated brown sugar should be packed firmly in the measuring spoon so that the measurements will be consistent from batch to batch.

HONEY

If you have ever tasted honey-cured ham or bacon, you already know the special flavor that only honey can impart. Use honey as a sweetener for seasoning sausage if you think it will help to achieve your flavor goal. Keep in mind, however, that honey is the sweetest of the sweeteners; a one-to-one substitution for another sweetener might make your product a little too sweet. If honey is substituted for granulated sugar, reduce the amount by 20 percent.

If honey has crystallized, liquefy it by putting the honey jar in a pan of hot water for a few hours. If you need to liquefy it faster than that, use a microwave oven at full power, and zap it for 15 seconds at a time until the honey is clear. Of course, if the honey jar is not made of glass, you will need to use a microwave-proof dish.

CORN SYRUP
In this book, corn syrup is often used as a sweetener and a binder in sausage making. Corn syrup also helps to retain moisture in sausage. The major sweetening component of corn syrup is dextrose (dextrose is also called glucose), but it contains maltose, as well. The colorless variety known as *light* corn syrup is preferred.

MAPLE SYRUP
Natural or artificially flavored maple syrup is occasionally used in sausage making.

To retard mold formation on either natural maple syrup or homemade maple-flavored syrup, store it in the refrigerator or freezer. If it crystallizes, liquefy it as you would liquefy honey (see above).

POWDERED DEXTROSE
Powdered dextrose is made from the starch of corn or, sometimes, of potatoes. Consequently, powdered dextrose is also called corn sugar. It is not as sweet as common sugar. In fresh sausages or in ordinary cured sausages, it is sometimes used in place of common sugar because it helps to prevent the sausage from losing moisture as well as reducing the harsh taste of salt. For such types of sausages, corn syrup may be substituted for dextrose; use 1.5 units of corn syrup for every unit of dextrose specified.

In fermented sausages, dextrose is the best sugar to use to feed the bacteria that produces the lactic acid responsible for the desired tartness.

The easiest way to obtain powdered dextrose is to order it from one of the suppliers mentioned in Appendix 5.

Twine

Cotton twine of the type used to tie rolled roasts is known as butcher's twine. You will find it useful for making ring sausages, tying links, and tying the ends of sausage ropes. It is particularly useful when stuffing fibrous casings or collagen casings.

The diameter of the twine need not be large; I use 1 mm (0.04 inch—between $\frac{1}{32}$ and $\frac{1}{16}$ inch) twine for everything. You can get butcher's twine at a culinary supply shop, but you might discover that a large spool of cotton twine is cheaper at a hardware store—that is where I buy my twine.

Vitamin C and Related Chemicals

Ascorbic acid (vitamin C) and two chemicals related to this acid are permitted by the USDA for use in meat processing. All of these substances function to *accelerate the color development*. They also *stabilize the color* during storage. These two effects can be very important for commercial processors. Rapid color development may lead to reduced processing time. Greater color stability can result in a product remaining attractive, even after days of storage in refrigerated display cases that are struck with artificial light. Without the use of one of these chemicals, the color may fade rapidly, and the product will not be marketable.

The chemicals referred to above that are related to vitamin C are sodium erythorbate and sodium ascorbate. You will often see vitamin C or one of these two chemicals listed as an ingredient on packages of cured sausage and meat.

A person who makes sausage as a hobby has little need for these chemicals, so they are not specified for use in this book. Nevertheless, their mention is deserved because some people have the mistaken impression that vitamin C (ascorbic acid) will function as a color developer (color fixer) in place of nitrites or nitrates. There is at least one book on sausage making and one book on food smoking that says ¼ teaspoon of vitamin C per 5 pounds of ground pork or ground beef will cause the pink or reddish color of the meat to be fixed. It won't; I've tried it.

Apparently, someone in the past thought that a color accelerator was the same thing as a color developer. It is not. None of these chemicals will function as a color developer (color fixer). Furthermore, it must be emphasized that neither vitamin C nor the two related chemicals will provide protection against botulism.

If you need accelerated color development or improved color stability, you may, of course, use one of these three chemicals along with Cure #1. Vitamin C is the least desirable because it can cause depletion of nitrite. Either sodium erythorbate or sodium ascorbate is most often used.

Your pharmacist, or a chemical supply company, may be able to order some for you. Also, you are likely to find sodium erythorbate in the PS Seasoning & Spices catalogue (see Appendix 5). If you must use vitamin C, be sure to use pure crystalline powder. Regardless of which one of the three is used, you should add ⅛ teaspoon (0.625 ml) to 2½ pounds (1.135 kg) of meat. The ⅛ teaspoon of the chemical should not be added directly to the meat. It should be thoroughly mixed with the seasoning ingredients first; this will result in a uniform distribution of the chemical.

CHAPTER 4

Health Matters

In this age, the average adult in any modern country is aware of germs and the most common diseases related to food. We are aware that sanitation prevents the spread of disease, and we know that refrigeration retards spoilage. We are also aware that it is dangerous to eat raw or undercooked pork. This level of knowledge helps to keep us healthy.

The amateur sausage maker, however, needs to have a bit more knowledge about such matters than the average person does. This is because sausage making and sausage smoking involves subjecting the food to conditions that come close to the limits of safe food handling. For example:

- When fresh meat is ground to make sausage, the microbes that are normally on the surface of all meat become mixed with the particles of ground meat.
- Sausage is often smoked in a warm smoker for several hours.
- Some sausage, including some pork sausage, is eaten raw.
- Most sausage is cooked until it is safe to eat, but just barely safe.

Reading this chapter will not qualify a person to become a public health specialist, and it does not cover all the health hazards related to food, but it will provide the basic information that a sausage maker needs know.

Some of the following information may cause concern because it deals with potential health problems related to food. I hope that it will be reassuring for me to mention that in all of the years that I have made sausage and smoked food, not once has the product spoiled during processing, and not once has a product caused food poisoning or any other health-related problem. If safe food-handling guidelines are practiced, sausage making poses no more of a health risk than common cooking.

Trichinosis

The parasitic disease known as trichinosis is most often associated with eating undercooked pork. A little less than 1 percent of hogs in the United States are infected, and one of the main causes of the disease is that pigs are sometimes fed uncooked garbage containing raw pork scraps. Well-informed hunters usually know that bear meat can also harbor these nasty little larvae. Trichinae may be present in the meat of any warm-blooded omnivorous animal, and they exist even in the meat of some carnivorous animals and warm-blooded marine animals such as the seal.

The larvae in consumed meat will mature into adult roundworms in the small intestine of the host animal—or human host. Some of the females will bore a hole in the small intestine of the host and deposit eggs. The resulting larvae enter the bloodstream and burrow into the tissue of various voluntary muscles. The host, as a defense mechanism, forms a coating around each larva. This coating, with the roundworm larva inside, is known as a cyst. In time, the cysts usually become calcified on the outside. The larvae, inside the cysts, remain in the muscles in a dormant condition. If the raw or undercooked flesh of this animal is eaten, the cycle repeats itself.

The cysts, each containing a coiled larva, are about $\frac{1}{50}$ inch (0.51 mm) long. That is about half the length of the comma in this sentence, more or less. Therefore, they are essentially invisible to the naked eye. The U. S. INSPECTED AND PASSED stamp means nothing as far as trichinosis is concerned: The inspection does not include microscopic inspection of the flesh of each hog. Furthermore, even if the flesh of each animal were to be inspected by microscope, cysts may be overlooked.

A drug has been developed to treat trichinosis, but it is much better to avoid contracting the disease in the first place. Intestinal disorders followed by chronic muscular pain are two of the many possible symptoms. This is the bad news. The good news is that it is very easy to kill trichinae before they cause problems. There is no danger in eating pork that has been treated by cooking it properly or by freezing it according to USDA (United States Department of Agriculture) instructions that are described below.

The common way to protect positively against trichinosis is to heat all meat (from susceptible animals) to a *minimum* internal temperature of 137° F

(58.4° C) *throughout.* To be even safer, commercially produced "fully cooked" meats, such as hams and sausages, are usually heated to a minimum internal temperature of between 152° and 154° F (between 67° and 68° C). When we cook pork in the oven or in a frying pan, the internal temperature usually climbs even higher than this.

Another way to kill trichinae in pork is to freeze it according to USDA regulations. Any one of the following USDA approved freezing procedures will definitely kill all the trichinae in pork:

- -20° F (-28.9° C) for 12 days
- -10° F (-23.4° C) for 20 days
- 5° F (-15° C) for 30 days

You may freeze the pork in your home freezer if your freezer temperature is cold enough, but most home freezers will not get that cold. Another consideration is that there are specifications on the thickness and stacking of the meat. Finally, if it is done according to USDA regulations, the temperature of the freezer must be accurately measured and monitored.

It is easier and safer to ask your butcher if he or she can order some *Certified Pork.* Certified Pork has been frozen according to the USDA regulations, and it will not cause trichinosis even if it is eaten raw.

Chain grocery stores may not be able to provide you with Certified Pork unless it is on the list of items for which the butchers can make a special order. However, local meat distributors or meat packers might be able to supply it, especially if they supply local sausage makers. An independently owned grocery store or butcher shop is another possible source. The most commonly available cut of Certified Pork is pork shoulder (Boston butt), and it is usually sold by the carton; one carton contains several frozen shoulders. Be sure that it has some kind of tag, label, or stamp that reads CERTIFIED PORK.

There is only one case where Certified Pork, or the equivalent, *must* be used: when the finished, ready-to-eat product contains uncooked pork. Examples of this are some varieties of fermented sausages. For all other products, use a meat thermometer to make sure that the pork is fully cooked.

Note that in the above discussions of freezing meat to kill trichinae, I used the word *pork.* Strains of trichinae found in some wild animals (especially those that live in cold or arctic climates) may be more resistant to freezing temperatures than the strains found in the domesticated swine. It is risky, therefore, to use the USDA freezing method to kill trichinae in the meat of susceptible *wild* animals such as bear. Kill the trichinae by making sure that the meat is heated to *at least 137° F (58.4° C) throughout.* Better yet—heat it to 160° F (71.1° C).

If you intend to process bear meat, you may be interested in the results of a study by a Montana State University researcher. The study was conducted from 1984 through 1989, and it consisted of inspecting the meat from 275 bears. *Bears infested with trichinae accounted for 15.6 percent of the total inspected.* In another study, this time by the University of Washington, it was reported that trichinae in bear meat might survive the USDA freezing regulations applied to pork. Be safe: *Cook* meat from potentially infested wild animals; don't depend on freezing to kill those insidious roundworm larvae.

You should never put raw or undercooked meat from susceptible animals in your mouth, even though you intend to just taste it and spit it out. Furthermore, always wash the cutting board and knives with hot water and dish detergent if they have been exposed to such meat.

Tularemia

Tularemia (also known as rabbit fever) is a disease of rodents. It is caused by a bacterium that can be transmitted to other animals and humans. If humans contract this disease, it is most often due to handling infected animals or eating the undercooked flesh of infected animals. Tick bites, or bites from bloodsucking flies, can also cause tularemia infection.

This disease can bring on a high fever, chills, headaches, vomiting, swollen lymph nodes, and various skin problems. Fortunately, it is not a fatal disease, and antibiotics will bring about dramatic recovery.

Wild rabbits are the greatest source of tularemia infection for a person who hunts wild game. If you handle wild rabbits, be sure to wear rubber or plastic gloves with no holes in them; it is believed that these bacteria can penetrate even healthy and uncut human skin.

It is perfectly safe to use wild rabbit to make sausage, but it must be cooked as well as pork: 160° F (71° C).

Food Poisoning

SALMONELLA

Salmonella food poisoning is common. (It is sometimes mistakenly called ptomaine poisoning.) The United States Public Health Service estimates that there are as many as 2,000,000 cases of salmonella food poisoning every year in the United States, and the incidence of this kind of poisoning is increasing. It is rarely fatal, but it can cause death in infants, older people, and people who are in poor health. With a little care by those who handle, prepare, and process food, there is little need to fear this disease.

Salmonella has no connection with salmon. The physician who did most of the initial research on these bacteria was named Dr. Daniel E. Salmon, and the bacteria were named in his honor. There are about 400 kinds of bacteria in the salmonella family, and several of them cause the common salmonella food poisoning.

These salmonella bacteria cause gastrointestinal infection. The symptoms may range from mild intestinal cramps to very severe diarrhea. Symptoms usually begin 6 to 48 hours after eating the contaminated food, and they persist for 4 to 16 hours. The right type of antibiotic for this bacterial infection can provide a very effective cure.

The salmonella organisms that cause food poisoning most often occur in eggs (especially in eggs that have a crack in their shell). It also occurs in poultry, meat, and in other kinds of animal products such as whipped cream, as well as in contaminated water. The bacteria cannot be detected by odor, and they can survive in frozen and dried foods. If salmonella bacteria are present, they will multiply at temperatures between 40° F (4.4° C) and 140° F (60° C). Temperatures that approximate the temperature of the human body are most favorable for their proliferation.

Salt and sugar help to prevent the growth of salmonella and other microorganisms. Salt inhibits spoilage and the proliferation of pathogens by reducing the amount of water available for microbial growth. Sugar inhibits spoilage and the proliferation of pathogens by creating an unfavorable environment. Consequently, if a product is smoked at temperatures between 40° and 140° F (4.4° and 60° C), it should contain a substantial amount of salt and sugar, and it should not be smoked with humid air. Do not smoke sausage or other foods in a water smoker below 140° F (60° C).

To prevent salmonella poisoning:

- Keep all utensils clean, especially the cutting boards. Be sure to wash them after they are exposed to raw meat.
- Avoid cracked eggs, unless they will be heated to an internal temperature of 165° F (74° C).
- Store food at 40° F (4° C) or below.

- Thaw meat in a refrigerator, or use the cold water thawing method. Microwave thawing is safe, but it is not recommended for the thawing of meat that will be used to make sausage.
- Do not let raw meat touch other foods.
- Keep hot foods hot.
- Refrigerate or discard leftovers immediately.

Following these simple precautions from the first stage of processing to the point of consumption will greatly reduce the risk of salmonella poisoning and poisoning from other varieties of bacteria. To reduce the risk to zero is impossible, even if you become a strict vegetarian.

The following are other bacteria that cause food poisoning: staphylococcus aureus, campylobacter, listeria monocytogenes, clostridium perfringens, clostridium botulinum, and Escherichia coli O157. A few of these bacteria can also form toxins if the food is stored between 40° F (4° C) and 130° F (54° C) for an extended time, and these toxins cannot be destroyed by normal cooking. Consequently, proper storage not only helps to prevent spoilage, it helps to prevent food poising from pathogens and the toxins that some of them produce.

Clostridium botulinum and E. coli O157 require additional explanation.

BOTULISM

Botulism is a word that was coined by Dr. Emile van Ermengem in 1896 when she was investigating the cause of food poisoning related to the eating of German sausages. *Botulus* means sausage in Latin.

Botulism is an often-fatal form of food poisoning caused by clostridium botulinum. Eating improperly canned foods is the common cause. Another cause is eating preserved foods that have been improperly processed and packed in an airtight plastic package or in an airtight casing. Commercially prepared foods rarely cause botulism because of the precautions taken by commercial processors. Foods improperly processed at home, particularly home-canned foods, are the main culprits.

No food-processing procedures in this book will lead to the formation of botulin, the toxin that causes botulism. However, the processing of smoked sausage could result in botulism if the specified nitrite curing powder is not used.

Clostridium botulinum spores are everywhere. They are in the soil, on fruit and vegetables, and on meat and fish. Consequently, they are also found in the human intestines. The spores themselves are harmless; the poison, called *botulin*, is created only when the spores reproduce. In order for the spores to multiply, several conditions must exist *at the same time*: an airtight environment, a certain temperature range, a favorable chemical environment (non-acidic, for example), and a period of storage favorable for reproduction. The processed food will be free of the toxin if *any one* of these required conditions is eliminated.

None of the processes mentioned in this book specify packing the food in a perfectly airtight container, such as a can or a sealed canning jar. Tightly sealed plastic bags or vacuum packs are suggested for use while cooking, refrigerating, or freezing the product; nevertheless, they are never suggested for storing or processing foods under conditions that might cause spores to reproduce. However, sausage casing that is packed tightly and sealed tightly can approximate an airtight container, so caution is prudent for sausages that will be smoked. The smoking temperature and lengthy smoking time could encourage spore reproduction.

Fortunately, there is a very easy way to make the smoked sausage perfectly safe: Change the chemical composition of the sausage in a way that will positively prevent toxin formation.

There are several ways to do this, but most of these approaches would make the sausage taste awful. There is one way, however, to change the chemical composition of the sausage and make it taste even better: Add a very small amount of sodium nitrite ($NaNO_2$). Toxin formation is positively prevented if a specified amount of this chemical is mixed with the raw sausage. *Not one person has ever been known to contract botulism after eating sausage properly treated with sodium nitrite.* You can feel confident that sausage properly treated with this chemical will be free of the toxin.

One of the commercially produced curing powders known as Prague Powder #1, Instacure #1, or Modern Cure is recommended for treating the sausage. Used as directed, any one of these products will impart exactly the right amount of sodium nitrite into the sausage. The sausage will be wholesome and free of botulin. (Commercial meat processors are required to use sodium nitrite in cooked sausage and luncheon meats, as mandated by the Federal Drug Administration.)

If you decide that you will not use chemical additives for processing your sausage products, you should also decide that you will not make smoked sausage. Untreated raw sausage (also called *fresh sausage*) can be made, cooked, and eaten safely—even if it is stuffed in casings. However, smoked sausage made without the above-mentioned nitrite may be deadly because, as mentioned above, the sausage is usually smoked for a long time in the temperature range that encourages spore reproduction and toxin formation.

E. COLI O157

I had never heard of this bacterium until the summer of 1996. I was living in Japan then, and it became headline news in that country. Almost 10,000 Japanese became ill, and at least eleven people died. Later, I found out that 700 people suffered the same kind of food poisoning in the U. S. in 1993; they ate undercooked ground beef at a hamburger sandwich chain.

E. coli O157 is a new strain of the intestinal bacteria that are known collectively as E. coli. Most of these E. coli bacteria are either harmless or cause temporary intestinal discomfort and diarrhea. However, one of them acquired genes that enabled it to cause severe illness in human beings. In 1982, U. S. scientists isolated it and labeled this new strain. They called it Escherichia coli O157:H7 (E. coli O157 is an abbreviation of the technical name).

Food poisoning caused by E. coli O157 is much more severe than that caused by salmonella food poisoning, and it is very difficult for doctors to treat; antibiotics can worsen the condition. Symptoms appear several days after consuming the contaminated food.

In a technical report published in March of 1995, it is reported that there are a minimum of 20,000 cases of E. coli O157 infection each year, and about 250 of these cases result in death.

Continuing research will clarify much of the mystery surrounding this new health threat, but there are some useful facts available at this time. It appears that non-chlorinated water and almost any food can become contaminated with E. coli O157 bacteria, but meat—particularly beef—deserves special attention. About 1 percent of healthy cattle have E. coli O157 in their intestines. Improper slaughtering can cause contamination of the meat. If this contaminated meat touches other meat or other food—directly or indirectly—contamination can spread.

One outbreak of E. coli O157 infection is especially important for the home sausage maker. From November 16 through December 21, 1994, there were twenty cases of E. coli O157 infection in the state of Washington, and three more cases were identified in northern California. Investigation and testing confirmed that all cases resulted from eating a certain brand of dry-cured salami purchased from the delicatessen counter of a specific chain grocery store. The suspected product was recalled—all 10,000 pounds.

The salami involved in this incident was traditionally dry-cured salami. This type of salami is fermented while it is being slowly dried under controlled temperature and humidity conditions. It is never cooked, and it is intended to be eaten raw. The combination of the lactic acid produced by fermentation and the loss of moisture preserves the sausage and kills the harmful microbes. This dry-cure process has had an excellent safety record for hundreds of years. In this case, however, the *E. coli* O157 present in the sausage were not killed.

Subsequent tests by the USDA have confirmed that *E. coli* O157 can survive the process of fermenting and dry curing. The USDA is currently doing research to develop processing techniques that will insure the destruction of this bacterium in dry-cured sausage. In the meantime, the producers of dry-cured sausage of any variety are being required to validate (prove) that their process results in a sausage that will be safe to eat. Some processors accomplished this by using a longer fermentation process; other processors used thermal treatment. (Thermal treatment means heating the sausage to a certain temperature and maintaining that temperature for a certain number of minutes.) However, many processors of dry-cured sausage have gone out of business; some refuse to change the traditional curing process to a process that will result in an inferior product, and other producers have found the validation requirements to be too burdensome or too expensive.

What does all this mean for people who make sausage at home? It seems to be clear that it is no longer safe for the average person to make dry-cured sausage. The meat that we might use for dry-cured sausage today, or next week, may not be contaminated by *E. coli* O157, but there is a chance that we will unwittingly use contaminated meat sometime in the future. If we use that meat to make dry-cured sausage using traditional methods, the people who eat that product could become very ill, or even die. If that same meat is used to make fully cooked sausage, the sausage will be perfectly safe because the *E. coli* O157 will be killed. The same precautions used to reduce the risk of salmonella food poisoning, or any other food poisoning, are equally effective for *E. coli* O157; cooking sausage to an internal temperature of 160° F (71° C) will kill *E. coli* O157.

In this book, there are recipes for salami, summer sausage, Thuringer, and the like, but they will be of the fully cooked variety. Instead of fermenting the sausages, a product called Fermento will be suggested. This commercially prepared product contains lactic acid, and gives the sausage a taste similar to fermented sausage. Some of these products will be *semi*dry-cured, but they will be fully cooked.

Although we can no longer make dry-cured sausages at home safely, I do not think that it is a great loss. In the culinary world, it is commonly believed that making dry-cured sausages is the most difficult task that can be attempted with meat. Special rooms or enclosures with round-the-clock temperature and humidity control are required. But even with these special rooms or enclosures, failure must be expected because it occurs as often as success. Dry-curing sausage is so difficult that many chefs with excellent credentials will not attempt it.

Nitrites and Nitrates

At least as early as ancient Rome, impure salts that were mined from certain locations were used to cure meats. The salts from some of these locations were prized for their ability to flavor meats and to give the meats a reddish or pink color, even when fully cooked. A few hundred years ago, it was realized that nitrates were the impurities in those salts that caused the unique flavor and the color fixing effect noted by the ancients. Since then, nitrates have been added to pure salt to cure meats and sausage. The most commonly used nitrate was potassium nitrate (KNO_3, commonly called saltpeter), but sodium nitrate ($NaNO_3$, also known as saltpeter or, less confusingly, as Chile saltpeter) has also been widely used. The Federal Meat Inspection Act of 1906 officially authorized the use of nitrates for the curing of commercial meat products.

Later on in the early 1900s, scientists discovered that the nitrates used for curing would slowly break down into nitrites. It was also discovered that those nitrites were the chemicals that led to the color fixing and flavor changes. Consequently, the U. S. government permitted the direct use of nitrites to cure meats, but placed a limit on the amount that could be used.

In the late 1960s, it became clear that the use of nitrates and nitrites could cause nitrosamines to be formed under certain conditions, and nitrosamines in substantial amounts were known to act as carcinogens in test animals. Therefore, in the early 1970s, there was much research and discussion about this. Tentative conclusions and a set of guidelines regarding nitrite and nitrate usage were issued in 1975, and there have been no significant changes in the guidelines since that time—this is in spite of continuing research.

Several problems confound this research: Nitrates and nitrites occur naturally in human saliva, in vegetables, and quite often in drinking water. For example, celery, beets, and radishes contain between 2700 and 1600 PPM (parts per million) of nitrites. The ham and sausages commonly available at a grocery store will contain not more than 156 PPM of nitrites.

Below is a summary of the most important considerations and conclusions made by researchers and government policymakers:

- The risk of botulism in some kinds of cured meat is very great. Nitrates and nitrites are the only palatable additives presently available that will positively prevent this often-deadly form of food poisoning.
- Though nitrosamines can cause cancer in test animals, it is not clear whether they will cause cancer in humans.
- Tests on commercially prepared products occasionally show trace amounts of nitrosamines, but the amounts detected are much lower than the amount that would be required to cause cancer in test animals.

The net result is that the danger from botulism is a real danger if these chemicals were to be banned. The degree of danger from nitrosamines posed by the continued use of these chemicals is unknown. Actually, there may be no danger at all. Considering these points, it was decided to continue to permit these chemicals to be used in some products (bacon, for example), and to mandate that they be used when there is a clear botulism hazard (smoked sausage in casing, for example). At the same time, however, they placed many restrictions on the usage of these chemicals in order to minimize the risk of exposure to nitrosamines. This approach allowed the continued production of traditionally cured products, preserved the protection against botulism offered by nitrates and nitrites, and minimized the exposure to carcinogens.

One significant restriction is that nitrates (not nitrites) are banned for all products, except fermented sausage and products cured with traditional dry cure. (Such products undergo a lengthy curing process, so the slower dissipation rate of nitrates is required.) Another change was that the amount of nitrites permitted in various categories of foods was reduced.

Of course, the U. S. government cannot prevent an amateur sausage maker from using nitrates and, furthermore, can't regulate the amount of *any* additive he or she uses. Nevertheless, since the federal regulations for the commercial use of nitrites and nitrates are for protecting our health, it is in our interest to follow those regulations to the extent possible. Consequently, nitrates are not specified for use in any sausage curing procedure in this book because fermented sausage formulations and processes are not presented.

Government regulations for commercial products specify nitrite content in *parts per million* (PPM), and the required or permissible amount differs according to the product. For example, more nitrite is required in sausage than is allowed in bacon. Since few of us have the equipment or expertise to measure nitrite in PPM, we will rely on the commercial curing powders—these curing powders must also meet federal regulations. Used as directed, they are formulated to give you a product that will be within government regulations—a product that will positively prevent botulism and pose zero to minimal risk from nitrosamine exposure.

CHAPTER 5

Grinding, Mixing, and Stuffing

Preparing the Meat

Note: Before reading this section, it might be helpful to review the "Meat" section in Chapter 3.

The meat to be ground for sausage should be fresh and well chilled—but not frozen. A little more meat than the recipe requires should be prepared to allow for trimming waste.

Trimming and cutting should be done on a clean plastic cutting board; cutting boards made of wood can harbor bacteria. With a boning knife, remove all blood clots, bone, and as much connective tissue as possible. It is impossible and unnecessary to remove all connective tissue, but try to cut out and discard tissue that is gristly, or tissue that might jam the cutting knife of the grinder.

Most sausage formulas suggest that the meat should contain about 25 percent fat. Here are two ways to get the fat-to-lean ratio you want:

- After the meat has been trimmed, cut the fat away from the lean. Precision cutting is not required here; if the fat and lean are roughly separated, that is fine. Now you can easily weigh the amount of fat and lean you want. This is a fast and reasonably accurate way for a home sausage maker to get the desired ratio.
- Probably the most widely used method for home sausage making is to look at the meat and make a guess as whether fat needs to be added or

removed. Experience will improve accuracy of judgment. Pork shoulder butt (also called Boston butt) contains about the correct amount of fat. For beef, selected beef chuck usually contains the proper ratio of lean to fat.

It is best to cut a large hunk of meat into slabs about ¾ inch (2 cm) thick, and then proceed to cut the slabs into ¾-inch (2 cm) cubes. A medium or large chef's knife with a stepped blade works best for cubing. The size and shape of the cut meat is not critical; the sole purpose of cutting the meat is to prepare pieces that will go into the hopper of the grinder easily. It is not important for the pieces of meat to have a cubical shape.

After weighing and preparing the correct amount of each kind of meat and fat, return the cubes to the refrigerator until they are thoroughly chilled. In fact, anytime the meat is not being worked on in some way (trimming, cutting, grinding, stuffing, smoking, etc.), it should be chilling in the refrigerator. Because this is so important, most recipes in this book suggest that the meat should be refrigerated after certain steps. *Here is a hint that is not mentioned in most of the recipes*: If you want to proceed to the next step soon, and you want the chilling to be accomplished as fast as possible, put the meat in the freezer rather than in the fridge. It should not stay in the freezer long enough to freeze, but no harm will be done if the bulk meat, the cubes, or the ground meat is a little crunchy on top.

Pork shoulder being cubed.

Grinding the Meat

Note: It might be helpful to review the section "Meat grinders (meat choppers or meat mincers)" in Chapter 2.

A food processor can be used to shred the meat. If you have a powerful food processor, you might wish to try it. However, if a food processor is used, small amounts of meat should be shredded at a time; this will reduce the strain on the machine. Be careful not to process the meat too long—the particles will be too fine.

Even though a food processor will do the job quickly, a meat grinder will provide a better texture because it will mince or chop the meat instead of shredding it. A meat grinder will also allow the fat to be ground finer or coarser than the red meat; this is necessary for some sausages.

All meat grinders work in the same way, whether they are powered by arm muscle or electricity. The desired plate (fine, medium, or coarse) is placed in front of the knife (chopping blades), the collar is screwed on tightly, cubed meat is stuffed into the hopper, and the handle is rotated—or the switch is turned on. That is about all there is to it, but a few pointers may be helpful, and a few techniques may be useful.

Meat being ground with a manual grinder.

When the meat is ground and the particles are extruded from the holes in the plate, the stream of particles coming out of each hole should be distinct from the other streams. If the streams blend into a sticky mass or look mushy, this is called *smear*, and grinding should stop until the problem is corrected. There are three possible causes for smear:

- The meat is too warm. It should been chilled to almost the freezing point. However, fat can be ground when it is frozen. Chill the meat and try again.
- The collar that holds the plate and chopping blades together is not tight. Tighten the collar.
- Sinew and other connective tissues are clogging the holes in the plate, or they are tangled around the chopping blades and plate. Unscrew the collar, clean the plate and chopping blades, and reassemble. Make sure the sharp edges of the blades are flat against the plate.

Some sausage makers separate the fat and the red meat, and they grind the fat a little finer than the muscle meat. The theory is that if the fat is fine, it will be more evenly distributed in the sausage, and less fat can be used to achieve the same taste. The theory sounds plausible, but when fat is ground without being mixed with muscle meat, the ground fat tends to clump together, and separating the clumps into particles is tedious. Techniques for dealing with this problem will be explained a little later.

There is another reason for grinding the fat finer than the muscle tissue. Coarsely ground muscle meat has less surface area than the same weight of finely ground muscle meat. Consequently, less fat is required to moisten the surface of the muscle meat particles if the particles are large.

The technique I use for most sausage grinding is easier than grinding the fat separately, and I think it gives about the same results. I roughly separate the meat and the fat, cut the meat into ¾-inch (2 cm) chunks, and cut the fat into smaller chunks. Then I mix the meat and the fat together and grind it. This technique helps to reduce the tendency of the fat to clump, and distributes the fat very well. After grinding, however, the meat and fat particles are the same size.

For common sausages, most people use neither one of the techniques mentioned above; they grind all the fat and muscle meat together without making any special effort with the fat grinding or distribution.

However, for some sausages, a very special effort must be made when working with the fat. Salami and some Asian sausages must have very noticeable

The plate collar on both mechanical and electrical grinders may be difficult to loosen after grinding cold meat. Loosen the collar by tapping gently with a wooden dowel and hammer.

specks of white fat. Mortadella has cubes of fat mixed with a sausage paste that looks much like the sausage paste for bologna. This highly visible fat in certain varieties of sausage helps to define the kind of sausage. If it does not have the white specks, for example, it is not salami. If it does not have cubes of fat mixed with the sausage paste, it is not mortadella.

No matter how you are grinding the meat, when you get to the end of the grinding session, there may be hunks of meat and fat just behind the plate that the auger was not able to push into the path of the chopping blades. Ignoring this meat and discarding it is the easiest thing to do, but it may be wasteful. If there is some useable meat behind the chopping blades (much of this will be unusable gristle and sinew), it can be minced with the chef's knife and added to the sausage mixture.

Mixing the Meat and Ingredients

After the meat has been ground and is chilling in the refrigerator or freezer, the seasoning and other ingredients are prepared and blended.

It is important that the finished sausage paste be perfectly blended and uniform before it is made into patties or stuffed. This goal is likely to be accomplished if all the seasoning ingredients are uniformly blended before the ground meat is added. Also, it is easier to accomplish this if at least one of the ingredients is a fluid: water, wine, broth, beer, juice, etc. The fluid dissolves, or partially dissolves, most of the other ingredients, and it acts as a carrier to spread the ingredients uniformly throughout the ground meat.

All the sausages in this book are prepared in this way; all ingredients except the ground meat are blended first, and this blend is always a thin paste or a viscous liquid. This seasoning should be prepared in a mixing bowl large enough to mix in the meat—at least a 5-quart (5 liter) bowl if 2½ lbs. (1,150 g) of sausage will be made. No matter where a recipe is obtained, it is an easy matter to change the recipe so that all seasoning ingredients are mixed with water or some other liquid before blending with ground meat. If this procedure is followed and the meat is blended properly, the taste of the entire batch of sausage will be uniform. If a recipe from another book, from the Internet, or wherever says to sprinkle the seasoning on the ground meat and mix it, this may result in some sausages tasting differently from other sausages in the same batch. For best results, change the recipe so that the spices and other ingredients are mixed together with a liquid before the ground meat is added.

The fluid-seasoning blend should be chilled before the ground meat is mixed with it. While the ground meat and the seasoning blend are being chilled, it is a good time to take a well-deserved break. Or, if you still have energy, use this time to wash the meat grinder and put it away; final cleanup will be faster and easier if that is done.

After the seasoning mixture is thoroughly chilled in the large mixing bowl, add the ground meat to the same bowl. The ground meat and seasoning paste must be mixed with the hands or with a heavy-duty standing mixer. Mixing with a wooden spoon, or the like, requires much energy, is tedious, and it will not do the job.

After one or two mixing sessions, mixing up to 5 lbs. (2,270 g) of sausage by hand becomes very easy. For sanitary reasons, and to insulate the hands from the ice-cold meat, it is best to wear rubber gloves. First, flatten the mixture in the bottom of the bowl with your fists, then fold it in half, and flatten it again with your fists. Next, spin the bowl about 90 degrees clockwise by twisting the fists, fold the mass again, and flatten it again with your fists. (It is a type of kneading process—similar to kneading dough.) Continue doing this until the ground meat and seasoning mixture looks uniform. From start to finish, mixing by hand will require about three minutes.

Mixing ground meat with seasoning.

If a mixer is used, it should be something like an upright 5- or 6-quart (5 to 6 liter) KitchenAid mixer with a paddle attachment. (Please see *Food mixers* in Chapter 2.) Mix for about one minute at slow speed and one minute at medium speed.

The friction involved in mixing the sausage generates heat, so the sausage needs to be thoroughly chilled again in the freezer or refrigerator before making patties or stuffing into casings. The making of patties or stuffing should be done the same day, however. If the bulk sausage is allowed to set in the refrigerator overnight, the salt causes the mixture to become stiff, and it will be difficult to stuff.

Preparing the Natural Casings

For home use, it is best to purchase casings that have been packed in salt; such casings can be preserved for years under refrigeration. If, however, you are using casings that have been packed in a preservative solution, they can be used immediately after a brief rinse; the preparation steps below need not be followed. Unfortunately, these casings have a shelf life of only about one month.

Flushing the inside of a natural casing (hog casing).

Natural casings that have been packed in salt are prepared for use by the following steps.

1. Measure the length of casing required for stuffing the batch of sausage. About 7 feet (210 cm) of small-diameter hog casing is required for 2½ lbs. (1,150 g) of sausage, and about 14 feet (420 cm) of the large-diameter sheep casing will be required. It is best to cut a little more than you think you will need; leftover casing can be returned to the container and re-salted with plain salt for future use. (Using a ruler or a tape measure to measure the length of the casing is awkward. It is better to use some kind of gauge. For example, the distance from the left side of my kitchen sink to the center of the drain is 1 foot, and I use this as a gauge to measure natural casing.)
2. Tie a short piece of string around the cut end of the casing remaining in the casing container so that the end will be easy to find next time.
3. Place the measured casing in a bowl, dishpan, or pot. Fill the container with cold water, and rinse the salt from the surface of the casing. Change the water about three times.
4. Open one end of the casing, and let water flow through the inside of the casing for a minute or so—slowly at first—until the casing has fully opened

and the water is flowing through it freely. Occasionally, there will be a hole or a tear in the casing. Cut out this bad part.

5. Place the rinsed casing in a small, non-reactive container with a tight-fitting lid; add about a cup of water and refrigerate for use the next morning. *Optional:* Add 1 tablespoon of vinegar per each cup of water before refrigerating. *Note: The acid in the vinegar causes the casing to become puffy and rubber-like, and this results in a more tender cooked casing. However, most sausage makers, including myself, do not use vinegar in the water, so it would be wise to compare the two techniques. Two negative points about using vinegar are that the casing is a little more difficult to slide on the stuffing horn, and that leftover casing should be discarded because the vinegar causes profound changes in the casing.*

Note: If there is not enough time to rinse the casing the day before and refrigerate it overnight, it may be rinsed very well and soaked in lukewarm water for only 30 minutes. The casing might not be as tender and will not be as slippery, but it will be useable.

Making Sausage Patties

Generic bulk sausage that is purchased in a grocery store is usually sold in a Styrofoam tray. However, a nationally known brand of bulk breakfast sausage—such as Jimmy Dean's breakfast sausage—is usually sold in a plastic ground-meat tube. If it is sold in a ground-meat tube, the raw sausage can be sliced into patties by cutting through the tube at approximately ⅜-inch (10 mm) intervals.

Similar ground meat tubes (also called *bags*) can be purchased wherever sausage casings are sold, but making patties using a mold is a cheaper and better option. A metal ground-meat mold that will make one patty at a time can be purchased, but the homemade patty mold described below is better; the homemade mold will make four patties at a time. I made the mold shown in the photographs in 1993, and I have used it countless times since then. The mold was cut from ⅜-inch (1 cm) plywood, and the diameter of each hole is 2½ inches (6.3 cm). Because it is coated with polyurethane varnish, it will withstand washing in hot, soapy water for a lifetime. In fact, it will certainly last long enough for me to pass it along to my grandchildren. It is very easy to use, and it produces patties of uniform size and thickness efficiently.

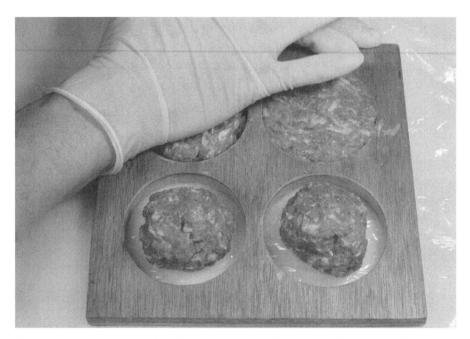

A homemade sausage mold is placed on a sheet of plastic food wrap, and balls of bulk sausage (sausage paste) are slapped with the palm of the hand to make patties.

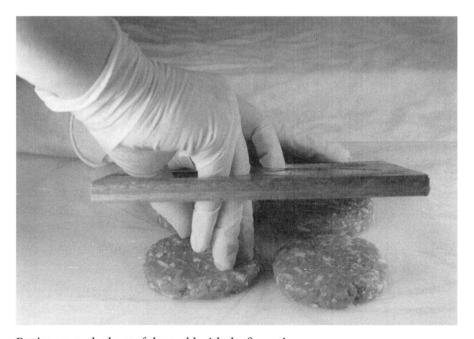

Patties are pushed out of the mold with the fingertips.

Four patties are wrapped together in plastic food wrap and frozen.

HOW TO USE A HOMEMADE SAUSAGE MOLD

1. Tear off about 18 inches (45 cm) of plastic food wrap, and spread it on the counter top. Place the homemade sausage mold in the middle of the food wrap.
2. Place an egg-sized ball of bulk sausage in the middle of each of the four mold holes.
3. Slap the top of each ball of bulk sausage repeatedly with the palm of your hand until the sausage fills the mold. Add or remove a small amount of sausage, if necessary.
4. Lift one edge of the mold, and gently push the patties out of each of the mold holes. Let the patties fall back down on the food wrap.
5. Remove the mold completely, and fold over the edges of the plastic food wrap—left, right, top, and bottom—to make an airtight package for the four patties.
6. Stack the sausage packages on a dinner plate or other flat surface, and place in the freezer.

Stuffing Hog and Sheep Casings

Note: Before stuffing hog or sheep casings for the first time, it might be helpful to review the section on "Natural casings" in Chapter 3, and the section "Preparing the natural casings" in this chapter (above).

The directions below assume that you are using a cast-iron, an upright, or another similar stuffer. If you are using a stuffer attachment for a manual or electric meat grinder, two people will be required, and the tasks indicated below will have to be divided so that one person feeds the sausage paste into the grinder, and the other person does the tasks associated with stuffing the casing.

The end of the hog or sheep casing is opened, and water (for lubrication) is dipped into the open end.

Stuffing natural sausage casing is easy to do, but there are a few pointers that should make the learning process go a little faster.

1. Remove the prepared casing from the refrigerator. Rinse the casing one more time, and allow it to set in lukewarm water for about 30 minutes. The final soaking in lukewarm water makes it a little easier to slide on the stuffing tube.
2. Just before the casing is slid onto the stuffing tube, open the end of the casing, and dip the open end below the surface of the water. When this open

end is raised, you will have scooped water into the casing. Do this several times so that there will be a puddle of water inside; this puddle will lubricate the casing interior as it is being slid onto the stuffing tube.

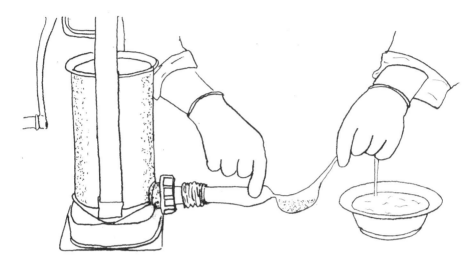

A puddle of water inside the casing provides lubrication as it is slid on the stuffing tube.

3. Attach the proper size stuffing tube to the stuffer. Use a ¾-inch (2 cm) tube for hog casings, and use a ½-inch or ⅝-inch (13 or 16 mm) tube for sheep casings. The main idea is that the casing should fit loosely on the tube, but not too loosely.

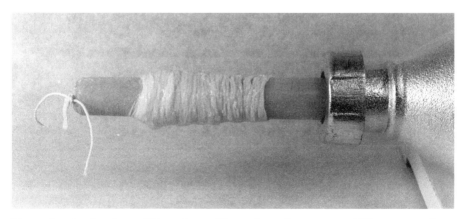

Natural casing has been slid on the stuffing tube and compressed like an accordion. Twine has been used to close the end of the casing.

4. Wet the entire length of the stuffing tube with water, and slide the wet casing onto the tube. Bunch the casing on the tube so that it looks something like a compressed accordion (see photo). If the casing will not slide on easily, the casing can be elevated so that the puddle of water will flow to the stuffing tube and lubricate it. If the puddle of water in the casing is used up, open the far end of the casing and add a little more water. Raise the far end of the casing so that the water flows to the stuffing tube and lubricates it.

5. The hog or sheep casing should be slid on the stuffing tube before the sausage paste is loaded into the stuffer. The reason is this: Sliding the entire length of casing on the stuffing tube takes time, especially for those of us who are learning the technique. And, during this time, the sausage paste will gradually become warmer if it has been put in the stuffer in advance; this is not good. Sausage paste should be stuffed in the casing quickly and efficiently while it is cold, and then the stuffed casings should be returned to the refrigerator immediately.

6. If you are using a lever-operated stuffer, filling the stuffer *half full* with the seasoned sausage mixture will allow the handle to provide greater force (greater leverage) to the pressure plate. If a gear-operated stuffer is used, the cylinder may be packed with as much sausage as it will hold. No matter which kind of stuffer is being used, it is important to pack the sausage paste in the stuffer a little at a time, using your fist to pound out the air pockets. The fewer the air pockets in the sausage paste, the fewer the air pockets in the sausage links.

7. Press the stuffer lever handle down (or rotate the gear crank) so that a small amount of sausage begins to emerge from the tube. Slide about 1½ inches (4 cm) of casing off the end of the tube. Force all the air out of the end of the casing, and tie a knot at the end. Alternatively, close the end of the casing by using twine. I find that twine is faster, easier, and wastes less casing, but most people tie a knot in the casing.

8. If you are right-handed, you will probably be most comfortable if you operate the stuffer handle (or crank) with your right hand. With the thumb and fingers of your left hand, slide the casing off the end of the tube as the sausage paste is being forced out. Keep your left hand cupped under the tube and toward the front of the tube; part of the palm should support the sausage casing as it is being filled. As you can see, your left hand will be very busy.

Hog casing being stuffed with a 5 pound Grizzly Industrial vertical stuffer, Model H6252. *Photo courtesy Grizzly Industrial, Inc.*

9. When the sausage mixture is forced into the casing, the goal is for the stuffed casing to have a uniform diameter and to be rather firm—but not so firm that the casing ruptures when you are twisting the sausage to form links. If an air pocket appears in the casing at any time, prick it right away with a sausage pricker or a large needle. When the stuffer will no longer force sausage paste into the casing, there will be a small amount of sausage remaining in the front of the stuffer body, and the stuffer tube (horn) will be full of sausage paste. Discarding this is wasteful. Remove the stuffing tube from the body of the stuffer and use the handle of a wooden spoon, or use a wooden dowel, to push the remaining paste into the casing. (I made three dowels of wood for this purpose. The three dowels' diameters match the internal diameters of the three sizes of stuffing tubes. The dowels were coated with polyurethane varnish to make them easy to clean.) Make a patty with sausage remaining in the stuffer, fry it, and treat yourself to a snack.

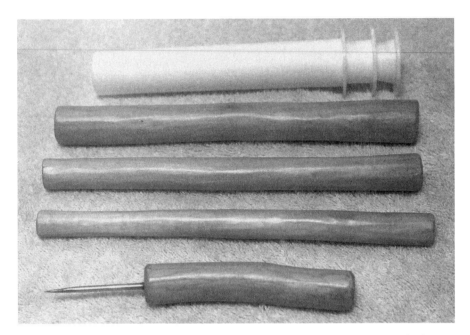

Three diameters of stuffing tubes and three diameters of homemade dowels that are used to push sausage paste into the casing when the stuffer has become empty. A homemade sausage casing perforator is at the bottom of the photo.

10. Links can be made any length. Start from either end of the sausage rope. To make 5-inch (13 cm) links, pinch the sausage 5 inches (13 cm) from the end of the rope with the thumb and index finger of one hand, and 10 inches (26 cm) from the end of the rope with the thumb and index finger of the other hand. Then, twist the link between your hands four or five revolutions clockwise. Pinch the rope again in two places that are located 5 and 10 inches (13 and 26 cm), respectively, from the last twist. Twirl this new link counterclockwise—or clockwise; the direction of the twist is not very important. Continue making links until the other end of the rope is reached. It is best to use some kind of gauge to make sure that the links are the same size; something like a measuring stick, masking tape stuck on the counter, or two marks on a sheet of paper will work well as a gauge. Masking tape works best for me.

Coiling the sausage rope conserves countertop space.

Measuring and making sausage links.

Stuffing Collagen Casings

Note: Before stuffing collagen casing sleeves for the first time, it might be helpful to review the section on "Collagen casing" in Chapter 3.

Stuffing collagen casing sleeves is no more difficult than stuffing natural casings, but there are several points that require caution and attention.

- Collagen casings sleeves are stuffed dry; they are never rinsed or soaked in water before using.
- If the collagen sleeve is longer than the stuffing tube, the sleeve must be cut in half, and half the sleeve is stuffed at one time.
- If there is a taper in the stuffing tube that prevents the sleeve from sliding all of the way on the stuffing tube, the sleeve must be cut in half, and half the sleeve is stuffed at one time.
- If collagen casing is twisted into links, the links will unwind easily. It is best to use butcher's twine to separate the links and to tie the ends of the sausage rope.
- Unlike natural casing, collagen casing is not elastic. Consequently, it is more difficult to stuff the right amount of sausage paste in the casing.

Except for the special considerations listed above, the stuffing of the collagen casing is much like the stuffing of a natural casing. The main difference is that collagen casing is not slid off the end of the tube as it is being stuffed. Instead, the accordion-like pleats near the end of the tube are gradually unfolded by gently pulling the casing as the sausage is being stuffed.

Stuffing Fibrous Casings

The common way to stuff fibrous casings is with the largest horn of the sausage stuffer. First, the fibrous casing is prepared for use by following the manufacturer's instructions. If the manufacturer's instructions are not available, soak it in warm water for 30 minutes. Be sure to put some warm water inside the casing.

Slide the casing on the stuffing horn, bunching the casing on the horn so it looks something like a compressed accordion—this is similar to the way natural casings are put on a stuffing horn, but the fibrous casing will be very loose. Initially, the bottom of the casing should be at the end of the stuffing tube.

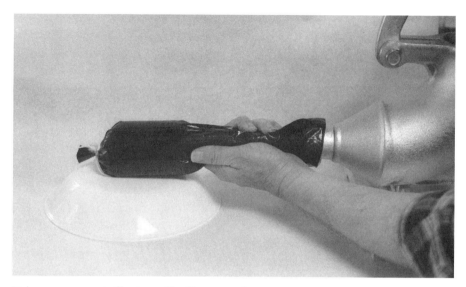

Using a sausage stuffer to stuff a fibrous casing.

One chub has been closed with spring-loaded hog ring pliers, and the other one was closed with twine.

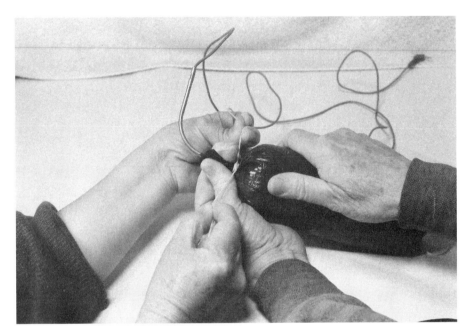

A cable probe for an electronic thermometer has been inserted into the top of the chub before closing it with twine.

Hold the casing tightly around the front part of the sausage horn with your left hand (if you are right-handed). Pump the sausage paste into the bottom of the casing, and let the casing slide off the horn as it fills with sausage paste. Take care that air pockets are not trapped inside. When the fibrous casing is almost full, twist the top closed, and seal it with a hog ring or butcher's twine. (Of course, butcher's twine must be used if a thermometer probe has been inserted into the top of the casing.)

Using a funnel with a very large diameter spout is another way to stuff fibrous casings—and it is very efficient. (I usually use a funnel because it is faster than using a sausage stuffer and—more importantly—cleanup is very easy.) Slide the casing on the funnel spout in the same way as described above, and pack the sausage into the casing with a large diameter dowel while the casing is held tightly around the spout with the left hand. Suitable funnels are difficult to find, however. Some kitchenware specialty shops stock them. Such funnels are probably intended for loading a container with solid foodstuffs such as dry beans or whole grain.

A large funnel for stuffing a fibrous casing.

CHAPTER 6

Cooking Sausage

The last step in making a great sausage is cooking it properly. It is just as important as carefully grinding, seasoning, and mixing it.

Most sausage is cooked (dry-cured sausage is the main exception), and if the cooking is done improperly, it can ruin an otherwise perfect sausage. Sausage is delicate, and no matter what method of cooking is used, it must be slow and gentle if the best result is desired. Overcooking is the most common mistreatment of sausage; it must be avoided.

Any method of cooking will accomplish the primary goals: to change the raw meat to cooked meat, to prevent parasitic diseases, and to kill pathogenic microbes. However, in addition to the primary goals, we want to prevent, to the extent possible, the escape of juices and melted fats. These fluids make the sausage delicious and succulent, and careful cooking helps to keep them in the sausage.

Important Note: The United States Department of Agriculture (USDA), together with the Food Safety and Inspection Service (FSIS), recommends that ground beef, pork, mutton, and similar ground meats be cooked until the internal temperature reaches a minimum of 160° F (71° C).

For ground poultry, 165° F (74° C) is the recommended minimum internal temperature. In April 2006, the recommended minimum internal temperature for ground poultry was changed from 160° F (71° C) to 165° F (74° C) because of the high risk of salmonella contamination and because of salmonella's acquisition of some resistance to being killed by heat.

If these recommended temperatures are reached for even one second, there is no risk of food poisoning. Actually, the temperatures could be 155° F (68° C) and 158° F (69° C), respectively, and there still would be no risk of food poisoning. (The recommended minimum temperatures have a safety factor of a few degrees for several reasons: thermometers are not always accurately calibrated; temperature measurements of one or two samples are not always representative of the entire lot; the thermometer is often not placed in the coolest part—usually the exact center—of the sausage.)

The recommended temperatures mentioned above are for the benefit of the average consumer like you and me. If we have a reasonably accurate thermometer and exercise care when measuring the internal temperature, the sausage should be safe to eat if heated to the recommended temperature.

Actually, the same level of pathogen kill can be accomplished at a lower temperature if that temperature is maintained for sufficient time; the microbes are not killed by temperature alone—they are killed by time and temperature working together. For example, the same level of safety can be accomplished by maintaining the internal temperature of the sausage at 145° F (63° C) for 4 minutes. The sausage will be just as safe to eat as sausage that has reached an internal temperature of 160° F (71° C). (The time that a certain temperature is maintained is called the "dwell time.") Below, *for reference only*, is a list of dwell times approved by USDA/FSIS for meat products that do not contain poultry:

- 130° F (54.4° C)….. 121 minutes
- 135° F (57.2° C)….. 37 minutes
- 140° F (60.0° C)….. 12 minutes
- 145° F (62.8° C)….. 4 minutes
- 150° F (65.6° C)….. 72 seconds
- 155° F (68.3° C)….. 23 seconds
- 160° F (71.1° C)….. 0 seconds

Most commercial sausage processors use the lower temperatures with appropriate dwell times when "fully cooked" sausage (or solid meat, such as ham, for example) is being produced. Unfortunately, the expensive processing equipment required for this is not available to the person who makes sausage in the kitchen at home. You may see sausage recipes in books, magazines, and on the Internet that specify lower internal temperatures, but I believe food safety is paramount. Consequently, in this book, cooking instructions follow the USDA recommendations for the normal consumer preparing food in a common residential kitchen.

Sausage Cooking Technology 101

Let's look at what is happening inside a sausage while it is cooking. This will help us to understand the best ways to cook it.

- Animal fats do not have a specific melting point. First, they soften as the temperature rises, and then they gradually turn to liquid. Poultry fats and wildfowl fats have low melting points, and if these fats are being used in the sausage, some of these bird fats will become semi-liquid when the internal temperature of the sausage reaches about 70° F (21° C). Medium hard fat, such as pork back fat, is more desirable because it melts at a higher temperature.

- The minced muscle-meat particles inside the sausage casing are coated with a protein called *myosin*; salt used in the sausage draws the *myosin* to the surface of each particle. When the temperature of the sausage mixture reaches 120° F (50° C), this protein begins to coagulate, causing these muscle-meat particles to stick together. This coagulation is complete at about 130° F (55° C), and the result is that the coagulated meat particles surround both fat particles and liquefied fat. When the fat continues to melt and juices are produced, the coagulated meat particles will help to retain them. This step is best accomplished slowly, with moderate heat.

- Pathogenic microbes, if any are present, will begin to be killed as the internal temperature rises above 130° F (55° C). The killing is faster as the temperature rises and the dwell time increases.

- If the sausage has been cured with a curing powder containing sodium nitrite, the pink or rosy color of the meat will be fixed when the sausage mixture reaches about 135° F (57° C).

- Trichinae in pork, and in meat from other susceptible animals, are killed when the sausage reaches 137° F (58° C).

- At 140° F (60° C), the sausage mixture begins to shrink, but it is unlikely that the juices and melted fats will be lost if there are no holes in the casing. If the sausage was not cured with a nitrite curing powder, the red meat in the mixture will begin to change to pink, and pink meat will begin to change to gray-brown.

- At 150° F (66° C), the meat in the sausage continues to shrink and a little fluid may be lost. Uncured meat that was originally red will begin to change from pink to gray-brown.

- Salmonella, *E. coli* O157, and all other pathogenic microbes are killed by the time the sausage reaches 155° F (68° C). At this point, the sausage is fully cooked and safe to eat. However, to provide an extra margin of safety, cooking should continue until an internal temperature of 160° F (71° C) is reached. However, the USDA recommends 165° F (74° C) for all sausage containing ground poultry. (Please use this temperature as the target temperature if the sausage contains fowl and you wish to follow the USDA recommendation.) There will be more shrinking, and there will be some loss of juices and melted fats.

- At 160° F (71° C)—or at 165° F (74° C) if the sausage contains bird meat—cooking should stop. Cooking beyond this point will cause the sausage to become increasingly dry and mealy. If excessive heat builds up in the casing, the casing might split open.

The information above provides a wealth of hints about the proper techniques for cooking. We can see, for example, that an important concern is the shrinkage of the meat that occurs from 140° F (60° C) until the cooking is finished; shrinkage is the primary cause of fluid loss. We can also see that overcooking will make the sausage dry and mealy, and may even cause the casing to split.

Another point that is perhaps less obvious is that the cooking heat surrounding the sausage should be as low as possible (just a little above the target temperature) to prevent overcooking of the sausage mixture just under the casing.

There is an important phenomenon related to the temperature of the cooking heat: The temperature at the center of the sausage will continue to rise even after it is removed from the heat source. This is caused by the fact (mentioned above) that the temperature of the sausage mixture just under the casing is higher than that at the center, and some of this heat will migrate to the center after the sausage is removed from the heat source.

The culinary jargon for this phenomenon is *afterheat*. What this means to us is that the sausage should be removed from the heat source *before* the internal temperature reaches the target temperature of 160° F (71° C)—or 165° F (74° C). The temperature at which the sausage should be removed from the heat source is dictated by many factors, so there is no formula to help make this decision. Two of the important factors are the temperature of the cooking heat and the diameter of the sausage. The higher the cooking heat temperature and the larger the diameter of the sausage, the greater the afterheat will be. For small-diameter sausages cooked with low heat, afterheat is so slight that it may be ignored.

Experience with your preferred cooking method and your favorite casing diameter for a particular sausage will allow you to make accurate predictions of the afterheat effect. In the beginning, record the sausage diameter. When the cooking temperature is known (when poaching, steaming, or roasting), record that as well. Remove the sausage from the heat when the internal temperature is between 155° F (68° C) and 160° F (71° C)—if your target is 160° F (71° C). The afterheat will likely bring the internal temperature to at least 160° F (71° C). If it is a little less than this target temperature, it is still safe to eat. If it begins to exceed the target temperature, try to arrest the afterheat with ice water if the casing is water resistant (unless it is to be eaten right away). The ice water helps to arrest afterheat, but it will not stop it immediately. The next time you cook the same diameter of sausage in the same way, you will be able to get closer to the target temperature.

Even if sausages are to be eaten soon after cooking, it is best to wait a few minutes after they are removed from the heat. When the sausages cool a few degrees, the muscle meat in the casing will begin to absorb some of the juices that had been squeezed out of the meat, but remain in the casing. As you probably know, roasted chickens, for example, should cool for 15 minutes or more before carving so that more juices will be retained; it is the same principle.

The method of cooking any specific kind of sausage is largely based on custom and personal preference. The various sausage-cooking methods are explained below. Cooking sausage by hot smoking will be discussed in Chapter 7.

Note: Sausage casings should never be pierced with a fork, or the like, before cooking.

COOKING BULK SAUSAGE

Bulk sausage is often used as an ingredient for pasta, rice, and potato dishes. It is also used in soups, stews, and sauces.

Place the bulk sausage in a frying pan, and break it up with a spatula or wooden spoon as it is cooking slowly. Continue to stir and cook the sausage until most of it has been browned. Place the cooked sausage in a wire mesh basket to drain the melted fat. Alternatively, place about two layers of paper towels on top of about four layers of newspaper, and drain the cooked meat on the paper. I use paper towels and newspaper; it is much easier to discard greasy paper placed in a plastic bag than it is to find a way to discard grease.

SAUTÉING PATTIES

The best and easiest way to cook sausage patties—either fresh or cured—is to sauté (fry) them. Any kind of frying pan will do. Preheat the frying pan and apply a thin film of cooking oil; this helps to prevent sticking. Usually, a medium-low setting is best, but the exact setting will depend on your kitchen range; use a setting that will cook the patties slowly. If they are about ⅜ inch (1 cm) thick, they will not dry out excessively when cooked with a medium-low setting, and the cooking time will be reasonable.

Turn them over frequently. Many kinds of patties contain some form of sugar (it may be common sucrose, or dextrose, or the lactose that is in powdered milk). When foods containing sugar are sautéed, the surface will caramelize: First, the surface will become an attractive reddish-brown, and then—if it is cooked too long—it will char and become black. Obviously, the goal is a reddish-brown surface. By turning patties over frequently, accidental charring will be avoided and the cooking will be uniform. The patties are done when they become this color on both sides. If you want to check for doneness, it is most easily accomplished by cutting a patty in half to make sure that the juices are clear and have no trace of pink coloration.

If the patties are covered with a lid while they are cooking, they may cook too fast and become fully cooked before the attractive reddish-brown color has developed. It is best to cook patties slowly, without a lid.

When the patties are first put in the frying pan, they may be pushed down gently with a spatula so that the meat makes good contact with the pan. However, after cooking is well underway, pushing down on the patties with a spatula will result in precious juices being wastefully squeezed out of the sausage.

SAUSAGE LOAF (LUNCHMEAT LOAF)

Sausage need not be made into patties or stuffed into casings—a common bread-baking pan can be used to mold and cook the sausage. The finished product will be a loaf that can be sliced into delicious and economical luncheon meat. The following instructions can be used to process and cook many varieties of sausage in a bread-baking pan:

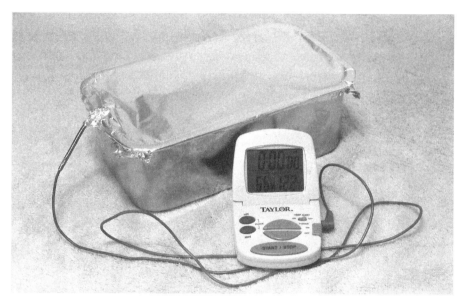

A bread-baking pan is filled with raw sausage. The probe of an electronic thermometer has been inserted, and the pan has been covered with aluminum foil.

1. Follow the instructions in the recipe for grinding the meat and blending the seasoning. Knead the mixture of ground meat and seasoning for about three minutes, or until it is uniform.

2. Rub the inside of a loaf pan with butter, margarine, or shortening, and pack the sausage paste into the pan. (Some sausage varieties are emulsified before the paste is packed in the loaf pan.) Cover the loaf pan tightly with aluminum foil or plastic food wrap—foil is preferred. (If available, use a loaf pan made of non-reactive material such as Pyrex, ceramic, Teflon coated metal, or stainless steel. If a non-reactive pan is not available, you might wish to line the loaf pan with plastic food wrap rather than rubbing the inside with grease. My loaf pan measures about 8¾ × 5 × 3 inches. In metric measurements: 22 × 13 × 8 cm.)

3. Refrigerate the sausage overnight to allow flavors to blend.

4. Lift the aluminum foil cover, insert the cable probe of an electronic thermometer into the center of the loaf, and reseal the aluminum foil. Steam the loaf at between 170° F (77° C) and 180° F (82° C) until the internal temperature is 160° F (71° C)—or 165° F (74° C) if the sausage contains poultry or wildfowl. (For steaming instructions, please see the section *Steaming Sausage* that appears later in this chapter.)

5. Remove the loaf from the bread-baking pan, let it cool in front of an electric fan for about one hour, and refrigerate it. The loaf should remain uncovered—or covered only with paper towels—while it is being chilled. The next morning the loaf may be sliced and wrapped with plastic wrap. Double wrap and freeze the portion that will not be consumed within a few days.

SAUTÉING SAUSAGE LINKS

Sausage links stuffed in either natural casings or collagen casings are excellent sautéed. Because sautéing causes the surface to brown, an extra level of flavor is added to the sausage. This is especially desirable for fresh sausage links, but cured—or cured and smoked links—also benefit from the extra flavor.

For maximum retention of the juices, always cook the sausages over medium-low heat. A little oil should be added to a frying pan that has been heated to the cooking temperature. A preheated pan with preheated oil will help prevent the sausages from sticking. Slowly brown one side of the links, turn them over and cover. Turn the links occasionally so that they will brown evenly. The cover over the links helps to retain the heat and creates a high humidity environment. The result is that the links cook faster and more uniformly, and the high humidity steams the links and helps to tenderize the casings. A few tablespoons of water or wine will help to insure high humidity.

When the sausages appear to be approaching the target temperature, the internal temperature should be checked with an instant-read thermometer. Insert the stem about 2½ inches (6.5 cm) into a sausage, and wait about 10 seconds until the needle becomes stable. At this point, you will need to decide whether to cover the links to get the internal temperature going up faster, or uncover and try to improve the browning.

The links are done when the internal temperature is between 155° F (68° C) and 160° F (71° C). Depending on the thickness of the links, afterheat should carry the temperature to 160° F (71° C). If the sausage contains poultry or wildfowl, the target temperature is 165° F (74° C), so you need to remove the sausages from the sauté pan when the internal temperature is between 160° F (71° C) and 165° F (74° C).

Another method of sautéing sausages is to precook them first by poaching or steaming. Since the sausages are fully cooked, they need only be heated and browned.

POACHING SAUSAGE

If stuffed sausage is cooked in hot water at a temperature well below the boiling point (or in other hot liquids such as broth, beer, or wine), it is called *poaching*.

Simmering also means cooking below the boiling point, but simmering implies a slightly higher temperature than that used for poaching. Poaching is a gentle and efficient way to cook sausage. It is gentle because the cooking temperature is just a little above the target temperature. It is efficient because water is a good conductor of heat. The water temperature is easy to control and provides uniform and gentle cooking with little effort.

The disadvantages are that poaching in plain water does not add flavor or color. In fact, there will be some loss of flavor due to some salt and other seasonings being dissolved by the liquid. Poaching is often used to cook smoked sausage and large lunchmeat-type sausages. It is also used to reheat sausages that have already been cooked—emulsified sausages, for example. If poaching is used for fresh sausages, it is usually used for fresh sausages that will be fried, grilled, or broiled later.

To minimize loss of flavor when poaching sausage stuffed in fibrous casing, each chub of sausage should be wrapped in at least two layers of plastic food wrap, and the food wrap should be twisted and sealed at both ends with wire bread-ties. This will provide water resistant properties comparable to that of a plastic casing.

Poaching is easy. Heat the water, or other liquid, to 180° F (82° C). A stockpot is an ideal vessel for cooking a large quantity. There should be enough liquid to cover the sausages completely. If water is being used, add ½ teaspoon of salt for each quart (liter). When the sausages are placed in the water, they will

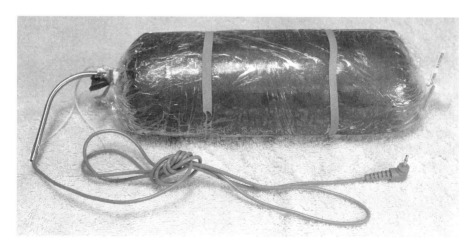

Sausage stuffed in fibrous casing should be wrapped in about two layers of plastic food wrap before poaching or steaming. Bread-bag wire ties on the ends and rubber bands around the circumference help to secure the plastic wrap.

lower the temperature. Bring the temperature back up to 175° F (79° C). While the sausages are cooking, try to maintain the liquid temperature between 170° F (77° C) and 180° F (82° C). It is best to use something like a round straining basket to hold the sausages under the water. Stir the sausages from time to time to ensure uniform exposure to the hot water.

The links, or fibrous casing chubs, are done when the internal temperature is between 155° F (68° C) and 160° F (71° C). Depending on the thickness of the sausage, afterheat should carry the temperature to 160° F (71° C). If the sausage contains poultry or wildfowl, the target temperature is 165° F (74° C), so you need to remove the sausages from the hot water when the internal temperature is between 160° F (71° C) and 165° F (74° C).

If sausages stuffed in natural casings will not be eaten soon, immerse them in ice water until the internal temperature is 110° F (43° C). Refrigerate immediately.

Sausage stuffed in fibrous casing should be air-cooled at room temperature for about one hour. The use of an electric fan will help cool the chubs. After one hour of cooling at room temperature, refrigerate the chubs, uncovered. Cooling these sausages in ice water might cause a loss of flavor when the sausage cools and shrinks. This shrinkage can cause cold water to be sucked into the fibrous casing, and the water will dilute the flavor.

The cooking and chilling of sausage packed in fibrous casings can cause the casing to wrinkle. This wrinkling is harmless, but many of the wrinkles will disappear if the chilled chub is dipped into boiling water for a short time.

Control of both cooking temperature and internal temperature is most easily accomplished by using two thermometers—one inserted in a sausage, and the other in the hot liquid. Electronic thermometers with a cable probe or instant-read dial thermometers work well for these tasks.

STEAMING SAUSAGE

When professional cooks steam food, they usually turn the heat high enough to produce a rolling boil, and they cover the steamer with a tight-fitting lid. Under these conditions, the temperature of the steam will be essentially the same as that of the boiling water. Cooking sausage in such a hot environment is unnecessarily harsh; low-temperature steaming is perfect for sausage. For many years, I used this low temperature steaming technique for cooking Chinese-style marinated-and-steamed fish, and later I discovered that it is also very good for steaming sausage. In fact, I rarely poach sausage nowadays; I steam it.

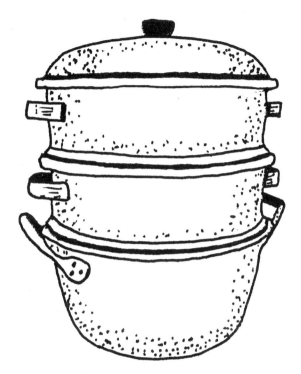

A three-tier Chinese-style steamer. The bottom tier is for water. Stacked on the water pan are two steamer baskets and a lid.

Low-temperature steaming, I believe, produces better results than poaching. When sausages are poached, they are immersed in hot water. The hot water seems to extract more favor from the sausages than does steam. Also, when sausages are steamed, the use of plastic food wrap gives even more protection against loss of flavor; they are bathed in their own juices while being cooked. Wrapping sausage links stuffed in natural casing may be a little troublesome—and probably unnecessary—but it is no trouble at all to wrap the larger fibrous casings with plastic food wrap.

A Chinese-style aluminum steamer works very well. The 12-inch (30 cm) diameter size is adequate for home use, and it can be purchased by mail order, or at most Asian grocery stores, for about $45. A stockpot with improvised steaming racks inside works equally well. When a steamer is used, it is best to have two electronic thermometers with cable probes—one probe continuously measures the internal temperature of the sausage, while the other probe continuously measures the temperature inside the steamer.

Sausage links in a steamer basket.

Sausage chubs in a steamer basket.

Professional sausage makers often use a special steam cabinet to cook sausages. Surprisingly, however, steaming—for some reason that is a mystery to me—is not a commonly suggested cooking method for sausages made at home.

Steaming sausage is simple:

1. Fill the bottom of the steamer with enough water to finish the steaming without going dry.
2. Place the cable probe of an electronic cable thermometer in the top rack of the steamer, and locate it so that the pointed half of the probe will touch neither the sausage nor the inside wall of the steamer.
3. Cover the steamer and heat it until the thermometer reads about 180° F (82° C). Place the sausages on the racks in such a way that the sausages do not touch the sides of the steamer and do not touch each other. Insert the cable probe of another electronic thermometer into a sausage to a depth of about 2½ inches (6.5 cm). Replace the tight-fitting lid on top. *Note: To minimize loss of flavor when steaming sausage stuffed in fibrous casing, each chub of sausage should be wrapped in at least two layers of plastic food wrap, and the food wrap should be twisted and sealed at both ends with wire bread-ties. This will provide water-resistant properties comparable to that of a plastic casing.*
4. Monitor and adjust the heat so that the steam temperature stabilizes somewhere between 170° F (77° C) and 180° F (82° C). Monitor both thermometers until the cooking is complete; remember to allow afterheat to raise the internal temperature after the sausages are removed from the steamer.
5. The links, or fibrous casing chubs, are done when the internal temperature is between 155° F (68° C) and 160° F (71° C). Depending on the thickness of the sausage, afterheat should carry the temperature to 160° F (71° C). If the sausage contains poultry or wildfowl, the target temperature is 165° F (74° C), so you need to remove the sausages from the steamer when the internal temperature is between 160° F (71° C) and 165° F (74° C).
6. If the sausages stuffed in natural casings will not be eaten soon, immerse them in ice water until the internal temperature is 110° F (43° C). Refrigerate immediately. Sausage stuffed in fibrous casing should be air-cooled at room temperature for about one hour; it is best to use an electric fan. After one hour of cooling, refrigerate the chubs, uncovered. (Cooling these sausages in ice water might cause a loss of flavor when the sausage cools and

shrinks while immersed in water; the shrinking can suck cold water into the casing, and the water will dilute the flavor of the sausage.)

After a few steaming sessions, the proper setting of the kitchen range required to maintain the 170° F (77° C) to 180° F (82° C) temperature will be learned. If the alarms on the thermometers are used, most of the sausage steaming can be accomplished while you are watching TV or reading a novel.

ROASTING SAUSAGE

Roasting sausages is an easy way to cook them. Heat the oven to 300° F (150° C). While the oven is heating, put a little oil in an ovenproof pan and heat it over medium-low heat. When the pan is hot, place the sausages in the pan, making sure that the links do not touch. If you have an electronic thermometer with a cable probe, insert the probe about 2½ inches (6.5 cm) into one of the links. Set the temperature alarm of the electronic thermometer to ring a few degrees before the target temperature is reached. The target temperature is normally 160° F (71° C), but it is 165° F (74° C) if the sausage contains poultry. If a cable probe thermometer is not available, use an instant-read thermometer to check the internal temperature from time to time.

There are two negative points about roasting sausages: They will not be browned as attractively as sausages cooked by grilling or sautéing, and the 300° F (150° C) temperature is rather harsh.

SMOKING SAUSAGE AND GRILLING SAUSAGE OUTSIDE

Please see Chapter 7 for information about smoking sausage and grilling sausage outside on a barbecue.

Sausage Smoking and Food Smokers

About Cold Smoking and Hot Smoking

WARNING: Do not smoke fresh, uncured sausage; it could result in a potentially fatal form of food poisoning called botulism. To be sure you have prevented botulism, all sausages to be smoked must have been properly cured with a sausage curing powder (Cure #1) such as Prague Powder #1, Modern Cure, or Instacure #1. For additional information, please see the section on Botulism in Chapter 4, HEALTH MATTERS.

Sausage does not need to be smoked, but most people like the unique and incomparable flavor imparted by hardwood smoke, and this is the main reason for smoking sausage; the smoke gives only a little protection against spoilage. The smoke deposited on the casing has anti-bacterial properties, but significant drying would have to occur to retard spoilage. And, in most cases, the goal is to give a smoke flavor to the sausage without drying it excessively.

The smoke flavor is most effectively imparted to the sausage when the sausage links are raw and the outsides of the casings are dry. If the smoking is done at a relatively low temperature, the sausage remains raw and the sausage casing tends to remain dry because very little juice and melted fat appear on the surface. This is called *cold smoking*. Under these conditions, the sausage will be infused with a rich, smoky flavor. The longer the sausage is cold smoked, the stronger the smoke flavor. The ideal intensity of the smoke flavor is purely a matter of taste. Try two hours for your first smoking session, and then increase the time, if desired, for future smoking sessions.

The exact definition of cold smoking is not carved in stone. Depending on the "expert," it can mean smoking at less than 85° F (29° C), or smoking at less than 120° F (49° C)—or anything between these temperatures. Actually, the definition of cold smoking often depends on the product being smoked. When I smoke cheese, for example, I consider cold smoking to be less than 80° F (27° C). Consequently, it might be said that the product being smoked influences the definition of cold smoking.

What does all this mean to a sausage maker? It means the following:

When the goal is to impart a smoky flavor to the sausage, keep the chamber temperature as low as possible—preferably below 100° F (38° C). The absolute maximum chamber temperature for cold smoking sausage is 120° F (49° C); if the temperature rises above 120° F (49° C), the sausage will begin to cook. Cooking is not bad, but when cooking begins, cold smoking has ended, and the ability of the sausage to absorb a smoky flavor will be reduced.

After the sausage is cold smoked, it needs to be cooked. One of several methods of cooking is to leave the sausage in the smoker, raise the chamber temperature, and *hot smoke* it. The details of how to do both cold smoking and hot smoking are given below.

HOW TO COLD SMOKE SAUSAGE

Sausages that are to be smoked should have been placed in the refrigerator overnight so that the Cure #1 (curing power) will have had time to migrate to all parts of the sausage mixture.

The first step is to dry the outside surface of the sausage so that the smoky aroma will adhere. Remove the sausage links or chubs from the refrigerator, and place them on a table (on wire racks or on paper towels). Direct an electric fan at them, and turn them over from time to time. (If there are pets in the house, it is best to use a room that can be secured against their entry.) At first, moisture will condense on the cold casings. Drying will be faster if this moisture is removed with a paper towel. The sausages are dry when the tips of the fingers slide easily on the surface of the casing and they do not feel clammy or tacky. This will require at least one hour.

Another way to dry the sausage is to place it in a 130° F (54° C) to 140° F (60° C) smoker with the smoker vents fully open.

When the surface is dry, place the sausages in the smoker by laying them on wire racks or hanging them on rods. If the sausages touch each other, smoke flavor cannot adhere at that point, and there will be no coloration at that point. If the sausages are on wire racks, it is best to turn them over from time to time to minimize the marks left by the racks.

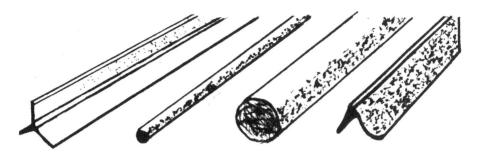

Four types of sausage hanging rods (also called smokehouse sticks).

Smoke at the lowest temperature possible for at least two hours—or as long as six hours if a stronger smoky flavor is desired. Do everything that can be done to keep the temperature below 100° F (38° C)—or to make the temperature as low as possible: Open the vent fully, direct a large fan at the smoker, place a shallow pan of ice in the chamber, and open the smoker door from time to time.

After this cold smoking is finished, raise the smoke chamber temperature to about 140° F (60° C)—with or without smoke—and hold this temperature for one or two hours until the sausages take on an attractive mahogany coloration. While smoking at this temperature, close the damper most of the way in order to reduce the airflow and, thereby, reduce dehydration. (The damper should never be closed all of the way, no matter what kind of food is being smoked. If the smoke becomes stagnant in the smoke chamber, it will impart an unpleasant taste to the product.) Holding the sausages at this temperature is done only to impart coloration, so it is optional.

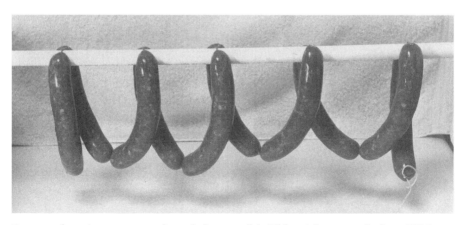

Sausages hanging on a round smokehouse stick. This stick was made from PVC plastic water pipe. Note that the links do not touch each other.

After the desired coloration has been accomplished, cool the sausages at room temperature for 30 minutes to one hour. During this time, the sausages will *"bloom"* (become darker)—blooming will make them even more attractive.

After this cooling and blooming period has been finished, refrigerate them immediately, overnight, to allow the smoke flavor to mellow. Do not cover the sausages—or cover them with paper towels only. If they are tightly covered, they will "sweat" and their appearance will suffer.

The next morning, these smoked, raw sausages may be cooked by any method explained in Chapter 6, or they may be frozen for up to two months for later use. They should be eaten or frozen within two days. If they will be frozen, it is best to wrap each link or chub in plastic food wrap before placing it in a sealed plastic bag.

HOW TO HOT SMOKE SAUSAGE

Two things should be kept in mind when deciding whether to hot smoke sausage instead of cooking it by another method. The first consideration is that hot smoking takes more time than cooking by any other method. The reason for this is that hot, dry air is a very poor conductor of heat; it does not impart heat into the sausage effectively. The second consideration is that hot air continuously flowing past the sausage removes moisture from the sausage. The loss of moisture is not significant for sausage stuffed in fibrous casing, but it is significant for sausage stuffed in sheep casing. When sheep or hog casing is used, the loss of moisture needs to be considered. In general, if juicy sausage is the goal, hot smoking may not be a good option for cooking; it might be better to cold smoke the sausage and then cook it by some other method. If, however, your goal is to make semi-dried sausage such as pepperoni sticks, drying in the smoker is the best way process it.

Hot smoked sausages are first cold smoked, or at least smoked at the lowest possible temperature for a while, and then the temperature is raised until they are fully cooked.

In order to have the entire hot smoking process all in one place, much of the initial cold smoking step, explained above, is repeated here.

Sausages that are to be smoked should have been placed in the refrigerator overnight so that the Cure #1 (curing power) and seasoning will have had time to migrate to all parts of the sausage mixture.

The first step is to dry the outside surface so that the smoky aroma will adhere to it. Remove the sausage links or fibrous casing chubs from the refrigerator, and place them on a table (on wire racks or paper towels). Direct an electric fan at them, and turn them over from time to time. (If there are pets in the house, it is best to use a room that can be secured against their entry.) At first, moisture will condense on the cold casings. Drying will be faster if this moisture is removed with a paper towel. The sausages are dry when the tips of the fingers slide easily on the surface of the casing, and it does not feel clammy or tacky. This will require at least one hour.

Another way to dry the sausage is to place it in a 130° F (54° C) to 140° F (60° C) smoker with the smoker vents fully open.

When the surface is dry, place the sausages in the smoker by laying them on wire racks or hanging them on rods. If the sausages touch each other, smoke flavor cannot adhere at that point, and there will be no coloration at that point. If the sausages are on wire racks, it is best to turn them over from time to time to minimize the marks left by the racks.

Smoke at the lowest temperature possible for at least two hours—or as long as six hours if a stronger smoky flavor is desired. Do everything you can to keep the temperature below 100° F (38° C)—or, to keep the temperature as low as possible: Open the vent fully, direct a large fan at the smoker, place a shallow pan of ice in the smoker, and open the smoker door briefly from time to time.

After this cold smoking is finished, raise the smoke chamber temperature to about 140° F (60° C)—with or without smoke—and hold this temperature for one or two hours until the sausages take on an attractive mahogany coloration. While smoking at this temperature, close the damper most of the way in order to reduce the airflow and, thereby, reduce dehydration. (The damper should never be closed all of the way, no matter what kind of food is being smoked. If the smoke becomes stagnant in the smoke chamber, it will impart an unpleasant taste to the product.)

Raise the temperature gradually (over a one hour period) to somewhere between 170° F (77° C) and 180° F (82° C). (During the period of hot smoking, the generation of smoke is usually continued, but it is optional.) Check the smoke vent again; it should be only about ¼ open to reduce drying. Insert the cable probe of an electronic thermometer 2½ inches (6.5 cm) into a sausage. Hot smoke at this temperature until the internal temperature is between 155° F (68° C) and 160° F (71° C). Depending on the thickness of the sausage, the afterheat should bring the internal temperature to 160° F (71° C). If the sausage contains poultry, the target temperature is 165° F (74° C), so you need to remove the sausages from the smoker when the internal temperature is between 160° F (71° C) and 165° F (74° C).

If the sausages have been stuffed in natural casings, remove them from the smoker, and immerse them in cold water (or spray them with cold water) until the internal temperature is below 110° F (43° C). (The cold water helps to re-solidify the fats and minimize shriveling.) Cool the sausages a little more at room temperature for 30 minutes to 1 hour. During this time, the sausages will "*bloom*" (become darker). Blooming will make them even more attractive. Refrigerate the links overnight; this allows the smoke flavor to mellow.

If the sausages have been stuffed in synthetic fibrous casings, remove the chubs from the smoker when they are fully cooked, and place them in front of an electric fan for about one hour to cool. (If sausages stuffed in fibrous casings are cooled in ice water, water will enter the casing and dilute the flavor.) Refrigerate them overnight to allow the smoke flavor to mellow.

When refrigerating the sausage, cover them with paper towels only. If they are tightly covered, they will "sweat" and their appearance will suffer.

The next morning, these smoked sausages may be re-heated by any cooking method explained in Chapter 6, or they may be frozen for up to two months for later use. If they will be frozen, it is best to wrap each link or chub in plastic food wrap before placing it in a sealed plastic bag. Because they have been fully cooked, sausages left in the refrigerator will keep well for at least a week.

PARTIAL HOT SMOKING

Instead of fully cooking the sausage in the smoker, it can be partially hot smoked and then poached, steamed, grilled, or sautéed. This method will reduce the dehydration caused by hot smoking.

Follow the instructions for hot smoking, including raising the chamber temperature to somewhere between 170° F (77° C) and 180° F (82° C). However, instead of fully cooking the sausages, remove them from the smoker when the internal temperature is at about 125° F (52° C).

Cool the sausages at room temperature for 30 minutes to 1 hour. During this time, the sausages that have been stuffed in natural casings will "*bloom*" (become darker), and blooming will make them even more attractive. Refrigerate the links or chubs overnight—uncovered, or covered with paper towels—to allow the smoke flavor to mellow.

The next morning, these smoked sausages may be cooked by any method explained in Chapter 6, or they may be frozen for up to two months for later use. If they will be frozen, it is best to wrap each link or chub in plastic food wrap before placing it in a sealed plastic bag.

Manufactured Smokers

Manufactured smokers are sold at prices that range from less than $100 for a small amateur model, to thousands of dollars for a large, fully automated, professional model. Descriptions of manufactured smokers will be limited to smokers that are designed for amateurs and have a modest price tag. The more elaborate and expensive smokers will have a built-in thermometer and automatic or manual devices to control factors such as temperature, airflow, humidity, and the feeding of smoking fuel.

PORTABLE ELECTRIC SMOKERS

Almost everyone can afford a portable electric smoker, and they are very easy to use. Although they employ electricity, there are no electrical controls to operate or adjust. They are lightweight and compact (some of them even have a knockdown design). Depending on the size, electric smokers are capable of holding anywhere from 20 pounds (9 kg) to 100 pounds (45 kg) of product. These smokers are designed to operate on the electrical power system used in all households in the United States and Canada. (Any appliance that specifies 110, 117, or 120 volts will work properly on this system.)

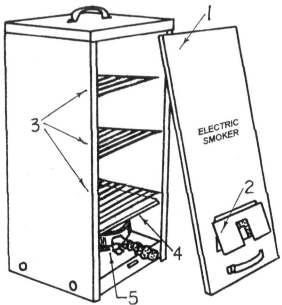

1. Front panel, removable.
2. Front flap—for removing and inserting the smoking chip pan.
3. Food racks.
4. Drip tray.
5. Smoking chip pan and heater.

Portable electric smoker—front loading type.

The electric heating element in the bottom will simultaneously provide heat to produce the smoke and heat to cook (or partially cook) the product. A small pan of hardwood chips is placed on this heating element to produce the smoke. Smoke-laden hot air rises to the top and escapes through vents. If the external (ambient) temperature is more than 70° F (21° C) and there is no strong wind, the internal temperature of the smoke chamber should reach at least 150° F (66° C).

The proliferation of these inexpensive manufactured smokers is the most important reason for the popularization of smoking as a hobby. These units are capable of producing a first-class smoked product, but they do have a few limitations and disadvantages; these are summarized below.

- Because these aluminum smokers are not insulated, and because there is no easy way to provide supplementary heat, the maximum temperature produced (if the smoker is used according to the manufacturer's instructions) depends on the outside temperature and the strength of the wind blowing on the smoker. The resulting temperature may not be hot enough to cook the sausage thoroughly; in order to hot smoke sausage, the temperature needs to be maintained somewhere between 170° F (77° C) and 180° F (82° C).
- There is no easy way to lower the internal temperature for cold smoking, except to partially open the door, to open the flap near the bottom, or to use an electric fan directed toward the smoker.
- These smokers do not have a thermometer to measure the smoke chamber temperature.

In summary, these portable smokers cannot be used for hot smoking unless the ambient temperature is very high, but—if used correctly—they will do a superb job of cold smoking sausages. Before a batch of product is smoked, the smoker should be tested. Follow the manufacturer's instructions for setting up and using the smoker, and then measure the internal temperature of the smoke chamber under various ambient temperature and wind conditions. The smoker can be used for cold smoking under any conditions that permit a temperature of 120° F (49° C), or below, to be maintained in the chamber. You might find, for example, that sausage can be cold smoked in your smoker if the ambient temperature is 60° F (16° C), or lower, provided there is an electric fan blowing on it.

Most of these portable smokers are not large enough to improvise a way to hang sausages, so the sausages must be placed on the wire racks provided with the smoker. Turn the sausages over from time to time to minimize the rack marks on the links.

BRADLEY SMOKERS

A little less than a year after my first book was published (*Mastering the Craft of Smoking Food*), I received a phone call from the Bradley Smoker Company in British Columbia, Canada. My book had come to their attention and they were selling it as an accessory on their website. The reason for the phone call was to ask me if I would join a special Bradley team that was developing several curing mixtures. (Curing mixtures are blends of salt, flavoring, sweeteners, and sodium nitrite to cure meat in preparation for smoking it.) I joined their team as a consultant, helped them formulate four curing mixtures, and I did all of the testing.

After the formulation and testing was finished, they asked me to write instructions for making various smoked products using the new Bradley curing mixes. Instructions for 23 products were written: ham, bacon, smoked salmon, pastrami, smoked duck, jerky, several smoked sausages, etc. To test these products, they gave me a deluxe Bradley smoker that they call the *Bradley Digital Smoker*. This was my introduction to the Bradley smokers.

The Bradley Digital Smoker was very impressive; the smoking fuel "bisquettes" are fed into the smoker automatically onto a small hotplate where they smolder and produce smoke. These bisquettes are disks of compressed hardwood chips (hickory, apple, oak, etc.) with a diameter of 2¼ inches (5.7 cm) and a thickness of ⅝ inch (1.6 cm). Each bisquette smolders for 20 minutes and is replaced with a fresh bisquette automatically. If extra heat for hot smoking is desired, a built-in heater can be used. The desired temperature can be selected, and the heater is controlled automatically, much like a kitchen oven.

I could find no fault with the smoke generator or the automatic feed of the smoking fuel. These features worked perfectly. However, if extra heat for hot smoking were used, the smoke chamber temperature would swing about 15° F (9° C) above and below the selected temperature. For example, if the temperature were set to 140° F (60° C), the temperature might swing between 125° F (52° C) and 155° F (68° C). The temperature swings were worrisome, but I hot smoked many solid-muscle products (non-sausage products) such as ham, pastrami, and chicken; the results were perfectly acceptable.

The digital smoker was acceptable for cold smoking, but the ambient temperature had to be low. For example, if the ambient temperature were 40° F (4.5° C) to 50° F (10° C), the temperature inside the chamber would remain under 120° F (49° C). Cold smoking of many products, including sausage, is possible at this temperature. If the chamber temperature climbs higher than 120° F (49° C), the Bradley Digital Smoker can still be used for cold smoking if a tray of ice is placed on the lower rack (between the smoking fuel hotplate and the food). Opening the door from time to time, and opening the smoke vent all of the way, also help to keep the heat down.

As indicated above, the Bradley Digital Smoker works fairly well for cold smoking sausage, and it works well for cold smoking and hot smoking solid-muscle products. Nevertheless, the wide temperature swings of the heater make it unsuitable for hot smoking sausage or for making semi-dried sausage. When I began writing this book on making sausage, I explained that problem to my contact, George Radke, at the Bradley Smoker Company. Mr. Radke offered to provide me with an *Original* Bradley Smoker to use for testing smoked sausage formulas. The Original Bradley is about the same as the Bradley Digital, except that the heater is manually controlled on the Original. I accepted his offer.

Approximately 75 percent of the cold smoked, hot smoked, and semi-dried sausages that I included in this book were processed in the Original Bradley smoker during the colder months of the year, and the remainder were processed and tested in my homemade smoker. (My homemade smoker has an offset smoke generator and a long flue to cool the smoke, so I used it when the ambient temperature was too high to use the Original Bradley smoker.)

In my opinion, the Original Bradley Smoker is the best modestly priced smoker on the market for the home sausage maker. I have not seen any other affordable brand of smoker for home use that will smoke at temperatures as low as the Bradley. The low temperature smoking is possible because the small hotplate that smolders the bisquette smoking fuel consumes only 125 watts, so it generates only a little more heat than a large light bulb. Moreover, the heater

The Original Bradley Smoker. *Photo courtesy Bradley Smoker, Inc.*

for the chamber is independent of the hotplate and can be controlled manually. The automatic feeding of the smoking fuel is another feature that you will not find on other smokers in this price range. I have not been able to find another brand of a reasonably priced smoker with these important features. The Original Bradley Smoker is not the cheapest smoker available, but at about $399, or less, it is affordable for most serious hobbyists. The only way you might get a better smoker for the same amount of money is to build a homemade smoker with an external smoke generator and a long smoke flue. (Please see Appendix 5 for the Bradley website.)

Recently, the Bradley Smoker Company has offered an accessory that they call the Cold Smoke Adaptor (please see photo). This accessory is useable on all Bradley smokers, and it can be attached easily without tools. The adaptor is very effective at reducing the internal temperature of the smoker when products are being cold smoked. To use the adaptor, the smoke generator is removed from the smoker and attached to the Cold Smoke Adaptor; this act creates an offset

The Bradley Cold Smoke Adaptor Accessory. This adaptor will attach to all Bradley smokers. The flexible aluminum flue cools the smoke. *Photo courtesy Bradley Smoker, Inc.*

The Bradley Smoke Generator has been removed from the smoker and attached to the Bradley Cold Smoke Adaptor. *Photo courtesy Bradley Smoker, Inc.*

smoke generator. An aluminum smoke tube cools the smoke as it flows to the smoke chamber. The Cold Smoke Adaptor sells for about $99, and it is available wherever Bradley Smokers are sold.

WATER SMOKERS

Since ancient times, the Chinese have used steam cookers. These cookers have a pan of water that is placed between the food and the heat source. Cooking food in this way results in slow and moist cooking. Indeed, this is a simple but ingenious way to reduce moisture loss while cooking foods. Properly used, this cooking method produces food of unsurpassed succulence with minimal shrinkage. A minor negative point is that the lower cooking temperature results in a cooking time about twice as long (or longer) as cooking in a kitchen oven. This Chinese method of cooking stood the test of time, and it eventually found its way to a place as distant as North America.

The southern portion of the United States, particularly, had a many devotees of this style of cooking. Some of these Americans made a habit of putting hardwood chunks on the charcoal fire. The entire system was put in a single enclosure to ensure that the food was exposed to steam from the water pan and smoke from the hardwood. By doing this, water smoking was invented!

A typical water smoker will hold a maximum of approximately 50 pounds (22 kg) of food. The smokers come in various shapes, but they are often round, have a dome-shaped lid, and their height is about twice that of their diameter. In addition to the traditional charcoal-burning units, some manufacturers offer the easier-to-use propane and electric models. The propane models have a control knob to control the heat by regulating the flow of propane. I use a Brinkmann propane water smoker, and I am very satisfied with it. It is easier to use than the charcoal fired type, and it is more durable than water smokers with electric heaters. I fitted my Brinkmann with an adapter hose so that a common propane tank can be used instead of the small, disposable propane cylinders.

No matter whether charcoal, propane, or electricity is used, the sausage will taste the same if it is seasoned and processed in the same way. Many of these water smokers can be used as barbecue grills if the water pan is not used.

Heat is produced in the bottom of the unit directly under the water pan. There are chrome- or nickel-plated cooking racks above the water pan. Wire mesh baskets can be purchased separately, and they are particularly useful for cooking small sausages.

For the charcoal burners, putting water-soaked chunks of hardwood near the charcoal produces smoke. The propane and electric models require that the

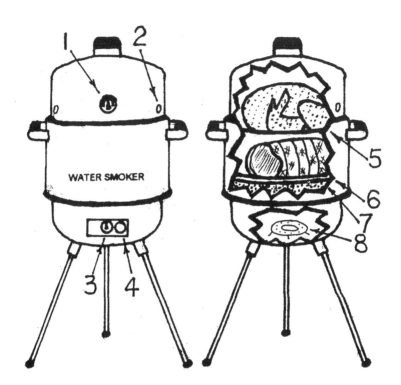

Water smoker—propane type.

1. Heat gauge.
2. Smoke vent.
3. Temperature control (regulates the flow of propane).
4. Igniter (for propane).
5. Upper food rack.
6. Lower food rack.
7. Water pan.
8. Propane burner.

water-soaked wood be put on a special tray or in another designated place. In some cases, the instructions will suggest wrapping the chunks of smoking fuel in aluminum foil to promote smoldering and to contain the ashes.

Hot water is put into the water pan, and the chamber is preheated. When the heat gauge or thermometer indicates that the correct temperature has been reached, the sausage links are put on the racks or in the baskets and hot smoked. You need to check the heat chamber thermometer and the water pan from time to time to make sure everything is progressing properly. Make sure that the water pan is always filled with *hot* water, and make sure that the water pan never goes dry. If the water pan goes dry and the residue in the bottom begins to scorch, the food will be tainted by that odor. Avoid raising the lid frequently to peek; this will cause excessive heat loss. Every peek will add about 10 or 15 minutes to the cooking time. Try cooking sausages at 180° F (82° C)— this will give the best results. If the cooking is too slow to suit you, boost the temperature up to 190° F (88° C) or 200° F (93° C).

In spite of all of the wonderful characteristics of manufactured water smokers, there are a few negative features:

- If the water smoker is electric, the same precautions as for the portable electric smokers must be taken; it should be used on a concrete surface and protected from rain.
- Because the units are not insulated, wind, precipitation, and external temperatures can affect the cooking time.
- Too much heat is produced for smoke cookers, such as water smokers, to be used as cold smokers.
- It is difficult to maintain a steady flow of smoke because the heat that is produced to maintain the correct cooking temperature may not be optimal to smolder the smoking fuel slowly. The wood will fail to produce any smoke if it is not heated enough, and it will burst into flames if it is heated too much.
- Most water smokers have a built-in heat gauge, but these heat gauges are not accurate and not consistent. The heat gauge may indicate such ranges as "WARM," "IDEAL," and "HOT," but sometimes the "IDEAL" range is not ideal. The ideal temperature to cook solid meat and poultry in the water smoker is between 225° F (107° C) and 275° F (135° C). Fish should not be water smoked at more than 225° F (107° C). The hot smoking of sausage should be done at about 180° F (82° C). However, the temperature in some water smokers may be 280° to 300° F (138° to 149° C) when the needle of the heat gauge is in the middle of the "IDE-AL" range. Consequently, it is best to use a real thermometer to measure the smoker's internal temperature. Try an instant-read dial thermometer with a stem. Wrap a small cloth around the stem, and plug it into one of the vent holes. Better yet, drill a small hole just above the heat gage, and then insert a short-stemmed dial thermometer.

- Smoking food in a water smoker produces a less intense smoke flavor than smoking it in other kinds of smokers. One reason for this is that the steam absorbs the smoke aroma that would otherwise be imparted to the food. But the main reason is that the steam condenses on the food; a dry surface is required for the smoke flavor to adhere and penetrate.

It was mentioned above that the "IDEAL" range of many water smokers is often too hot to get the best results. Unfortunately, turning down the heat to 180° F (82° C) might cause another problem: It could cause the water to stop simmering, and that might lower the humidity. To prevent this problem, you may wish to alter your smoker so that more heat will hit the water pan directly. If your water smoker uses lava rock to spread the heat, you need to move all the lava stones away from the center, and pile them around the edge. This will allow more heat to strike the water pan directly. If your smoker has a metal heat deflector, you may be able to remove it or have some large holes punched in it. If it can be done easily, try to move the water pan closer to the heat source. However, before any changes are made, it is best to get to know your water smoker well. Try to avoid making irreversible changes.

BARBECUE-TYPE SMOKE COOKERS

Cooking sausages by grilling them outside on a barbecue is the most festive way to prepare them. This is also one of the tastiest ways to cook sausages because a slightly smoky taste is added. However, grilling is more of an art than a science, so experience can be expected to improve the results.

There are many shapes and sizes of hot smokers on the market, and they will all do a good job if used properly. The manufacturer's instructions together with your experience will enable you to learn the techniques quickly. Whatever brand or type you use, it should always be used outside, and it will probably be necessary to soak the smoking fuel in water so that it will produce smoke rather than flames.

Both of the methods listed below have many devotees.

- Precook the sausages by poaching or steaming them. They are fully cooked when you put them on the grill, so you need only concentrate on browning them to add new levels of flavor and attractiveness. The heating should be just enough to make them hot all the way through. This is accomplished by placing them near—but not over—the flame, or the medium-hot charcoal, for part of the time in order to brown them slowly and evenly. The rest of the time, they are covered and heated a little further away from the heat source. When precooked sausages are being grilled, the internal temperature is not usually measured.

- Grilling raw sausages is a little more difficult because they have to be cooked to the target temperature in addition to browning them attractively. The key is gentle heat and slow cooking. The browning is done in the same way as indicated above, but the cooking should be done very slowly. After the links are browned, keep them covered, and place them in a position on the grill where the internal temperature will climb gradually. On some types of grills, placing the sausages in a covered cast-iron frying pan helps to provide uniform and gentle heat. The links are done when the internal temperature is between 155° F (68° C) and 160° F (71° C). Depending on the thickness of the sausage, afterheat should carry the temperature to 160° F (71° C). If the sausage contains poultry, the target temperature is 165° F (74° C), so you need to remove the sausages from the grill when the internal temperature is between 160° F (71° C) and 165° F (74° C).

CHAPTER 8

Fresh Sausage

In the world of sausage making, some expressions have a special meaning. The expression *fresh sausage* is one case in point. Fresh sausage means sausage that does not contain nitrites or nitrates. The opposite of fresh sausage is *cured sausage*. Sausage makers tend to use the word *cured* whenever nitrates or nitrites have been used. However, food smokers (not sausage makers) will often use the word *cured* even if only dry salt or common brine has been used. It is confusing, but we can't change the ways that people use the English language. We have to live with it.

Fresh sausage can be used as bulk sausage for seasoning, made into patties, or stuffed in casings. If it is stuffed in casings, it is still called fresh sausage, but some people prefer to call it *stuffed fresh sausage*.

Note: The sausages in this chapter have been arranged in alphabetical order. WARNING: Fresh sausage must be fried, grilled, roasted, poached, or steamed. Smoking stuffed fresh sausage, or cooking it at low heat for a long time, could cause botulism, a potentially fatal form of food poisoning.

Andersonville Brown Sugar and Honey Breakfast Sausage

The Johnsonville Sausage Company makes a very unusual and very tasty sausage called *Brown Sugar and Honey Breakfast Links*. The combination of sweeteners makes it unusual and tasty. This sausage is not exactly the same as that made by Johnsonville, but it is remarkably similar.

THE CASING

Make the sausage into patties, or use natural casings. If 24 to 26 mm (1 in. to 1¹⁄₁₆ in.) sheep casing is to be used, prepare about 14 feet (420 cm) of casing. If small-diameter hog casing will be used, prepare 7 feet (210 cm). Rinse the casing, and refrigerate it in water overnight. Rinse again, and soak in warm water a few minutes before using.

MEAT FOR 2½ LBS. (1,150 G) OF SAUSAGE

Prepare 2½ lbs. (1,150 g) of pork shoulder butt that contains about 20 percent fat, or use 2 lbs. (910 g) of lean pork and ½ lb. (225 g) of back fat; cut the meat into ¾-inch (2 cm) cubes. Refrigerate the meat, and put the meat grinder in the refrigerator, too. If the sausage stuffer will be used, refrigerate it, as well.

SEASONINGS AND OTHER INGREDIENTS

2½ tsp. (12.5 ml) salt
6 Tbsp. (90 ml) brown sugar—packed in the spoon
2 Tbsp. (30 ml) honey
2 Tbsp. (30 ml) maple syrup
2 Tbsp. (30 ml) lemon juice
2 tsp. (10 ml) mild-flavored unsulfured molasses
1 tsp. (5 ml) Mapleine (imitation maple flavor)
1 tsp. (5 ml) white pepper
½ tsp. (2.5 ml) MSG (optional)
½ tsp. (2.5 ml) marjoram
½ tsp. (2.5 ml) onion granules
2 Tbsp. (30 ml) cold water
½ cup (120 ml) finely powdered skim milk

MIXING AND STUFFING

1. Grind the pork with a ¼-inch (6.4 mm) or smaller plate, and refrigerate it for 30 minutes.
2. Mix the seasoning, powdered skim milk, and water in a 5-quart (5 liter) mixing bowl. Refrigerate this seasoning mixture for about 15 minutes.
3. Blend the meat and the seasoning well by kneading for about three minutes. Shape the mixture into ³⁄₈-inch (10 mm) thick patties, and wrap them in plastic food wrap. Alternatively, stuff the sausage into collagen, sheep, or hog casings.

4. Refrigerate the sausage that will be eaten within the next two days, and freeze the remainder.

Please see Chapter 6 for cooking suggestions.

Basic Turkey Sausage

This turkey sausage formula was developed by an organization that promotes the consumption of turkey meat. They assume that the ground turkey available at grocery stores will be used. Vegetable oil is added to the seasoning mixture to compensate for the insufficient amount of fat in commercially ground turkey. The oil is not required if the amount of fat in the ground turkey is about 20 percent of the total meat.

This sausage is pleasantly seasoned, and it is suitable for breakfast, lunch, or dinner. It may be made into patties, stuffed into natural casings, or even stuffed into synthetic fibrous casings to make luncheon meat. However, it cannot be smoked because it is not a cured sausage.

CASINGS

If 24 to 26 mm (1 in. to 1¹⁄₁₆ in.) sheep casing is to be used, prepare about 14 feet (420 cm) of casing. If small-diameter hog casing will be used, prepare 7 feet (210 cm). Rinse the casing, and refrigerate it in water overnight. Rinse again, and soak in warm water a few minutes before using.

THE MEAT FOR 2½ LBS. (1,150 G) OF SAUSAGE

Prepare 2½ lbs. (1,150 g) of turkey. Use the skin and fat, too. (Ground turkey available at a grocery store is also usable. If this ground meat has an inadequate amount of fat, add the vegetable oil listed below.) Cut into ¾-inch (2 cm) cubes. Refrigerate. While this meat is being prepared, chill the grinder and sausage stuffer in the refrigerator.

SEASONINGS AND OTHER INGREDIENTS

2½ tsp. (12.5 ml) salt
1 cup (240 ml) onion, minced
2 tsp. (10 ml) parsley, dried
1½ tsp. (7.5 ml) black pepper
1 tsp. (5 ml) thyme
1 tsp. (5 ml) nutmeg

1 tsp. (5 ml) ginger powder

1 tsp. (5 ml) red pepper flakes

2 cloves of garlic, minced

¼ cup (60 ml) vegetable oil (if required—see above)

¼ cup (60 ml) cold water

½ cup (120 ml) finely powdered skim milk

MIXING AND STUFFING

1. Grind the well-chilled turkey with a medium plate. Refrigerate the ground fowl for about 30 minutes.

2. Measure the seasoning and other ingredients (everything except for the ground turkey) into a large mixing bowl, and mix well. Refrigerate for at least 15 minutes.

3. Add the chilled ground turkey to the seasoning mixture, and knead until it is thoroughly mixed and uniform. This will require about three minutes. Chill this sausage paste while the sausage stuffer and casings are being prepared.

4. Make the sausage into patties, or stuff it into casings and twist into links. Refrigerate the sausage overnight to permit the seasoning to be absorbed by the meat. Use a covered container.

5. Sausages that will not be eaten within two days should be wrapped in plastic food wrap individually, placed in a plastic bag, and frozen.

Please see Chapter 6 for cooking suggestions.

Bockwurst

To me, this light colored sausage is elegant and delicate. In Germany, however, bockwurst is considered a two-fisted beer-drinker's sausage. It is commonly eaten while drinking a strong, dark beer called bock beer; hence, the name *bockwurst* was given to this sausage. In some parts of the United States, bockwurst is also known as *white sausage* because of its light color. The formula is complex, but the numerous and unusual ingredients complement each other very well. It is one of my favorite sausages, and I make it several times during the spring when wild chives appear in my backyard.

THE CASINGS

Prepare 7 feet (210 cm) of hog casings. Rinse the casings, and soak them in water overnight. Rinse the casings again, and soak them in warm water 30 minutes before using.

THE MEAT

Prepare the following meats. Refrigerate the meat, and put the meat grinder and sausage stuffer in the refrigerator, too.

- 1¾ lbs. (800 g) fatty pork butt
- ¾ lb. (340 g) veal, chicken thighs, or turkey thighs (veal is traditional)

SEASONINGS AND OTHER INGREDIENTS

¼ cup (60 ml) fresh milk
2 tsp. (10 ml) salt
1 Tbsp. (15 ml) onion granules
1 tsp. (5 ml) chopped parsley, dehydrated
¾ tsp. (3.75 ml) white pepper, finely ground
¼ tsp. (1.25 ml) celery seed, ground
¼ tsp. (1.25 ml) mace
1 Tbsp. (15 ml) lemon juice
1 Tbsp. (15 ml) light corn syrup
¼ cup (60 ml) green onions or chives, minced
2 eggs
½ cup (120 ml) powdered skim milk

MIXING AND STUFFING

1. Grind the meats with a ⅜-inch (9.5 mm) or smaller plate, and refrigerate them for 30 minutes.
2. Except for the meat, mix the seasonings and other ingredients well in a large mixing bowl. Chill this mixture for at least 15 minutes.
3. Add the ground meat, and knead at least three minutes until the seasoning and ground meat blend is uniform.
4. Stuff the sausage, and make the rope into 5-inch (13 cm) links. It is best for the stuffed sausage to be refrigerated overnight, or for a few hours at least.
5. Steam the links until the internal temperature is 160° F (71° C)—or 165° F (74° C) if chicken or turkey was used. Spray the sausage with cold water for one or two minutes, or cool in front of an electric fan. Refrigerate, uncovered, until chilled. Package the sausage in plastic bags, and freeze the portion that will not be consumed within two days. Bockwurst is traditionally eaten with mild mustard.

Cajun Boudin Blanc

Several distinctly different Cajun sausages use the word *boudin* in the name. If *blanc* is used in the name, the sausage is whitish because it does not contain blood in the formula. Not only are there many formulations for boudin blanc, there are many approaches to blending, preparing, and cooking the sausage. The list of ingredients, below, is typical, but the processing method of the sausage in this recipe is one of the easiest I have seen.

It is certainly an unusual sausage. In addition to meat, it contains vegetables and rice. It is truly a meal in one, and it is very popular in Louisiana as a snack food.

The way that Cajun boudin blanc is eaten is also unusual. Because there is cooked rice and vegetables inside the sausage, the sausage is not firm and the teeth will not cut through the casing when it is bitten. Because of this, almost no one will try to eat the casing. Instead, they will squeeze the contents out of the casing into their mouth and discard the casing when it is empty.

THE CASINGS

Prepare 12 feet (360 cm) of hog casings. Rinse the casings, and soak the casings in water overnight. Rinse again the next morning.

THE MEAT

Prepare 2½ lbs. (1,150 g) of minced pork butt. The sausage will be less greasy if the fat content of the meat is about 15 percent rather than 25 percent. Use a ¼-inch (6.4 mm) plate to grind the pork.

OTHER INGREDIENTS AND SEASONINGS

6 cups (1,440 ml) cooked rice, long grain preferred, cooled
¾ cup (180 ml) onions, finely chopped
¾ cup (180 ml) parsley, finely chopped
¾ cup (180 ml) green onions, chopped
⅓ cup (80 ml) green bell pepper (or 1 jalapeño), finely chopped
⅓ cup (80 ml) celery, finely chopped
4 tsp. (20 ml) salt
1 tsp. (5 ml) minced garlic
1 tsp. (5 ml) red pepper flakes
1 tsp. (5 ml) black pepper
1 tsp. (5 ml) cayenne

½ tsp. (2.5 ml) sage—packed in the spoon
¼ tsp. (1.25 ml) bay leaf powder
¼ tsp. (1.25 ml) allspice
¼ tsp. (1.25 ml) thyme

MIXING AND STUFFING

1. Except for the meat, mix the seasonings and all other ingredients in a large mixing bowl. Next, add the ground meat and mix again. Before stuffing, chill the sausage mixture for at least 30 minutes—longer is better.

2. Stuff the sausage. Make 6-inch (15 cm) links. Wrap the sausage links in plastic food wrap and put them in plastic bags, expelling as much air as possible. Freeze or refrigerate immediately; this sausage is very perishable. If it is frozen, it will keep for 2 months, but refrigerated sausage should be eaten within two days.

3. To cook, steam the thawed sausage links at 180° F (82° C) until the internal temperature is 160° F (71° C). Continue steaming the links at the same temperature for an additional 30 minutes. This additional steaming will tenderize the vegetable ingredients.

Carl's Italian Sausage

A friend of Italian ancestry helped me tailor this sausage so that it closely matches the flavor of the sausage that he ate so often as a child. Carl Preciso was raised on a farm near the Columbia River in Northern Oregon, and his grandfather, a farmer who was born in Northern Italy, raised hogs on this farm. Whenever a hog was butchered, Grandpa made sausage of the type presented below.

The following is the mild version that is popular in Northern Italy; it is also called sweet Italian sausage. To make the hot type, add more cayenne and, if you like, more paprika.

This sausage is traditionally stuffed into hog casings, but it can also be processed as bulk sausage, made into patties, or used as a pizza topping.

THE CASINGS

Prepare 7 feet (210 cm) of hog casings. Rinse the casings and soak them in water overnight. Before using, rinse the casings again, and soak in warm water for a few minutes.

THE MEAT FOR 2½ LBS. (1,150 G) OF SAUSAGE

Prepare 2½ lbs. (1,150 g) of pork shoulder butt that contains about 20 percent fat, or use 2 lbs. (910 g) of lean pork and ½ lb. (225 g) of back fat; cut the meat into ¾-inch (2 cm) cubes. Refrigerate the meat, and put the meat grinder and sausage stuffer in the refrigerator, too.

OTHER INGREDIENTS AND SEASONINGS

2¼ tsp. (11.25 ml) salt
2 tsp. (10 ml) black pepper, coarsely ground
2 tsp. (10 ml) ground coriander—packed in the spoon
2 tsp. (10 ml) anise seeds, cracked
2 tsp. (10 ml) fennel seeds, cracked or powdered
1 tsp. (5 ml) garlic powder
1½ tsp. (7.5 ml) paprika
¼ tsp. (1.25 ml) cayenne
¾ tsp. (3.75 ml) thyme, powdered
⅛ tsp. (0.625 ml) bay leaf powder
¼ cup (60 ml) lemon juice
3 Tbsp. (45 ml) light corn syrup
½ cup (120 ml) powdered skim milk
¼ cup (60 ml) cold water

MIXING AND STUFFING

1. Grind the pork with a ¼-inch (6.4 mm) or smaller plate, and refrigerate it for 30 minutes.
2. Except for the ground pork, mix the seasoning and other ingredients in a 5-quart (5 liter) mixing bowl. Refrigerate this seasoning mixture for about 15 minutes.
3. Add the chilled ground meat to the seasoning mixture, and knead until it is thoroughly mixed and uniform. This will require about three minutes. Chill this meat and seasoning mixture again while the sausage stuffer and hog casings are being prepared.
4. Stuff the sausage into the hog casings, and twist into 5-inch (13 cm) links. Refrigerate the links overnight to permit the seasoning to be absorbed by the meat. Use a covered container.
5. Sausages that will not be eaten within two days should be wrapped in plastic food wrap individually, placed in a plastic bag, and frozen.

6. Please see Chapter 6 for cooking suggestions. (Sometimes Italian sausage is browned in a frying pan, and then a little red wine is added; the sausage is covered and steamed in the wine until fully cooked. This is one of Carl's favorite methods of preparation.)

Chaurice (Creole)

This sausage probably came to Louisiana with the Spaniards. It is also believed that its name is related to *chorizo,* the well-known family of sausages popular in Spain and Mexico.

Chaurice has many variations and different levels of heat. The ingredient formula below is typical. The level of heat in this formula will be considered hot by most of us. However, a native of Louisiana would consider this sausage only moderately hot. If it needs to be hotter, increase the amount of cayenne and crushed red pepper flakes. This is an easy-to-make and flavorful sausage; the challenge is to get the heat adjusted to suit your taste.

Chaurice is good on a hoagie roll, and it works well for seasoning beans, potatoes, and sauerkraut. Louisiana natives say it goes well with eggs for breakfast.

CASINGS

This sausage is sometimes made into patties, but stuffing it into hog casings is more common. If small-diameter hog casing are used, prepare 7½ feet (225 cm) of casing. Rinse the casing, and refrigerate it in water overnight. Rinse again, and soak in warm water a few minutes before using.

THE MEAT FOR 2½ LBS. (1,150 G) OF SAUSAGE

Prepare 2½ lbs. (1,150 g) of fatty pork shoulder. Cut into ¾-inch (2 cm) cubes. Refrigerate. While this meat is being prepared, chill the grinder and sausage stuffer in the refrigerator.

SEASONINGS AND OTHER INGREDIENTS

2½ tsp. (12.5 ml) salt
½ cup (120 ml) onion, minced
¼ cup (60 ml) parsley, finely chopped
2 Tbsp. (30 ml) chili powder
2 tsp. (10 ml) garlic, minced
1 tsp. (5 ml) thyme

1 tsp. (5 ml) red pepper flakes
1 tsp. (5 ml) cayenne
1 tsp. (5 ml) sugar
½ tsp. (2.5 ml) black pepper
½ tsp. (2.5 ml) allspice
¼ tsp. (1.25 ml) bay leaf powder
cold water to make a seasoning slurry

MIXING AND STUFFING

1. Grind the well-chilled pork with a coarse plate. A coarse grind will give the sausage an authentic bite texture. Refrigerate the ground meat for about 30 minutes.
2. Except for the ground pork, measure the seasoning and other ingredients into a large mixing bowl, and add enough cold water to make a slurry. Stir until it is uniformly mixed. Refrigerate for at least 15 minutes.
3. Add the chilled ground meat to the seasoning mixture, and knead until it is thoroughly mixed and uniform. This will require about three minutes. Chill this sausage paste while the sausage stuffer and casings are being prepared.
4. Stuff the sausage paste into the casings, and twist into 5-inch (13 cm) links. Refrigerate the links overnight to permit the seasoning and flavors to be absorbed by the meat. Use a covered container.
5. Sausages that will not be eaten within two days should be wrapped in plastic food wrap individually, placed in a plastic bag, and frozen.

Sautéing or grilling the links is suggested. Please see Chapter 6 for cooking details.

Cheeseburger Sausage

This sausage is perfect for cheeseburger lovers. Grill, or cook in a covered frying pan. Serve on a hotdog bun with your favorite hamburger garnish.

CASINGS

Rinse 8 feet (240 cm) of small-diameter hog casing, and refrigerate it overnight in water. Rinse it again, and soak the casing in warm water a few minutes before using.

THE MEAT AND CHEESE FOR 2 LBS. 11 OZ. (1,200 G) OF SAUSAGE

Prepare the meat listed below; cut into ¾-inch (2 cm) cubes and refrigerate. Cut the cheese into ¼-inch (6 mm) cubes. (Any kind of cheese is acceptable, but many people prefer American cheese for use in this sausage.) While this meat and cheese is being prepared, chill the grinder and sausage stuffer in the refrigerator.

- 2 lbs. (910 g) of lean beef and ½ lb. (225 g) of beef or pork fat— or 2½ lbs. (1,150 g) of fatty beef. (Part of the beef may be replaced with wild game or pork.)
- 6 oz. (170 g) of cheese

SEASONINGS AND OTHER INGREDIENTS

1 tsp. (5 ml) salt
1 tsp. (5 ml) seasoned salt
¼ cup (60 ml) onion, minced
1 tsp. (5 ml) ground black pepper
½ tsp. (2.5 ml) ground mustard—packed in the spoon
2 tsp. (10 ml) dried parsley flakes
½ tsp. (2.5 ml) liquid smoke (optional)
½ tsp. (2.5 ml) garlic granules
½ cup (120 ml) finely powdered skim milk
¼ cup (60 ml) water

MIXING AND STUFFING

1. Grind the meat with a ³⁄₁₆-inch (4.8 mm) or smaller plate. Refrigerate the ground meat and cheese cubes for about 30 minutes.
2. Mix the seasoning, powdered skim milk, and water in a large mixing bowl. Refrigerate this seasoning mixture for about 15 minutes.
3. Add the chilled ground meat to the seasoning mixture, and knead until it is thoroughly mixed and uniform. This will require about three minutes. Fold in the cheese cubes. Chill this meat, cheese, and seasoning mixture again while the sausage stuffer and hog casings are being prepared.
4. Stuff the sausage into the hog casings, and twist into 6-inch (15 cm) links. Refrigerate the links overnight to permit the seasoning to be absorbed by the meat. Use a covered container.

5. Sausages that will not be eaten within two days should be wrapped in plastic food wrap individually, placed in a plastic bag, and frozen.

Please see Chapter 6 for cooking suggestions.

Chicken Breakfast Patties

Boned chicken thighs or turkey thighs will make the best sausage, but it will be good even if it is made with ground turkey sold at supermarkets.

THE CASING

This sausage is best made into patties, but if it will be stuffed into 24 to 26 mm (1 in. to 1¹⁄₁₆ in.) sheep casing, prepare about 14 feet (420 cm) of casing. Rinse the casing, and refrigerate it overnight in water. Rinse again, and soak it in warm water a few minutes before using.

MEAT FOR 2½ LBS. (1,150 G) OF SAUSAGE

Prepare 2½ lbs. (1,150 g) of boned chicken or turkey thighs; be sure to use the skin and the fat. (If commercially ground poultry is used, and it appears to be deficient in fat, be sure to use the optional vegetable oil listed below.) Cut the meat into ¾-inch (2 cm) cubes. Refrigerate the poultry and put the meat grinder in the refrigerator. If the sausage stuffer will be used, refrigerate it as well.

SEASONINGS AND OTHER INGREDIENTS

2½ tsp. (12.5 ml) salt
¼ cup (60 ml) dry breadcrumbs
2 tsp. (10 ml) dried parsley
1 tsp. (5 ml) poultry seasoning—packed in the spoon
½ tsp. (2.5 ml) garlic granules
½ tsp. (2.5 ml) ground ginger
½ tsp. (2.5 ml) thyme
½ tsp. (2.5 ml) white pepper
½ tsp. (2.5 ml) cayenne
1 egg, beaten
2 Tbsp. (30 ml) olive oil or vegetable oil (optional—see above)
¼ cup (60 ml) water
½ cup (120 ml) powdered skim milk

MIXING AND MAKING PATTIES OR STUFFING

1. Grind the poultry with a medium plate, and refrigerate it for 30 minutes.
2. Mix the seasoning and other ingredients (except for the meat) in a 5-quart (5 liter) mixing bowl. Refrigerate this seasoning mixture for about 15 minutes.
3. Blend the meat and the seasoning well by kneading for about three minutes. Shape the mixture into ⅜-inch (10 mm) thick patties, and wrap them in plastic food wrap. Alternatively, stuff the sausage into sheep casings.
4. Refrigerate the sausage that will be eaten within the next two days, and freeze the remainder.

Please see Chapter 6 for cooking suggestions.

Chinese-Style BBQ Pork Sausage

Almost everyone has eaten *cha shu*—flavorful Chinese-style barbecued pork that originated in the Hong Kong area of China. This delicacy is usually colored red on the outside. As an appetizer, it is thinly sliced and served in Chinese restaurants with a small dish of hot mustard and toasted sesame seeds. A small amount of hot Chinese mustard is smeared on the pork, and then it is dipped in toasted sesame seeds. *Cha shu* is also used in fried rice, or in other dishes, as a seasoning ingredient.

This sausage is based on a recipe for Chinese barbecued pork that appeared in a cookbook published in China. However, instead of barbecuing the marinated pork, we will grind it coarsely, stuff it in synthetic fibrous casing, and cook it by steaming or poaching.

The pork is marinated for a rather long time before it is ground and stuffed. This marinating imparts the unique flavor of Chinese barbecued pork. If you like pork, this product will probably become one of your favorites. My friends appreciate the taste imparted by the ingredients listed below.

Cha shu is traditionally used as an appetizer, but this sausage can also be used for gourmet sandwiches, or it can be used to season stir-fried vegetables. Cooks with an active imagination will use it as an ingredient in other dishes.

In China, red-orange powdered food color is used in the marinade. However, the red food color liquid available anywhere in the United States works perfectly. Large bottles of this food color can be obtained at restaurant-supply food stores inexpensively. Chinese cooks here in the United States usually use the American liquid food color.

Below, you will see that *clear* honey is required. If your honey has crystal-lized, it may be clarified quickly in a microwave. Put the required amount of honey in a small bowl, and zap it for 15 seconds at a time repeatedly in the microwave oven until it is clear.

CASINGS

The casings should not be prepared until the marinating is finished and the marinated meat is ground. Fibrous casings 2½-inch (6.35 cm) in diameter are recommended. For 2½ pounds (1,150 g) of sausage, two fibrous casings—12 inches (30 cm) long—will be required. Prepare the fibrous casings by soaking them in lukewarm water for about 30 minutes. Be sure to put warm water in-side the casings.

MEAT FOR 2½ LBS. (1,150 G) OF SAUSAGE

Prepare 2½ lbs. (1,150 g) of pork shoulder butt that contains about 20 percent fat. Cut the meat into ¾-inch (2 cm) cubes. Refrigerate the pork while the mari-nade is being prepared.

THE MARINADE FOR 2½ LBS. (1,150 G) OF SAUSAGE

⅓ cup (80 ml) honey (clear)
¼ cup (60 ml) sugar
¼ cup (60 ml) sherry, or *shao hsing* wine
3 Tbsp. (45 ml) soy sauce
1 Tbsp. (15 ml) grated fresh ginger, or 1 tsp. (5 ml) powdered ginger
1½ tsp. (7.5 ml) salt
½ tsp. (2.5 ml) red food color (liquid)
¼ tsp. (1.25 ml) white pepper, finely ground
2 cloves garlic, minced, or ¼ tsp. (1.25 ml) garlic powder

MARINATING, MIXING AND STUFFING

Day 1, morning

Prepare the marinade. Marinate the cubes of pork until the morning of Day 3. Stir the pork cubes or shake the container several times a day.

Day 3, morning

1. Remove the meat from the marinade and drain. Do not rinse. Discard the marinade. Grind the well-chilled pork with a coarse plate. A coarse plate will give the sausage a country-style bite texture. Refrigerate the ground meat for about 30 minutes.

2. Stuff the sausage into fibrous casings. Insert the cable probe of an electronic thermometer in the open end of one of the sausages. Close the casing around the probe with butcher's twine.

3. This sausage is a type of fresh sausage, so it should not be smoked. Steaming is recommended. Steaming and other cooking options are explained in Chapter 6.

Chipolata Sausage

Because this sausage has a Spanish-sounding name, I was surprised to learn that chipolata has been made in England for such a long time that the English consider it a British sausage. In fact, many people believe that the famous English banger is based on this sausage. The chipolata sausage, it seems, originated in Mexico, and somehow found its way to England; hence the Spanish-sounding name.

These mild, unassertive sausages are stuffed into sheep casings and twisted into short links—2 inches (5 cm) or less. The links have the nickname "little fingers." They are often used as cocktail sausages.

Powdered skim milk is not used in this formula. It is not required because the breadcrumbs function to retain moisture and plump the sausage links.

THE CASINGS

Sheep casing must be used if the sausages are to have the proper appearance. If 24 to 26 mm (1 in. to 1¹⁄₁₆ in.) sheep casing is to be used, prepare at least 14 feet (420 cm) of casing. Rinse the casings, and soak them in water overnight. Rinse them again, and soak in warm water a few minutes before using.

MEAT FOR 2½ LBS. (1,150 G) OF SAUSAGE

Prepare 2½ lbs. (1,150 g) of pork shoulder butt that contains about 20 percent fat. Cut the meat into ¾-inch (2 cm) cubes. Refrigerate the meat, and chill the meat grinder and the sausage stuffer in the refrigerator.

OTHER INGREDIENTS AND SEASONINGS

2½ tsp. (12.5 ml) salt
1½ tsp. (7.5 ml) onion granules
½ tsp. (2.5 ml) white pepper, finely ground
¼ tsp. (1.25 ml) ground coriander—packed in the spoon
¼ tsp. (1.25 ml) paprika

¼ tsp. (1.25 ml) nutmeg
¼ tsp. (1.25 ml) thyme
⅛ tsp. (0.625 ml) cayenne
¼ cup (60 ml) dry breadcrumbs, *not* packed in the cup
⅓ cup (80 ml) cold water

MIXING AND STUFFING

1. Grind the well-chilled pork with a fine plate. Refrigerate the ground meat for about 30 minutes.
2. In a large mixing bowl, mix all the seasoning and other ingredients except for the ground pork. Place this mixture in the freezer to cool rapidly.
3. Add the chilled ground meat to the seasoning mixture, and knead until it is thoroughly mixed and uniform. This will require about three minutes. Chill this sausage paste while the sausage stuffer and casings are being prepared.
4. Stuff the sausage paste into the casings, and twist into 2-inch (5 cm) links. (Because the sausage rope will be twisted into many short links, it is best to stuff the casings a little more loosely than normal to prevent ruptures.) Refrigerate the links overnight to permit the seasoning to be absorbed by the meat. Use a covered container.
5. Sausages that will not be eaten within one day should be wrapped in plastic food wrap, placed in a plastic bag, and frozen.

Sauté or grill the links. Please see Chapter 6 for cooking suggestions.

Classic Breakfast Sausage

This is not a clone of the popular Jimmy Dean brand breakfast sausage, but the taste is similar. It is good made into patties or stuffed into sheep casings.

THE CASING

If 24 to 26 mm (1 in. to 1¹⁄₁₆ in.) sheep casing is to be used, prepare at least 14 feet (420 cm) of casing. Soak it in water, in the refrigerator, overnight. Rinse again, and soak it in warm water before using.

MEAT FOR 2½ LBS. (1,150 G) OF SAUSAGE

Prepare 2½ lbs. (1,150 g) of pork shoulder butt that contains about 20 percent fat, or use 2 lbs. (910 g) of lean pork and ½ lb. (225 g) of back fat; cut the meat into ¾-inch (2 cm) cubes. Refrigerate the meat, and put the meat grinder in the refrigerator. If the sausage stuffer will be used, refrigerate it as well.

SEASONINGS AND OTHER INGREDIENTS

2½ tsp. (12.5 ml) salt
1½ tsp. (7.5 ml) sage, rubbed—packed in the spoon
1 tsp. (5 ml) parsley, dried, crushed
½ tsp. (2.5 ml) coriander, ground—packed in the spoon
½ tsp. (2.5 ml) MSG (optional)
½ tsp. (2.5 ml) black pepper
½ tsp. (2.5 ml) thyme
½ tsp. (2.5 ml) cayenne
2 Tbsp. (30 ml) water
¼ cup (60 ml) powdered skim milk

MIXING AND STUFFING

1. Grind the pork with a ³⁄₁₆-inch (4.8 mm) or smaller plate, and refrigerate it for 30 minutes.
2. Mix the seasoning, powdered skim milk, and water in a 5-quart (5 liter) mixing bowl. Refrigerate this seasoning mixture for about 15 minutes.
3. Blend the meat and the seasoning well by kneading for about three minutes. Shape the mixture into ⅜-inch (10 mm) thick patties, and wrap them in plastic food wrap. Alternatively, stuff the sausage into sheep casings.
4. Refrigerate the sausage that will be eaten within the next two days, and freeze the remainder.

Please see Chapter 6 for cooking suggestions.

Cumberland Sausage

The Cumberland sausage is one of the oldest and most popular in England. As with all famous sausages, there is no definitive recipe; each of the butchers and sausage makers has his/her own secret recipe. But no matter which recipe is used, there are certain things that they have in common. For example, breadcrumbs are mixed with the meat, and the sausage is always stuffed in hog casings. The British claim that there are several good reasons for using breadcrumbs in sausage: When the sausage is cooking and the juices are being squeezed out of the shrinking meat, the breadcrumbs absorb and retain these juices inside the casing; and, because the juices are retained in the casing, the link does not shrink or change its shape.

All the recipes I have seen call for nutmeg and black pepper, and most call for mace, as well. Many of the recipes have belly bacon (the common bacon in the United States) in the list of ingredients, and insist that the pork must be coarsely ground. In some of the recipes, small amounts of marjoram and/or sage are used.

The sausage mixture is traditionally stuffed into pork casings as long as 20 inches (50 cm), and is coiled and roasted in an oven. In modern times, however, the sausage rope is often twisted into shorter links and sautéed.

The traditional and common way to cook a Cumberland sausage coil is to roast it in a 300° F (150° C) oven for about 30 minutes (longer for medium- to large-diameter hog casings), basting from time to time. The cooked coil is cut into serving lengths, placed on a bed of mashed potatoes, and smothered with onion gravy. This makes a great stick-to-your-ribs meal, British style. Onion gravy mix is available in many United States grocery stores, but you may have to search a little.

CASINGS
Rinse 7 feet (210 cm) of small-diameter hog casing, and refrigerate it in water overnight. Rinse again before using.

THE MEAT FOR 2½ LBS. (1,150 G) OF SAUSAGE
Prepare the meats listed below and refrigerate them. While these meats are being prepared, chill the grinder and sausage stuffer in the refrigerator.

- 2 lbs. (910 g) of lean pork and ¼ lb. (115 g) of back fat—or 2¼ lbs. (1020 g) of fatty pork shoulder. Cut into ¾-inch (2 cm) cubes.
- ¼ lb. (115 g) of common belly bacon. Chop roughly.

SEASONINGS AND OTHER INGREDIENTS
2½ tsp. (12.5 ml) salt
1 tsp. (5 ml) black pepper
½ tsp. (2.5 ml) ground nutmeg
¼ tsp. (1.25 ml) mace
1 oz. (30 g) plain breadcrumbs, dry—about 6 Tbsp. (90 ml)
6 Tbsp. (90 ml) boiling water
¼ cup cold water

MIXING AND STUFFING

1. If fatty pork is being used, separate the fat from the pork to the extent possible—complete and perfect separation is not possible and not required. Grind the lean pork with a coarse plate, and grind the well-chilled—or partially frozen—fat and bacon with a fine plate. Refrigerate the ground meat for about 30 minutes.
2. In a small bowl, mix the breadcrumbs with the boiling water. Stir well and let set one minute. Add the cold water, stir again, and place in the freezer.
3. Mix the seasoning in a large mixing bowl. Remove the wet breadcrumbs from the freezer and add to the seasoning mixture. Refrigerate for about 15 minutes.
4. Add the chilled ground meat to the seasoning mixture, and knead until it is thoroughly mixed and uniform. This will require about three minutes. Chill this meat and seasoning mixture again while the sausage stuffer and hog casings are being prepared.
5. Stuff the sausage into the hog casings, and twist into four very long links— each about 20 inches (50 cm) long. Form each of these links into a coil. Or, if you want to sauté or grill the sausage instead of baking it, twist the rope into whatever sized links you desire. Refrigerate the coils and/or links overnight to permit the seasoning to be absorbed by the meat. Use a covered container.
6. Sausages that will not be eaten within one day should be wrapped in plastic food wrap individually, placed in a plastic bag, and frozen.

Please see Chapter 6 for cooking suggestions.

Curry Flavored Sausage

Most sausages have a cultural base, but Curry Flavored Sausage does not. Someone conceived the idea of seasoning sausage with curry powder and made the sausage. Several versions appeared, and this is one of the simple ones.

The tablespoon of curry powder in this recipe gives the sausage a mild and pleasant curry flavor. Even people who are not particularly fond of curry are likely to enjoy this sausage. Curry aficionados will want to increase the amount of curry powder and add some more heat in the form of pepper or cayenne.

CASINGS

If 24 to 26 mm (1 in. to 1$\frac{1}{16}$ in.) sheep casing is to be used, prepare about 14 feet (420 cm) of casing. If small-diameter hog casing will be used, prepare 7 feet

(210 cm). Rinse the casing, and refrigerate it in water overnight. Rinse again, and soak in warm water 30 minutes before using.

THE MEAT FOR 2½ LBS. (1,150 G) OF SAUSAGE

Prepare 2½ lbs. (1,150 g) of pork shoulder. Cut into ¾-inch (2 cm) cubes. Refrigerate. While this meat is being prepared, chill the grinder and sausage stuffer in the refrigerator.

SEASONINGS AND OTHER INGREDIENTS

2½ tsp. (12.5 ml) salt
1 Tbsp. (15 ml) curry powder, mild
1 tsp. (5 ml) white pepper
¼ cup (60 ml) cold milk
½ cup (120 ml) powdered skim milk

MIXING AND STUFFING

1. Grind the well-chilled pork with a medium or fine plate. Refrigerate the ground meat for about 30 minutes.
2. Mix the seasoning, powdered skim milk, and milk in a 5-quart (5 liter) mixing bowl. Refrigerate this seasoning mixture for about 15 minutes.
3. Add the chilled ground meat to the seasoning mixture, and knead until it is thoroughly mixed. This will require about three minutes. Chill this sausage paste while the sausage stuffer and casings are being prepared.
4. Stuff the sausage paste into the casings, and twist into links. Refrigerate the links overnight to permit the seasoning to be absorbed by the meat. Use a covered container.
5. Sausages that will not be eaten within two days should be wrapped in plastic food wrap individually, placed in a plastic bag, and frozen.

Any cooking method described in Chapter 6 may be used for these links.

Currywurst Sauce

Since World War II, currywurst has gradually become the most popular fast food item in Germany. The sausage for currywurst is grilled or sautéed, cut into bite-sized pieces about ⅜ inch (1 cm) thick, and topped with a curry flavored tomato sauce; it is usually served with French fries and a roll. The sausage used for this fast food item is usually the common uncured bratwurst, but any kind of stuffed sausage may be used—even cured Polish sausage.

Consequently, instructions for making currywurst are *not* instructions for making a unique sausage; they are directions for making the curry flavored tomato sauce that is splashed on top of any kind of sausage link.

Each of the currywurst vendors usually has his or her secret recipe for the currywurst sauce, but many amateur recipes are available. Most of the amateur recipes are very simple and use tomato ketchup as a base. The sauce below is a little more sophisticated, and it is similar to the sauce served by the professionals; yet, it is easy to make. This sauce will serve six to eight people.

While the sauce is being prepared, sauté, roast, or grill bratwurst, or your favorite sausage. If you wish to serve it in the authentic German fast-food style, you should also prepare French fries and hot rolls. Instead of the German fast-food style, my wife and I like to eat it with steamed medium-grain rice and a salad.

If onion granules and garlic granules are used in place of the fresh items, the preparation time for this sauce is much faster.

INGREDIENTS
2 cans (15 oz./425 g size cans) of tomato sauce
1 onion, medium, chopped—or 2 tsp. (10 ml) onion granules
3 Tbsp. (45 ml) honey
¾ tsp. (3.75 ml) white pepper, finely ground
2 cloves garlic, sliced—or ¾ tsp. (3.75 ml) garlic granules
1 Tbsp. (15 ml) paprika
1 to 3 tsp. (5 to 15 ml) chili sauce (season to taste)
1 to 3 Tbsp. (15 to 45 ml) mild curry powder (season to taste)

SAUCE PREPARATION
1. Pour the tomato sauce in a medium-size saucepan. (Because tomato sauce is somewhat acidic, a stainless steel or enameled saucepan is best.) Add all other ingredients except the chili sauce and curry powder. Bring to a boil. Simmer for 20 to 30 minutes if the sauce was made with fresh onion and garlic. Simmer for 5 minutes if onion and garlic granules are being used.
2. Strain the sauce, and discard the chopped onions and sliced garlic. Return the sauce to the pan.
3. Slowly add the chili sauce to taste, and then add the curry powder to taste. Simmer about five minutes more to bring out the flavor of the curry powder.

4. Slice the sautéed, roasted, or grilled sausage, and place the slices on the individual plates with the French fries and roll. The slices should be about ⅜ inch (1 cm) thick. (If hog casings were used for the links, the casings may be removed before the links are sliced.)

5. Let each person drench the sausage in the desired amount of sauce.

Duck Sausage

This sausage has a variety of seasonings and spices that are commonly used for sausage, but the main ingredient—duck—makes this an exotic sausage. Domesticated duck works as well as wild duck. However, if domesticated duck is used, be sure to use duck that has not been pumped with brine (salt water).

Save the duck carcass. At the end of this sausage recipe, there are easy-to-follow instructions on how to use the carcass to make delicious duck soup.

If you happen to have a lot of duck meat on your hands, you might wish to try the cured duck sausage, *Duckwurst*, in the next chapter.

CASINGS

If 24 to 26 mm (1 in. to 1¹⁄₁₆ in.) sheep casing is to be used, prepare about 14 feet (420 cm) of casing. If small-diameter hog casing will be used, prepare 7 feet (210 cm). Rinse the casing, and refrigerate it in water overnight. Rinse again, and soak in warm water a few minutes before using.

THE MEAT FOR 2½ LBS. (1,150 G) OF SAUSAGE

Prepare 2 lbs. (910 g) of duck meat; the skin and fat should not exceed about 20 percent of the total meat. Cube the duck. Prepare ½ lb. (250g) of bacon; cut into squares. Refrigerate these meats for at least 30 minutes. While the meats are being prepared, chill the meat grinder and stuffer in the refrigerator.

Mince the meats with the smallest plate available. It would be best to mince the meats two times; mincing twice provides a finely textured sausage. Chill the meat between each grinding. After the grinding is finished, chill the meat again for about 30 minutes.

SEASONINGS AND OTHER INGREDIENTS

2¼ tsp. (11.25 ml) salt
1½ tsp. (7.5 ml) black pepper
1 tsp. (5 ml) paprika
½ tsp. (2.5 ml) cayenne
½ tsp. (2.5 ml) coriander seed, ground—packed in the spoon

¼ tsp. (1.25 ml) thyme
¼ tsp. (1.25 ml) garlic granules
¼ tsp. (1.25 ml) celery seed, ground
¼ tsp. (1.25 ml) sage, rubbed—packed in the spoon
⅛ tsp. (0.625 ml) summer savory
⅛ tsp. (0.625 ml) allspice
1 Tbsp. (15 ml) light corn syrup
2 Tbsp. (30 ml) cold water
2 Tbsp. (30 ml) finely powdered milk
2 Tbsp. (30 ml) red wine

MIXING AND STUFFING

1. Except for the ground duck and ground bacon, measure the seasoning and other ingredients into a large mixing bowl, and mix well. Refrigerate for at least 15 minutes.
2. Add the chilled ground meat to the seasoning mixture, and knead until it is thoroughly mixed and uniform. This will require about three minutes. Chill this sausage paste while the sausage stuffer and casings are being prepared.
3. Stuff the sausage paste into the casings, and twist into links. Refrigerate the links overnight to permit the seasoning to be absorbed by the meat. Use a covered container.
4. Sausages that will not be eaten within two days should be wrapped in plastic food wrap individually, placed in a plastic bag, and frozen.

It is suggested that the links be sautéed in a small amount of vegetable oil or grilled. Please see Chapter 6 for detailed cooking instructions.

Duck Soup

It takes only a little work to make a very delicious and unique soup using the bones left after carving the meat from them.

INGREDIENTS

duck bones
1 each: duck heart, gizzard, and neck
1½ quarts (1½ liters) water
4 green onions, roughly chopped

1 Tbsp. (15 ml) sherry or *shao hsing* (optional)
¼ tsp. (1.25 ml) ginger powder (optional)
5 bouillon cubes, chicken flavor

1. Put all the ingredients in a pot, and simmer about one hour.
2. Strain the soup into another pot. (There will be scum on the sides of the first pot.) If froth or scum is on the surface, skim it off. Save the heart, gizzard, and neck to use as a snack—or mince this meat and add it to the strained broth. Discard the bones and the green onions.
3. Add 1 cup (240 ml) of very thinly sliced celery to the broth, and simmer a few minutes until the celery is barely tender. If desired, the soup may be thickened with 1 tablespoon of cornstarch mixed with 3 tablespoons of water; add the cornstarch and water mixture to the soup slowly while stirring. Boil gently for one minute. Check the seasoning. Serve.

English Bangers

This sausage is stuffed in hog casings, and it is very popular in the United Kingdom. The special feature of this sausage is the use of breadcrumbs as one of the main ingredients. The breadcrumbs retain moisture, and they cause a significant amount of steam to be generated in the sausage when it is cooked. The pressure generated by the steam is often enough to make the sausages rupture or explode; they are called bangers for this reason.

You may use the prepared, unseasoned breadcrumbs available in all grocery stores in the United States, the coarse Japanese-style breadcrumbs available in Asian food stores and even in common grocery stores (known as *panko*), or you may make your own breadcrumbs by raking dried bread with the tines of a fork. I prefer *panko*, the Japanese-style breadcrumbs. Depending on the kind and amount of breadcrumbs you use, you may have to adjust the moisture content of the stuffing mixture.

Powdered skim milk is not used in this formula. It is not required because the breadcrumbs function to retain moisture and plump the sausage links. Pork broth is often used in bangers. However, I find that chicken consommé powder mixed with water is more convenient, and it tastes just as good.

THE CASINGS

Prepare 8 feet (240 cm) of hog casings. Rinse the casings, and soak them in water overnight. Rinse them again, and soak in warm water for a few minutes before using.

MEAT FOR 2½ LBS. (1,150 G) OF SAUSAGE

Prepare 2½ lbs. (1,150 g) of pork shoulder butt that contains about 20 percent fat. Cut the meat into ¾-inch (2 cm) cubes. Refrigerate the meat, and chill the meat grinder and the sausage stuffer in the refrigerator.

OTHER INGREDIENTS AND SEASONINGS

1½ tsp. (7.5 ml) chicken consommé powder
1 tsp. (5 ml) salt
½ tsp. (2.5 ml) black pepper, finely ground
½ tsp. (2.5 ml) sage—packed in the spoon
¼ tsp. (1.25 ml) ginger powder
¼ tsp. (1.25 ml) mace
1 egg
¾ cup (180 ml) dry breadcrumbs, *not* packed in the cup
½ cup (120 ml) cold water

MIXING AND STUFFING

1. Grind the well-chilled pork with a medium or coarse plate. A coarse plate will give the sausage a country-style bite texture. Refrigerate the ground meat for about 30 minutes.
2. In a large mixing bowl, blend the breadcrumbs, chicken consommé powder, water, and egg. Mix well, and set aside one minute. Add the seasoning ingredients and mix again. Place in the freezer to cool rapidly.
3. Add the chilled ground meat to the egg-and-seasoning mixture, and knead until it is thoroughly mixed and uniform. This will require about three minutes. Chill this sausage paste while the sausage stuffer and casings are being prepared.
4. Stuff the sausage paste into the casings, and twist into 5-inch (13 cm) links. Because the high water content of the sausage will create internal steam pressure, it is best to stuff the casings a little more loosely than normal. Refrigerate the links overnight to permit the seasoning to be absorbed by the meat. Use a covered container.
5. Sausages that will not be eaten within one day should be wrapped in plastic food wrap individually, placed in a plastic bag, and frozen.

Sauté or grill the links. Please see Chapter 6 for cooking suggestions.

French Country Sausage

The French use a blend of four spices to season various dishes. It is even used in some sausage formulations. They call it *quatre épices*, and it is used in this French Country Sausage. Quatre épices can be purchased, but it is very easy to blend it in your own kitchen; please see Appendix 1 for blending instructions and additional information.

THE CASING

Patties or natural casings are the best for French Country Sausage. If 24 to 26 mm (1 in. to 1¹⁄₁₆ in.) sheep casing is to be used, prepare about 14 feet (420 cm) of casing. If small-diameter hog casing will be used, prepare 7 feet (210 cm). Rinse the casing, and refrigerate it in water overnight. Rinse again, and soak in warm water a few minutes before using.

MEAT FOR 2½ LBS. (1,150 G) OF SAUSAGE

Prepare 2½ lbs. (1,150 g) of pork shoulder butt that contains about 20 percent fat, or use 2 lbs. (910 g) of lean pork and ½ lb. (225 g) of back fat; cut the meat into ¾-inch (2 cm) cubes. Refrigerate the meat, and put the meat grinder in the refrigerator. If the sausage stuffer will be used, refrigerate it, as well.

SEASONINGS AND OTHER INGREDIENTS

2½ tsp. (12.5 ml) salt
2 tsp. (10 ml) parsley, dried
1 tsp. (5 ml) black pepper
½ tsp. (2.5 ml) thyme
½ tsp. (2.5 ml) quatre épices (see Appendix 1)—packed in the spoon
¼ tsp. (1.25 ml) nutmeg
2 Tbsp. (30 ml) white wine

MIXING AND STUFFING

1. Grind the pork with a medium plate, and refrigerate it for 30 minutes.
2. Except for the ground pork, mix the seasoning and other ingredients in a 5-quart (5 liter) mixing bowl. Refrigerate this seasoning mixture for about 15 minutes.
3. Blend the meat and the seasoning well by kneading for about three minutes. Make patties, or stuff the sausage into sheep or hog casings.

4. Refrigerate the sausage that will be eaten within the next two days, and freeze the remainder.

Please see Chapter 6 for cooking suggestions.

French Garlic Sausage

Garlic and black pepper are the predominant seasonings in this sausage, but other seasonings—including the brandy or sherry—make a decided contribution to the flavor.

THE CASING

Small natural casings are the best for French Garlic Sausage. If 24 to 26 mm (1 in. to 1$\frac{1}{16}$ in.) sheep casing is to be used, prepare about 14 feet (420 cm) of casing. If small-diameter hog casing will be used, prepare 7 feet (210 cm). Rinse the casing, and refrigerate it in water overnight. Rinse again, and soak in warm water a few minutes before using.

MEAT FOR 2½ LBS. (1,150 G) OF SAUSAGE

Prepare 2½ lbs. (1,150 g) of pork shoulder butt that contains about 20 percent fat, or use 2 lbs. (910 g) of lean pork and ½ lb. (225 g) of back fat; cut the meat into ¾-inch (2 cm) cubes. Refrigerate the meat, and put the meat grinder in the refrigerator. If the sausage stuffer will be used, refrigerate it, as well.

SEASONINGS AND OTHER INGREDIENTS

2½ tsp. (12.5 ml) salt
1 Tbsp. (15 ml) black pepper, coarse grind
2 tsp. (10 ml) garlic, minced
1 tsp. (5 ml) nutmeg
¾ tsp. (3.75 ml) thyme
½ tsp. (2.5 ml) ginger powder
¼ tsp. (1.25 ml) allspice
2 eggs, large
3 Tbsp. (45 ml) brandy or sherry

MIXING AND STUFFING

1. Grind the pork with a medium plate, and refrigerate it for 30 minutes.

2. Except for the ground pork, mix the seasoning and other ingredients in a 5-quart (5 liter) mixing bowl. Refrigerate this seasoning mixture for about 15 minutes.
3. Blend the meat and the seasoning well by kneading for about three minutes. Stuff the sausage into sheep or hog casings.
4. Refrigerate the sausage that will be eaten within the next two days, and freeze the remainder.

Please see Chapter 6 for cooking suggestions.

Fresh Bratwurst

Bratwurst is one of the most popular sausages in North America, and it is available in almost all grocery stores. In the German language, *brat* means *roast* or *bake*, but this sausage is most often grilled or sautéed. Serve it between two halves of a roll—exactly like a hotdog. Garnish it with horseradish mustard, chopped onions, and dill pickle sticks. Served with cold beer, this will be an unforgettable meal.

CASINGS
Rinse 7 feet (210 cm) of small-diameter hog casing, and refrigerate it, in water, overnight. Rinse again in warm water before using.

THE MEAT FOR 2½ LBS. (1,150 G) OF SAUSAGE
Prepare the meats listed below; cut into ¾-inch (2 cm) cubes and refrigerate. While this meat is being prepared, chill the grinder and sausage stuffer in the refrigerator.

• 1½ lbs. (680 g) of lean pork and ½ lb. (225 g) of back fat—or 2 lbs. (910 g) of fatty pork shoulder.
• ½ lb. (225 g) of lean veal (beef, chicken thighs, or turkey thighs may be substituted).

SEASONINGS AND OTHER INGREDIENTS
2½ tsp. (12.5 ml) salt
1 tsp. (5 ml) white pepper
1 tsp. (5 ml) ground mustard—packed in the spoon
¾ tsp. (3.75 ml) ground nutmeg
½ tsp. (2.5 ml) garlic granules

½ tsp. (2.5 ml) sage—packed in the spoon

½ cup (120 ml) finely powdered skim milk

¼ cup (60 ml) water

1 Tbsp. (15 ml) light corn syrup

2 eggs

MIXING AND STUFFING

1. Grind the meats together with a ³⁄₁₆-inch (4.8 mm) or smaller plate. Refrigerate the ground meat for about 30 minutes.

2. Mix the seasoning and all other ingredients except for the ground meat in a large mixing bowl. Refrigerate this seasoning mixture for about 15 minutes.

3. Add the chilled ground meat to the seasoning mixture, and knead until it is thoroughly mixed and uniform. This will require about three minutes. Chill this meat and seasoning mixture again while the sausage stuffer and hog casings are being prepared.

4. Stuff the sausage paste into the hog casings, and twist into 6-inch (15 cm) links. Refrigerate the links overnight to permit the seasoning to be absorbed by the meat. Use a covered container.

5. Sausages that will not be eaten within two days should be wrapped in plastic food wrap individually, placed in a plastic bag, and frozen.

Please see Chapter 6 for cooking suggestions.

Goosewurst

In the past, domesticated goose was the traditional Christmas dinner fare in many households, but turkey and ham have replaced it. Goose, however, remains a popular wildfowl for hunting in Canada and the United States.

This recipe can be used for either domesticated or wild goose. However, domesticated geese sold at grocery stores are commonly pumped with a salt solution before freezing. If such geese are used to make this sausage, the sausage will be too salty. You might have to search for a goose that has not been pumped.

THE CASING

I always make patties with this sausage, but it can be stuffed in casings. If 24 to 26 mm (1 in. to 1¹⁄₁₆ in.) sheep casing is to be used, prepare about 14 feet (420 cm) of casing. If small-diameter hog casing will be used, prepare 7 feet (210 cm). Rinse the casing, and refrigerate it in water overnight. Rinse again, and soak in warm water a few minutes before using.

MEAT FOR 2½ LBS. (1,150 G) OF SAUSAGE

Prepare 2½ lbs. (1,150 g) of goose that contains about 20 percent fat. The skin may be used. Cut the meat into ¾-inch (2 cm) cubes. Refrigerate the meat, and put the meat grinder in the refrigerator. If the sausage stuffer will be used, refrigerate it as well.

SEASONINGS AND OTHER INGREDIENTS

2½ tsp. (12.5 ml) salt
¼ cup (60 ml) minced onions
2 Tbsp. (30 ml) prunes, finely chopped
2 Tbsp. (30 ml) sherry
1 Tbsp. (15 ml) honey
½ tsp. (2.5 ml) marjoram
½ tsp. (2.5 ml) rosemary
¼ tsp. (1.25 ml) cayenne
¼ tsp. (1.25 ml) garlic powder

MIXING AND STUFFING

1. Grind the goose flesh with a medium plate, and refrigerate it for 30 minutes.
2. Mix the seasoning and other ingredients, except for the ground goose, in a 5-quart (5 liter) mixing bowl. Refrigerate this seasoning mixture for about 15 minutes.
3. Blend the ground meat and the seasoning well by kneading for about three minutes. Shape the mixture into ⅜-inch (10 mm) thick patties, and wrap them in plastic food wrap. Alternatively, stuff the sausage into sheep or hog casings.
4. Refrigerate the sausage that will be eaten within the next two days, and freeze the remainder.

Please see Chapter 6 for cooking suggestions.

Greek Sausage (Loukanika)

Loukanika may not be found in a common grocery store, but it is a fairly well known sausage among sausage makers. This uniquely seasoned sausage is delicious as a snack food, a main course, or as an ingredient for various dishes.

CASINGS

Loukanika may be made into patties, or it may be stuffed into hog casings. If you intend to use small-diameter hog casing, rinse 7½ feet (210 cm) of the casing and refrigerate it, in water, overnight. Rinse again before using.

THE MEAT FOR 2½ LBS. (1,150 G) OF SAUSAGE

Prepare the meats listed below; cut into ¾-inch (2 cm) cubes and refrigerate. While this meat is being prepared, chill the grinder and sausage stuffer in the refrigerator.

- 1½ lbs. (680 g) of lean pork and ½ lb. (225 g) of back fat—or 2 lbs. (910 g) of fatty pork shoulder.
- ½ lb. (225 g) of lean lamb

NOTE: This sausage is also made with beef instead of lamb, and it is often made with 100 percent pork, as well.

SEASONINGS AND OTHER INGREDIENTS

2½ tsp. (12.5 ml) salt
1 Tbsp. (15 ml) olive oil
1 tsp. (5 ml) marjoram
½ tsp. (2.5 ml) thyme
½ tsp. (2.5 ml) black pepper
½ tsp. (2.5 ml) ground allspice
½ tsp. (2.5 ml) coriander—packed in the spoon
½ tsp. (2.5 ml) oregano
1 clove garlic, finely minced
¼ cup (60 ml) red wine
½ cup (120 ml) finely powdered skim milk
½ cup (120 ml) minced onion
2 Tbsp. (30 ml) cold water
grated orange peel from one orange (orange zest)

MIXING AND STUFFING

1. Grind the meats together with a medium-size plate. Refrigerate the ground meat for about 30 minutes.

2. Mix the seasoning and all other ingredients, except for the ground meat, in a large mixing bowl. Refrigerate this seasoning mixture for about 15 minutes.

3. Add the chilled ground meat to the seasoning mixture, and knead until it is thoroughly mixed and uniform. This will require about three minutes. Chill this meat and seasoning mixture again while the sausage stuffer and hog casings are being prepared.

4. Stuff the sausage into the hog casings, and twist into 6-inch (15 cm) links. Refrigerate the links overnight to permit the seasoning to be absorbed by the meat. Use a covered container.

5. Sausages that will not be eaten within two days should be wrapped in plastic food wrap individually, placed in a plastic bag, and frozen.

Please see Chapter 6 for cooking suggestions.

Irish Breakfast Sausage

This is one of those sausages that people never tire of eating. It is mildly seasoned, and it goes well with everything, anytime. Like most UK sausages, it contains breadcrumbs to hold the juices.

The sausage mixture is traditionally stuffed into sheep casings and twisted into 4-inch (10 cm) links. It would also be very good formed into patties or stuffed into hog casings.

CASINGS

If 24 to 26 mm (1 in. to 1$\frac{1}{16}$ in.) sheep casing is to be used, prepare about 14 feet (420 cm) of casing. If small-diameter hog casing will be used, prepare 7 feet (210 cm). Rinse the casing, and refrigerate it in water overnight. Rinse again before using.

THE MEAT FOR 2½ LBS. (1,150 G) OF SAUSAGE

Prepare 2 lbs. (910 g) of lean pork and ½ lb. (225 g) of back fat—or 2½ lbs. (1,150 g) of fatty pork shoulder. Cut into ¾-inch (2 cm) cubes. Refrigerate. While this meat is being prepared, chill the grinder and sausage stuffer in the refrigerator.

SEASONINGS AND OTHER INGREDIENTS

2½ tsp. (12.5 ml) salt

1½ tsp. (7.5 ml) black pepper

1 tsp. (5 ml) marjoram

½ tsp. (2.5 ml) mace

½ tsp. (2.5 ml) thyme

¼ tsp. (1.25 ml) rosemary

½ cup (120 ml) plain breadcrumbs, dry—*not* packed in the cup

1 egg, large

6 Tbsp. (90 ml) boiling water

½ cup (120 ml) cold water

1 Tbsp. (15 ml) whiskey *(optional)*—Irish whiskey, if you have it

MIXING AND STUFFING

1. Grind the well-chilled pork with a fine plate. Refrigerate the ground meat for about 30 minutes.

2. In a small bowl, mix the breadcrumbs with the boiling water. Stir well and let set 1 minute. Add the cold water, stir again, and place in the freezer.

3. Crack the egg into a large mixing bowl, and beat well. Add the seasoning, including the optional whiskey, and mix well. Remove the wet breadcrumbs from the freezer and add to the seasoning mixture. Stir until uniform. Refrigerate for at least 15 minutes.

4. Add the chilled ground meat to the seasoning mixture, and knead until it is thoroughly mixed and uniform. This will require about three minutes. Chill this meat and seasoning mixture again while the sausage stuffer and casings are being prepared.

5. Stuff the sausage paste into the casings, and twist into 4-inch (10 cm) links. Because the sausage will be twisted into short links, and because the high water content of the sausage will create internal steam pressure, it is best to stuff the casings a little more loosely than normal. Refrigerate the links overnight to permit the seasoning to be absorbed by the meat. Use a covered container.

6. Sausages that will not be eaten within one day should be wrapped in plastic food wrap, placed in a plastic bag, and frozen.

Sauté or grill the links. Please see Chapter 6 for cooking suggestions.

Irish Sausage

The Irish are not famous sausage makers, but all the Irish sausage that I have eaten has been delightful. Pleasant, unobtrusive flavor seems to be their hallmark. Like most UK sausages, Irish sausage usually contains breadcrumbs to hold the juices.

   This sausage is best stuffed into sheep casings and twisted into links. It would also be very good formed into patties or stuffed into hog casings.

CASINGS

If 24 to 26 mm (1 in. to 1¹⁄₁₆ in.) sheep casing is to be used, prepare about 15 feet (450 cm) of casings. If small-diameter hog casing will be used, prepare 7½ feet (225 cm). Rinse the casing, and refrigerate it in water overnight. Rinse again, and soak in warm water 30 minutes before using.

THE MEAT FOR 2½ LBS. (1,150 G) OF SAUSAGE

Prepare 2 lbs. (910 g) of lean pork and ½ lb. (225 g) of back fat—or 2½ lbs. (1,150 g) of fatty pork shoulder. Cut into ¾-inch (2 cm) cubes. Refrigerate. While this meat is being prepared, chill the grinder and sausage stuffer in the refrigerator.

SEASONINGS AND OTHER INGREDIENTS

2¾ tsp. (13.75 ml) salt
1½ tsp. (7.5 ml) black pepper
1 tsp. (5 ml) marjoram
1 tsp. (5 ml) thyme
½ tsp. (2.5 ml) garlic granules
½ tsp. (2.5 ml) basil
½ tsp. (2.5 ml) rosemary
6 Tbsp. (90 ml) plain breadcrumbs, dry—*not* packed in the spoon
2 eggs, beaten
6 Tbsp. (90 ml) boiling water
½ cup (120 ml) cold water

MIXING AND STUFFING

1. Grind the well-chilled pork with a medium or coarse plate. A coarse plate will give the sausage a country-style texture. Refrigerate the ground meat for about 30 minutes.

2. In a small bowl, mix the breadcrumbs with the boiling water. Stir well and let set one minute. Add the cold water, stir again, and place in the freezer.

3. Crack the eggs into a large mixing bowl, and beat. Add the seasoning ingredients, and mix well. Remove the wet breadcrumbs from the freezer, and add them to the egg-and-seasoning mixture. Stir until uniform. Refrigerate for at least 15 minutes.

4. Add the chilled ground meat to the egg-and-seasoning mixture, and knead until it is thoroughly mixed and uniform. This will require about three minutes. Chill this sausage paste while the sausage stuffer and casings are being prepared.

5. Stuff the sausage paste into the casings, and twist into links. Because the high water content of the sausage will create internal steam pressure, it is best to stuff the casings a little more loosely than normal. Refrigerate the links overnight to permit the seasoning to be absorbed by the meat. Use a covered container.

6. Sausages that will not be eaten within one day should be wrapped in plastic food wrap individually, placed in a plastic bag, and frozen.

Sauté or grill the links. Please see Chapter 6 for cooking suggestions.

Italian Farm-Style Sausage

Italian farmers in northern Italy use recipes similar to the one below. There is nothing in the recipe that identifies it as originating in Italy. Actually, this recipe is similar to the simple farm sausages made in countries all over the world—if that country has a culture based on European culture. The sausage is simple, mild, and pleasant tasting. It can be formed into patties or stuffed, and it can be cooked by any method other than smoking.

THE CASING

I usually make patties with this sausage, but it can be stuffed in casings. If 24 to 26 mm (1 in. to 1$\frac{1}{16}$ in.) sheep casing is to be used, prepare about 14 feet (420 cm) of casing. If small-diameter hog casing will be used, prepare 7 feet (210 cm). Rinse the casing, and refrigerate it in water overnight. Rinse again, and soak in warm water a few minutes before using.

MEAT FOR 2½ LBS. (1,150 G) OF SAUSAGE

Prepare 2½ lbs. (1,150 g) of pork shoulder butt that contains about 20 percent fat, or use 2 lbs. (910 g) of lean pork and ½ lb. (225 g) of back fat; cut the meat into ¾-inch (2 cm) cubes. Refrigerate the meat, and put the meat grinder in the refrigerator. If the sausage stuffer will be used, refrigerate it, as well.

SEASONINGS AND OTHER INGREDIENTS

2½ tsp. (12.5 ml) salt
2 tsp. (10 ml) granulated sugar
¾ tsp. (3.75 ml) black pepper
¼ tsp. (1.25 ml) ground coriander—packed in the spoon
¼ tsp. (1.25 ml) nutmeg
⅛ tsp. (0.625 ml) cayenne
1 clove garlic, minced
¼ cup (60 ml) water
½ cup (120 ml) powdered skim milk

MIXING AND STUFFING

1. Grind the pork with a ¼-inch (6.4 mm) plate, and refrigerate it for 30 minutes. (Because this is a country-style sausage, coarsely ground meat is appropriate.)
2. Mix the seasoning, powdered skim milk, and water in a 5-quart (5 liter) mixing bowl. Refrigerate this seasoning mixture for about 15 minutes.
3. Blend the meat and the seasoning well by kneading the two for about three minutes. Shape the mixture into ⅜-inch (10 mm) thick patties, and wrap them in plastic food wrap. Alternatively, stuff the sausage into sheep or hog casings.
4. Refrigerate the sausage that will be eaten within the next two days, and freeze the remainder.

Please see Chapter 6 for cooking suggestions.

Italian Sausage with Lemon Zest

Most of the spices used in traditional Italian sausage are used in this sausage, but less of these spices are used so that the lemon zest and white wine can impart a bright, tangy flavor.

THE CASINGS

Prepare 7 feet (210 cm) of hog casings. Rinse the casings, and soak them in water overnight. Rinse the casings again, and soak in warm water a few minutes before using.

THE MEAT FOR 2½ LBS. (1,150 G) OF SAUSAGE

Prepare 2½ lbs. (1,150 g) of pork shoulder butt that contains about 20 percent fat, or use 2 lbs. (910 g) of lean pork and ½ lb. (225 g) of back fat; cut the meat into ¾-inch (2 cm) cubes. Refrigerate the meat, and put the meat grinder and sausage stuffer in the refrigerator.

OTHER INGREDIENTS AND SEASONINGS

2¼ tsp. (11.25 ml) salt
2 tsp. (10 ml) parsley, dried
1 tsp. (5 ml) ground coriander—packed in the spoon
1 tsp. (5 ml) anise seeds, cracked
1 tsp. (5 ml) fennel seeds, cracked or powdered
1 tsp. (5 ml) garlic powder
1 tsp. (5 ml) grated lemon peel (lemon zest)
¼ cup (60 ml) white wine
¼ cup (60 ml) finely powdered skim milk

MIXING AND STUFFING

1. Grind the pork with a ¼-inch (6.4 mm) plate, and refrigerate it for 30 minutes.
2. Mix the seasoning, lemon zest, wine, and powdered milk in a 5-quart (5 liter) mixing bowl. Refrigerate this seasoning mixture for about 15 minutes.
3. Add the chilled ground meat to the seasoning mixture, and knead until it is thoroughly mixed and uniform. This will require about three minutes. Chill this meat and seasoning mixture again while the sausage stuffer and hog casings are being prepared.
4. Stuff the sausage into the hog casings, and twist into 5-inch (13 cm) links. Refrigerate the links overnight to permit the seasoning to be absorbed by the meat. Use a covered container.
5. Sausages that will not be eaten within two days should be wrapped in plastic food wrap individually, placed in a plastic bag, and frozen.

Please see Chapter 6 for cooking suggestions.

Italian Turkey Sausage

Much of the seasoning used in this sausage is typical of Italian sausage, but some of the seasoning—particularly the sage—is typical of American breakfast sausage. The variety of seasonings makes this a flavorful sausage, but the quantities of the various seasonings are modest, so it is not strongly flavored. However, one thing is certain: It is a versatile sausage that can be used as bulk sausage for seasoning, can be formed into patties, or can be stuffed into natural casings and used as a main course.

The meat specified in the original recipe was ground turkey sold at grocery stores, but boned turkey thighs together with the fat and skin would make better sausage, so they are suggested in this revised formula. Obviously, pork could replace part of the turkey.

THE CASINGS
Forming the sausage into patties is certainly an option, but if 24 to 26 mm (1 in. to 1¹⁄₁₆ in.) sheep casing is to be used, prepare about 14 feet (420 cm) of casing. If small-diameter hog casing will be used, prepare 7 feet (210 cm). Rinse the casing, and refrigerate it in water overnight. Rinse again, and soak in warm water 30 minutes before using.

THE MEAT FOR 2½ LBS. (1,150 G) OF SAUSAGE
Prepare 2½ lbs. (1,150 g) of boned turkey thighs. Cut the meat into ¾-inch (2 cm) cubes. (Alternatively, use ground turkey purchased at the grocery store.) Refrigerate the meat, and put the meat grinder and sausage stuffer in the refrigerator.

OTHER INGREDIENTS AND SEASONINGS
2½ tsp. (12.5 ml) salt
2 tsp. (10 ml) poultry seasoning—packed in the spoon
1 tsp. (5 ml) ginger powder
1 tsp. (5 ml) black pepper, ground
1 tsp. (5 ml) oregano
½ tsp. (2.5 ml) fennel seeds, cracked or powdered
½ tsp. (2.5 ml) sage—packed in the spoon
½ tsp. (2.5 ml) garlic powder
½ tsp. (2.5 ml) thyme, powdered
¼ tsp. (1.25 ml) cayenne
¼ tsp. (1.25 ml) anise seeds, cracked
⅛ tsp. (0.625 ml) ground coriander—packed in the spoon
1 Tbsp. (15 ml) light corn syrup
½ cup (120 ml) powdered skim milk
¼ cup (60 ml) cold water

MIXING AND STUFFING

1. Grind the meat with a ¼-inch (6.4 mm) or smaller plate, and refrigerate it for 30 minutes.
2. Mix the seasoning, powdered skim milk, and water in a 5-quart (5 liter) mixing bowl. Refrigerate this seasoning mixture for about 15 minutes.
3. Add the chilled ground meat to the seasoning mixture, and knead until it is thoroughly mixed and uniform. This will require about three minutes. Chill this meat and seasoning mixture again while the sausage stuffer and casings are being prepared.
4. Stuff the sausage into casings, and twist into 5-inch (13 cm) links. Refrigerate the links overnight to permit the seasoning to be absorbed by the meat. Use a covered container.
5. Sausages that will not be eaten within two days should be wrapped in plastic food wrap individually, placed in a plastic bag, and frozen.

Please see Chapter 6 for cooking suggestions.

Jewish Beef Sausage

This well-seasoned beef sausage makes an excellent main course. The seasonings enhance the beefy flavor of the meat. Be sure that these sausages are not overcooked.

CASINGS

If 24 to 26 mm (1 in. to 1¹⁄₁₆ in.) sheep casing is to be used, prepare about 14 feet (420 cm) of casing. Rinse the casing, and refrigerate it in water overnight. Rinse again, and soak in warm water a few minutes before using.

THE MEAT FOR 2½ LBS. (1,150 G) OF SAUSAGE

Prepare 2½ lbs. (1,150 g) of beef chuck. Cut into ¾-inch (2 cm) cubes. Refrigerate. While this meat is being prepared, chill the grinder and sausage stuffer in the refrigerator.

SEASONINGS AND OTHER INGREDIENTS

2½ tsp. (12.5 ml) salt (or 1 Tbsp./15 ml kosher salt)
2 tsp. (10 ml) whole mustard seed
1½ tsp. (7.5 ml) black pepper
1 tsp. (5 ml) ground coriander—packed in the spoon

¾ tsp. (3.75 ml) garlic granules
½ tsp. (2.5 ml) allspice
½ tsp. (2.5 ml) dry mustard
⅛ tsp. (0.625 ml) bay leaf powder
⅛ tsp. (0.625 ml) ground cloves
1 Tbsp. (15 ml) light corn syrup
¼ cup (60 ml) finely powdered milk
½ cup (120 ml) cold water

MIXING AND STUFFING

1. Grind the well-chilled beef with a medium plate. Refrigerate the ground meat for about 30 minutes.
2. Measure the seasoning, corn syrup, and powdered milk into a large mixing bowl, and stir with a whisk until well blended. Refrigerate for at least 15 minutes.
3. Add the chilled ground beef to the seasoning mixture, and knead until it is thoroughly mixed and uniform. This will require about three minutes. Chill this sausage paste while the sausage stuffer and casings are being prepared.
4. Stuff the sausage paste into the casings, and twist into links. Refrigerate the links overnight to permit the seasoning to be absorbed by the meat. Use a covered container.
5. Sausages that will not be eaten within two days should be wrapped in plastic food wrap individually, placed in a plastic bag, and frozen.

Please see Chapter 6 for cooking suggestions.

Krautwurst

Sausage with sauerkraut as an ingredient is popular in some areas of southern Germany. It is usually poached in beer, and then grilled or sautéed. Krautwurst is served on a roll with mustard, and is eaten while drinking dark beer.

As usual, this recipe uses 2½ pounds (1,150 g) of meat. However, because there is ½ pound (225 g) of sauerkraut used as an ingredient, the final product will weigh a little over 3 pounds (1,360 g), and a little more than the normal length of casing will be needed.

If the sauerkraut is sprayed with cold water briefly before it is mixed with the meat, the tartness of the sausage will be reduced. If it is thoroughly rinsed in water, the tart taste will be very mild. In any case, before it is chopped, the kraut should be squeezed to remove as much moisture as possible.

CASINGS

Rinse 8 feet (240 cm) of small-diameter hog casing, and refrigerate it overnight in a cup of water. Rinse again in warm water before using.

THE MEAT FOR 2½ LBS. (1,150 G) OF SAUSAGE

Prepare the meats listed below. Cut the pork into ¾-inch (2 cm) cubes, and cut the sliced bacon crosswise into squares. Refrigerate. While this meat is being prepared, chill the grinder and sausage stuffer in the refrigerator.

- 2 lbs. (910 g) pork shoulder
- ½ lb. (225 g) bacon

SEASONINGS AND OTHER INGREDIENTS

½ lb. (225 g) sauerkraut, rinsed (optional), drained and squeezed
2¾ tsp. (13.75 ml) salt
1½ Tbsp. (22.5 ml) light corn syrup
1 Tbsp. (15 ml) onion granules
1 tsp. (5 ml) marjoram
1 tsp. (5 ml) ground mustard—packed in the spoon
1 tsp. (5 ml) ground caraway seed
1 tsp. (5 ml) garlic granules
¾ tsp. (3.75 ml) white pepper
½ tsp. (2.5 ml) whole mustard seed
½ cup (120 ml) finely powdered skim milk
¼ cup (60 ml) water

MIXING AND STUFFING

1. Grind the pork and bacon together with a ³⁄₁₆-inch (4.8 mm) or larger plate. Refrigerate the ground meat for about 30 minutes.
2. Chop the rinsed (optional), drained, and squeezed sauerkraut with a stainless steel knife. (A carbon steel knife might impart a metallic taste to the acidic sauerkraut.) Transfer the chopped kraut to a large mixing bowl.
3. Add the seasoning, powdered skim milk, and water to the same bowl, and mix well. Refrigerate this seasoning mixture for at least 15 minutes.
4. Add the chilled ground meat to the seasoning mixture, and knead until it is thoroughly mixed and uniform. This will require about three minutes.

Chill this meat and seasoning mixture again while the sausage stuffer and hog casings are being prepared.

5. Stuff the sausage into the prepared hog casings, and twist into 6-inch (15 cm) links, or tie the sausage rope into four rings. (Rings are traditional for this sausage. See photo of sausage rings in Chapter 9, *Ring Bologna*.) Refrigerate the sausage overnight to permit the seasoning to be absorbed by the meat. Use a covered container.

6. Sausages that will not be eaten within two days should be wrapped in plastic food wrap individually, placed in a plastic bag, and frozen.

Please see Chapter 6 for cooking suggestions.

Lamb Sausage—Mild

This sausage has a variety of seasonings and spices, but the amount of each item is modest. The result is a flavorful, but mildly seasoned sausage. It works well as a breakfast sausage when it is made into patties. It makes a tasty appetizer when serving cocktails if it is stuffed into sheep casings and twisted into 2- to 3-inch (5 to 7.5 cm) links.

CASINGS

If 24 to 26 mm (1 in. to 1$\frac{1}{16}$ in.) sheep casing is to be used, prepare about 14 feet (420 cm) of casing. Rinse the casing, and refrigerate it in water overnight. Rinse again, and soak in warm water about 30 minutes before using.

THE MEAT FOR 2½ LBS. (1,150 G) OF SAUSAGE

Prepare 2½ lbs. (1,150 g) of lamb, or 2 lbs. (910 g) of lamb and ½ lb. (230 g) of beef. In either case, the total fat content should be about 20 percent. Cut into ¾-inch (2 cm) cubes. Refrigerate. While this meat is being prepared, chill the grinder and sausage stuffer in the refrigerator.

SEASONINGS AND OTHER INGREDIENTS

2½ tsp. (12.5 ml) salt
1 tsp. (5 ml) paprika
1 tsp. (5 ml) onion granules
½ tsp. (2.5 ml) garlic granules
½ tsp. (2.5 ml) black pepper
½ tsp. (2.5 ml) oregano

¼ tsp. (1.25 ml) coriander seed, ground—packed in the spoon
¼ tsp. (1.25 ml) rosemary
¼ tsp. (1.25 ml) allspice
2 Tbsp. (30 ml) cold water
1 Tbsp. (15 ml) white wine

MIXING AND STUFFING

1. Grind the well-chilled lamb and beef with a fine plate—⅛ inch (3.2 mm), if available. Refrigerate the ground meat for about 30 minutes.

2. Measure the seasoning and all other ingredients, except for the meat, into a large mixing bowl, and mix well. Refrigerate for at least 15 minutes.

3. Add the chilled ground meat to the seasoning mixture, and knead until it is thoroughly mixed and uniform. This will require about three minutes. Chill this sausage paste while the sausage stuffer and casings are being prepared.

4. Stuff the sausage paste into the casings, and twist into links. Refrigerate the links overnight to permit the seasoning to be absorbed by the meat. Use a covered container.

5. Sausages that will not be eaten within two days should be wrapped in plastic food wrap individually, placed in a plastic bag, and frozen.

Sauté the links in a small amount of olive oil, or grill them. Please see Chapter 6 for detailed cooking instructions.

Lincolnshire-Style Sausage

We never hear about, or see, Lincolnshire sausage here in the United States, but it is impossible to live in England without being introduced to it. Hardcore Lincolnshire sausage connoisseurs in the UK insist that Lincolnshire sausages must be made in Lincolnshire County, and must be made with pork from English pigs—and there are more requirements in addition to these!

This sausage is a very simple and conventional fresh sausage. Sage and black pepper are the predominant seasonings, and there is a bit of ginger and a hint of mace and allspice. That's about it. Nothing special. From the American standpoint, the only thing of special interest is that it has breadcrumbs in it, but this is common with United Kingdom sausages. Nevertheless, some of the most simple sausage formulations make excellent tasting sausages that you will want to eat repeatedly. You may find, as the Brits have found, that this is one of them.

THE CASINGS

Prepare 7½ feet (225 cm) of hog casings. Rinse the casings, and soak them in water overnight. Rinse them again, and soak in warm water for a few minutes before using.

MEAT FOR 2½ LBS. (1,150 G) OF SAUSAGE

Prepare 2½ lbs. (1,150 g) of pork shoulder butt that contains about 25 percent fat. Cut the meat into ¾-inch (2 cm) cubes. Refrigerate the meat, and chill the meat grinder and the sausage stuffer in the refrigerator.

OTHER INGREDIENTS AND SEASONINGS

2½ tsp. (12.5 ml) salt
1 Tbsp. (15 ml) sage—packed in the spoon
1½ tsp. (7.5 ml) black pepper, finely ground
1 tsp. (5 ml) ginger powder
¼ tsp. (1.25 ml) mace
¼ tsp. (1.25 ml) allspice
¼ cup (60 ml) dry breadcrumbs—*not* packed in the cup
½ cup (120 ml) cold water

MIXING AND STUFFING

1. Grind the well-chilled pork with a coarse plate. A coarse plate will give the sausage a traditional country-style bite texture. Refrigerate the ground meat for about 30 minutes.
2. In a large mixing bowl, mix all the seasoning and other ingredients except for the meat. Place this seasoning blend in the freezer to cool rapidly.
3. Add the chilled ground meat to the mixture, and knead until it is thoroughly mixed and uniform. This will require about three minutes. Chill this sausage paste while the sausage stuffer and casings are being prepared.
4. Stuff the sausage paste into the casings, and twist into 5-inch (13 cm) links. Refrigerate the links overnight to permit the seasoning to be absorbed by the meat. Use a covered container.
5. Sausages that will not be eaten within one day should be wrapped in plastic food wrap individually, placed in a plastic bag, and frozen.

Sauté or grill the links. Please see Chapter 6 for cooking suggestions.

Merquez—Lamb Sausage

This sausage is popular in northern African countries such as Tunisia and Libya. The name is often spelled *Merguez*, and there are, of course, variations in the formula.

This sausage is best stuffed into sheep casings and twisted into 3- to 5-inch (7.6 to 12.7 cm) links.

CASINGS

If 24 to 26 mm (1 in. to 1¹⁄₁₆ in.) sheep casing is to be used, prepare about 14 feet (420 cm) of casing. Rinse the casing, and refrigerate it in water overnight. Rinse again, and soak in warm water about 30 minutes before using.

THE MEAT FOR 2½ LBS. (1,150 G) OF SAUSAGE

Prepare 2½ lbs. (1,150 g) of lamb, or 2 lbs. (910 g) of lamb and ½ lb. (230 g) of beef. In either case, the total fat content should be about 20 percent. Cut into ¾-inch (2 cm) cubes. Refrigerate. While this meat is being prepared, chill the grinder and sausage stuffer in the refrigerator.

SEASONINGS AND OTHER INGREDIENTS

2½ tsp. (12.5 ml) salt
2 Tbsp. (30 ml) paprika
2 tsp. (10 ml) onion granules
1 Tbsp. (15 ml) parsley, dried
1 tsp. (5 ml) garlic granules
½ tsp. (2.5 ml) black pepper
½ tsp. (2.5 ml) oregano
½ tsp. (2.5 ml) ground coriander seed—packed in the spoon
½ tsp. (2.5 ml) cayenne
½ tsp. (2.5 ml) cumin
6 Tbsp. (90 ml) cold water

MIXING AND STUFFING

1. Grind the well-chilled meat cubes with a fine plate—⅛ inch (3.2 mm), if available. Refrigerate the ground meat for about 30 minutes.
2. Measure the seasoning and water into a large mixing bowl, and mix well. Refrigerate for at least 15 minutes.

3. Add the chilled ground meat to the seasoning mixture, and knead until it is thoroughly mixed and uniform. This will require about three minutes. Chill this sausage paste while the sausage stuffer and casings are being prepared.

4. Stuff the sausage paste into the casings, and twist into links. Refrigerate the links overnight to permit the seasoning to be absorbed by the meat. Use a covered container.

5. Sausages that will not be eaten within two days should be wrapped in plastic food wrap individually, placed in a plastic bag, and frozen.

Sauté the links in a small amount of olive oil, or grill them. Please see Chapter 6 for cooking instructions.

Midwest-Style Breakfast Sausage

In the Midwestern part of the United States, breakfast sausage seasoned as indicated below was made on small farms. In the towns, small butcher shops made it themselves and sold it in bulk.

THE CASING

If natural casing will be used, rinse it well and soak it in water overnight in the refrigerator. Rinse again, and soak in warm water a few minutes before using.

MEAT FOR 2½ LBS. (1,150 G) OF SAUSAGE

Prepare 2½ lbs. (1,150 g) of pork shoulder butt that contains about 20 percent fat, or use 2 lbs. (910 g) of lean pork and ½ lb. (225 g) of back fat; cut the meat into ¾-inch (2 cm) cubes. Refrigerate the meat, and put the meat grinder in the refrigerator. If the sausage stuffer will be used, refrigerate it, as well.

SEASONINGS AND OTHER INGREDIENTS

2½ tsp. (12.5 ml) salt
¼ cup (60 ml) minced onion
1 Tbsp. (15 ml) dried parsley flakes
1 Tbsp. (15 ml) rubbed sage—packed in the spoon
1½ tsp. (7.5 ml) dried ginger powder
1 tsp. (5 ml) black pepper
½ tsp. (2.5 ml) thyme
½ tsp. (2.5 ml) marjoram

½ tsp. (2.5 ml) cayenne
¼ tsp. (1.25 ml) garlic granules
¼ cup (60 ml) water
½ cup (120 ml) finely powdered skim milk

MIXING AND STUFFING

1. Grind the pork with a ¼-inch (6.4 mm) or smaller plate. Refrigerate.
2. Mix the seasoning, powdered skim milk, and water in a 5-quart (5 liter) mixing bowl. Refrigerate this seasoning mixture for about 15 minutes.
3. Blend the meat and the seasoning well by kneading for about three minutes. Shape the mixture into ⅜-inch (10 mm) thick patties, and wrap them in plastic food wrap. Alternatively, stuff the sausage into sheep or hog casings.
4. Refrigerate the sausage that will be eaten within the next two days, and freeze the remainder.

Please see Chapter 6 for cooking suggestions.

Minnesota Fresh Bratwurst

There are many recipes for bratwurst in North America. In particular, there are many for Sheboygan, Wisconsin style bratwurst. This Minnesota style is not as well known, but this formula is quite good.

CASINGS

Rinse 7 feet (210 cm) of small-diameter hog casing, and refrigerate it, in water, overnight. Rinse again in warm water before using.

THE MEAT FOR 2½ LBS. (1,150 G) OF SAUSAGE

Prepare the meats listed below; cut into ¾-inch (2 cm) cubes and refrigerate. While this meat is being prepared, chill the grinder and sausage stuffer in the refrigerator.

- 1½ lbs. (680 g) of lean pork and ½ lb. (225 g) of back fat—or 2 lbs. (910 g) of fatty pork shoulder.
- ½ lb. (225 g) of lean veal (beef, chicken thighs, or turkey thighs may be substituted).

SEASONINGS AND OTHER INGREDIENTS

2½ tsp. (12.5 ml) salt

1 tsp. (5 ml) white pepper

½ tsp. (2.5 ml) marjoram

¼ tsp. (1.25 ml) ground nutmeg

¼ tsp. (1.25 ml) garlic granules

¼ tsp. (1.25 ml) ground coriander—packed in the spoon

½ cup (120 ml) finely powdered skim milk

¼ cup (60 ml) milk

1 Tbsp. (15 ml) light corn syrup

1 egg

MIXING AND STUFFING

1. Grind the meats together with a ³⁄₁₆-inch (4.8 mm) plate. Refrigerate the ground meat for about 30 minutes.
2. Mix the seasoning and all other ingredients, except for the meat, in a large mixing bowl. Refrigerate this seasoning mixture for about 15 minutes.
3. Add the chilled ground meat to the seasoning mixture, and knead until it is thoroughly mixed and uniform. This will require about three minutes. Chill this meat and seasoning mixture again while the sausage stuffer and hog casings are being prepared.
4. Stuff the sausage into the hog casings, and twist into 6-inch (15 cm) links. Refrigerate the links overnight to permit the seasoning to be absorbed by the meat. Use a covered container.
5. Sausages that will not be eaten within two days should be wrapped in plastic food wrap individually, placed in a plastic bag, and frozen.

Please see Chapter 6 for cooking suggestions.

Mr. Mattson's Potato Sausage

When the Swedes immigrated to the United States, they usually settled in states like Minnesota, Wisconsin, and Michigan, which have climates similar to Sweden. They brought with them their love of potato sausage and the knowledge of how to make it. In those areas of the United States, potato sausage is available in grocery stores, but a few people still make it at home, and the homemade kind is best.

Pam Nordeen, the great granddaughter of an immigrant named John Matt-son, gave the following recipe to me. Her family is still treasuring his recipe; it is written faintly in pencil on paper yellowed with age. Mr. Mattson emigrated from Sweden and became a dairy and root crop farmer in Michigan. When he retired, he sold his farm to Henry Ford, and Mr. Ford built a power plant on it for a nearby motorcar factory. John Mattson passed away in about 1968 but his sausage recipe lives on.

The basic ingredients and the processing of his sausage are the same as for the Swedish *Potatis Prov,* but his seasoning is a little different. It is normal for the ratio of meat to potatoes to vary with the source of the recipe. His ratio of meat to potatoes is 1 to 2, and Mr. Mattson was adamant about this ratio. He complained frequently that the commercially prepared potato sausage con-tained too much meat.

The kind of seasoning in this sausage is clearly indicated in his handwritten recipe: salt, pepper, mace, savory, allspice, and sage. Unfortunately, the amount of each seasoning was not specified, so I made educated guesses, made a test batch, and then made changes according to the advice of Pam Nordeen and her sister.

The traditional version of *Potatis Prov* does not use savory and sage, and it usually calls for nutmeg and garlic instead.

Potatis Prov is often served for breakfast. It goes well with eggs prepared in any manner.

THE CASING

Hog casing must be used, and about 14 feet (420 cm) of casing will be required. Rinse it well, and soak it in water overnight in the refrigerator. Rinse again, and soak it in warm water for a few minutes before using.

THE MEAT, POTATOES, AND ONION

The meat: Prepare ¾ lb. (340 g) of pork shoulder butt and ¼ lb. (115 g) of beef chuck; cut the meat into ¾-inch (2 cm) cubes. Refrigerate the meat, and put the meat grinder and sausage stuffer in the refrigerator.

The potatoes: Weigh 2¼ lbs. (1020 g) of unpeeled potatoes, and peel them. After peeling, the weight will be about 2 lbs. (about 910 g)—just right. Cube the potatoes to about the same size as the meat cubes. Place the cubed potatoes in a stainless steel or plastic pan, cover with water, add 1 tablespoon of lemon juice, and refrigerate. (The acid in the lemon juice helps to retard the darkening of the peeled potatoes.)

The onion: Peel one medium onion and chop it coarsely. Refrigerate.

SEASONINGS AND OTHER INGREDIENTS
4 tsp. (20 ml) salt
1 tsp. (5 ml) white pepper
½ tsp. (2.5 ml) summer savory
½ tsp. (2.5 ml) allspice
½ tsp. (2.5 ml) sage
¼ tsp. (1.25 ml) mace
2 Tbsp. (30 ml) cold water

MIXING AND STUFFING
1. Grind the meat and chopped onions with a ³⁄₁₆-inch (4.8 mm) plate. Refrigerate.
2. Drain the cubed potatoes, but do not rinse them. Grind the cubes with a ¼-inch (6.4 mm) plate. Place the minced potatoes on paper towels that have been laid on several sheets of newspaper. Refrigerate for 30 minutes. (The paper towels and newspaper will absorb the excess moisture.)
3. Mix the seasoning ingredients and water in a 5-quart (5 liter) mixing bowl. After mixing, the seasoning mixture should be a thick liquid; if it is not liquid, add a little more water. Refrigerate this seasoning mixture for about 15 minutes.
4. Blend the meat and onion mixture, the ground potatoes, and the seasoning by kneading for about three minutes. Chill this mixture while the sausage stuffer and hog casings are being prepared.
5. Stuff the sausage into the hog casing and twist the sausage rope into 5-inch (13 cm) links. Refrigerate the links overnight to permit the seasoning to be absorbed by the meat and potatoes. (The sausages will darken; this is normal and harmless. The darkening is caused by oxygen passing through the casing and reacting with the potato particles lying just under the casing.)
6. Refrigerate the sausage that will be eaten within the next two days. (These sausages are very perishable; don't exceed two days of refrigerator storage.) Wrap the remaining sausages in plastic wrap. Place the wrapped links in a sealed plastic bag and freeze for up to two months.

COOKING
Cooking is accomplished by poaching the links in hot water or chicken broth until the minced potatoes are tender. It is best if the hot liquid is about 180° F

(82° C). The closer the temperature of the liquid comes to the boiling point, the more likely some of the sausage links will explode due to steam being generated in the casing.

Depending on the thickness of the links and the temperature of the water, cooking will require between 45 minutes and 1½ hours. To test, cut off a bite-sized hunk of sausage. If the minced potato is still raw, close the cut end with twine and continue to cook.

Oxford Bangers

In addition to the common English banger presented earlier in this chapter, England is noted for another banger known as the Oxford banger. The formulas are considerably different. The Oxford banger is spicier, and has much more sage in it. Another difference is that the common banger is made entirely of pork, whereas the Oxford banger is traditionally made of about half pork and half veal. (The formula below will suggest that chicken or turkey thigh be substituted for the veal.)

THE CASINGS

Prepare 7½ feet (225 cm) of hog casings. Rinse the casings, and soak them in water overnight. Rinse them again, and soak in warm water for a few minutes before using.

MEAT FOR 2½ LBS. (1,150 G) OF SAUSAGE

Grind the following meats with a ⅜-inch (9.5 mm) or smaller plate. Refrigerate the meat, and chill the meat grinder and the sausage stuffer in the refrigerator, too.

- 1¾ lbs. (800 g) fatty pork butt
- ¾ lb. (340 g) chicken thighs, or turkey thighs—boned, and with the skin and fat attached (veal is traditional)

OTHER INGREDIENTS AND SEASONINGS

2½ tsp. (12.5 ml) salt
2 tsp. (10 ml) sage—packed in the spoon
1 tsp. (5 ml) lemon juice
½ tsp. (2.5 ml) black pepper, finely ground
½ tsp. (2.5 ml) cayenne
½ tsp. (2.5 ml) marjoram

¼ tsp. (1.25 ml) mace
¼ tsp. (1.25 ml) thyme
¼ tsp. (1.25 ml) nutmeg
2 eggs
⅓ cup (80 ml) dry breadcrumbs, *not* packed in the cup
cold water to make a slurry

MIXING AND STUFFING

1. Measure seasoning, eggs, breadcrumbs, and water into a large mixing bowl, and add enough cold water to make a slurry. Mix well. Place in the freezer to cool rapidly.
2. Add the chilled ground meat to the chilled seasoning mixture, and knead until it is thoroughly mixed and uniform. This will require about three minutes. Chill this sausage paste while the sausage stuffer and casings are being prepared.
3. Stuff the sausage paste into the casings, and twist into 5-inch (13 cm) links. Refrigerate the links overnight to permit the seasoning to be absorbed by the meat. Use a covered container.
4. Sausages that will not be eaten within one day should be wrapped in plastic food wrap individually, placed in a plastic bag, and frozen.

Sauté or grill the links. Please see Chapter 6 for cooking suggestions.

Russian Farmer's Sausage

This is a coarse and hearty sausage with a simple, but strong, seasoning.

THE CASING

This sausage is good made into patties or stuffed into hog casings. If small-diameter hog casing will be used, prepare 7½ feet (225 cm) of casing. Rinse the casing, and refrigerate it in water overnight. Rinse again, and soak in warm water a few minutes before using.

MEAT FOR 2½ LBS. (1,150 G) OF SAUSAGE

Prepare 2½ lbs. (1,150 g) of pork shoulder butt that contains about 20 percent fat, or use 2 lbs. (910 g) of lean pork and ½ lb. (225 g) of back fat; cut the meat into ¾-inch (2 cm) cubes. Refrigerate the meat, and put the meat grinder in the refrigerator. If the sausage stuffer will be used, refrigerate it, as well.

SEASONINGS AND OTHER INGREDIENTS

2½ tsp. (12.5 ml) salt

1 cup (240 ml) chopped onions

¼ cup (60 ml) parsley, dried

1 Tbsp. (15 ml) caraway seeds

1 Tbsp. (15 ml) dill seeds

1 Tbsp. (15 ml) garlic, minced

1½ tsp. (7.5 ml) black pepper, ground

1 tsp. (5 ml) sugar

½ cup (120 ml) water

½ cup (120 ml) powdered skim milk

MIXING AND STUFFING

1. Grind the pork and onions with a coarse plate, and refrigerate the mixture for 30 minutes.

2. Mix the seasoning, powdered skim milk, and water in a 5-quart (5 liter) mixing bowl. Refrigerate this seasoning mixture for about 15 minutes.

3. Blend the ground meat and onion mixture with the seasoning by kneading for about three minutes. Shape the mixture into ⅜-inch (10 mm) thick patties, and wrap them in plastic food wrap. Alternatively, stuff the sausage into hog casings.

4. Refrigerate the sausage that will be eaten within the next two days, and freeze the remainder.

Please see Chapter 6 for cooking suggestions.

Scandinavian-Style Sausage

Potatoes or potato flour is traditionally used in some of the sausages made in Sweden, Norway, and Denmark. Certain elements of several Scandinavian sausages were combined to formulate the sausage below.

THE CASING

If hog casing is used, about 7½ feet (225 cm) will be required. Rinse it well, and refrigerate it in water overnight. Rinse again, and soak it in warm water a few minutes before using.

THE MEAT

Mince the following meats with a ³⁄₁₆-inch (4.8 mm) plate:

- 2 lbs. (910 g) of pork butt
- ½ lb. (225 g) beef chuck

THE SEASONING

2 Tbsp. (30 ml) granulated onion or onion powder
1½ tsp. (7.5 ml) salt
¼ tsp. (1.25 ml) white pepper
¼ tsp. (1.25 ml) allspice
¼ tsp. (1.25 ml) granulated sugar
½ tsp. (2.5 ml) chicken bouillon powder or chicken consommé powder
½ cup (120 ml) water
½ cup (120 ml) powdered skim milk
1 cup (240 ml) boiled and mashed potatoes, unseasoned, chilled

MIXING AND STUFFING

1. Blend all the seasoning ingredients, including the water and powdered milk—except for the mashed potatoes. Then add the mashed potatoes and blend again.
2. Blend the ground meat with the seasoning-and-potato mixture. Knead for about three minutes.
3. Stuff the sausage into the hog casing, and twist the sausage rope into 5-inch (13 cm) links. Refrigerate the links overnight to permit the seasoning to be absorbed by the meat and potatoes.
4. Refrigerate the sausage that will be eaten the next day. (This sausage is very perishable.) Wrap the remaining sausages in plastic wrap. Place the wrapped links in a sealed plastic bag, and freeze them for up to two months.

Please see Chapter 6 for cooking suggestions and instructions.

Toulouse Sausage

Toulouse is the city in southwest France where this sausage originated. The sausage formula is one of the most simple of all the sausages I have examined. One version of this sausage is seasoned with nothing more than salt, pepper, and nutmeg. The version here is a little more complex—it has six seasonings.

Traditionally, this sausage is coarsely ground, stuffed into hog casing, and twisted into links about 5 inches (13 cm) long.

THE CASING

If small-diameter hog casing will be used, prepare 7 feet (210 cm) of casing. Rinse the casing, and refrigerate it in water overnight. Rinse again, and soak in warm water a few minutes before using.

MEAT FOR 2½ LBS. (1,150 G) OF SAUSAGE

Prepare 2½ lbs. (1,150 g) of pork shoulder butt that contains about 20 percent fat, or use 2 lbs. (910 g) of lean pork and ½ lb. (225 g) of back fat; cut the meat into ¾-inch (2 cm) cubes. Refrigerate the meat, and put the meat grinder in the refrigerator. If the sausage stuffer will be used, refrigerate it, as well.

SEASONINGS AND OTHER INGREDIENTS

2½ tsp. (12.5 ml) salt
¾ tsp. (3.75 ml) white pepper
½ tsp. (2.5 ml) garlic granules
¼ tsp. (1.25 ml) nutmeg
1 Tbsp. (15 ml) light corn syrup
2 Tbsp. (30 ml) good-tasting white wine

MIXING AND STUFFING

1. Grind the pork with a coarse plate, and refrigerate it for 30 minutes.
2. Mix the seasoning, corn syrup, and wine in a 5-quart (5 liter) mixing bowl. Refrigerate this seasoning mixture for about 15 minutes.
3. Blend the meat and the seasoning well by kneading for about three minutes. Stuff the sausage into hog casings.
4. Refrigerate the sausage that will be eaten within the next two days, and freeze the remainder.

Please see Chapter 6 for cooking suggestions.

Turkey Breakfast Sausage

Turkey, chicken, or any kind of wild or domesticated fowl can be used to make sausage. In my opinion, dark meat makes the best sausage, and boned thigh meat is the easiest to use. Chicken drumsticks can be used, but turkey drumsticks are troublesome because of the numerous tendons. Below is a very simple but tasty breakfast sausage.

THE CASING
Breakfast sausage made into patties is good, but it can be stuffed in casings. If 24 to 26 mm (1 in. to 1$\frac{1}{16}$ in.) sheep casing is to be used, prepare about 14 feet (420 cm) of casing. If small-diameter hog casing will be used, prepare 7 feet (210 cm). Rinse the casing, and refrigerate it in water overnight. Rinse again, and soak in warm water 30 minutes before using.

MEAT FOR 2½ LBS. (1,150 G) OF SAUSAGE
Prepare 2½ lbs. (1,150 g) turkey, chicken, or other fowl. Use the skin and fat—up to 20 percent of the total amount of meat. Cut it into cubes. Refrigerate the meat, and put the meat grinder in the refrigerator. If the sausage stuffer will be used, refrigerate it, as well.

SEASONINGS AND OTHER INGREDIENTS
2½ tsp. (12.5 ml) salt
1 tsp. (5 ml) poultry seasoning—packed in the spoon
1 tsp. (5 ml) sage, rubbed—packed in the spoon
1 tsp. (5 ml) fresh ginger, grated or minced
¾ tsp. (3.75 ml) black pepper
¼ tsp. (1.25 ml) cayenne
¼ tsp. (1.25 ml) liquid smoke (optional)
1 Tbsp. (15 ml) light corn syrup
¼ cup (60 ml) water
½ cup (120 ml) powdered skim milk

MIXING AND STUFFING
1. Grind the poultry with a medium plate, and refrigerate it for 30 minutes.
2. Except for the meat, mix the seasoning and other ingredients in a 5-quart (5 liter) mixing bowl. Refrigerate this seasoning mixture for about 15 minutes.
3. Blend the meat and the seasoning well by kneading for about three minutes. Shape the mixture into ⅜-inch (10 mm) thick patties, and wrap them in plastic food wrap. Alternatively, stuff the sausage into sheep or hog casings.
4. Refrigerate the sausage that will be eaten within the next two days, and freeze the remainder.

Please see Chapter 6 for cooking suggestions.

Turkey or Waterfowl Italian Sausage

Turkey, chicken, or waterfowl—wild or domesticated—can be used to make this sausage. If turkey or chicken is used, dark meat with the skin and fat is best. This is a tasty, but mildly seasoned, Italian sausage with a little poultry seasoning added.

THE CASINGS

If 24 to 26 mm (1 in. to 1$\frac{1}{16}$ in.) sheep casing is to be used, prepare about 14 feet (420 cm) of casing. If small-diameter hog casing will be used, prepare 7 feet (210 cm). Rinse the casing, and refrigerate it in water overnight. Rinse again, and soak in warm water 30 minutes before using.

THE MEAT FOR 2½ LBS. (1,150 G) OF SAUSAGE

Prepare 2½ lbs. (1,150 g) of fowl that contains about 20 percent fat, cut the meat into ¾-inch (2 cm) cubes. Refrigerate the meat, and put the meat grinder and sausage stuffer in the refrigerator.

OTHER INGREDIENTS AND SEASONINGS

2½ tsp. (12.5 ml) salt
1 tsp. (5 ml) black pepper, coarsely ground
1 tsp. (5 ml) poultry seasoning—packed in the spoon
1 tsp. (5 ml) oregano, powdered
½ tsp. (2.5 ml) fennel seeds, cracked or powdered
½ tsp. (2.5 ml) garlic powder
½ tsp. (2.5 ml) thyme, powdered
¼ tsp. (1.25 ml) cayenne
¼ tsp. (1.25 ml) anise seeds, cracked
¼ tsp. (1.25 ml) ground coriander—packed in the spoon
1 Tbsp. (15 ml) light corn syrup
½ cup (120 ml) powdered skim milk
¼ cup (60 ml) cold water

MIXING AND STUFFING

1. Grind the fowl with a medium plate, and refrigerate it for 30 minutes.
2. Mix the seasoning, powdered skim milk, and water in a 5-quart (5 liter) mixing bowl. Refrigerate this seasoning mixture for about 15 minutes.
3. Add the chilled ground meat to the seasoning mixture, and knead until it is thoroughly mixed and uniform. This will require about three minutes.

Chill this meat and seasoning mixture again while the sausage stuffer and hog casings are being prepared.

4. Stuff the sausage into the hog casings, and twist into 5-inch (13 cm) links. Refrigerate the links overnight to permit the seasoning to be absorbed by the meat. Use a covered container.

5. Sausages that will not be eaten within two days should be wrapped in plastic food wrap individually, placed in a plastic bag, and frozen.

Please see Chapter 6 for cooking suggestions.

Warren's Country-Style Bulk Breakfast Sausage

I made this sausage for the first time almost thirty years ago when I was living in Japan, and it was the first sausage I ever made. The wife of a Christian missionary gave the recipe to me. It continues to be one of my favorite fresh sausages. The use of poultry seasoning in a 100 percent pork sausage makes this an unusual formulation.

THE CASING

I always make patties with this sausage, but it can be stuffed in casings. If 24 to 26 mm (1 in. to 1¹⁄₁₆ in.) sheep casing is to be used, prepare about 14 feet (420 cm) of casing. If small-diameter hog casing will be used, prepare 7 feet (210 cm). Rinse the casing, and refrigerate it in water overnight. Rinse again, and soak in warm water a few minutes before using.

MEAT FOR 2½ LBS. (1,150 G) OF SAUSAGE

Prepare 2½ lbs. (1,150 g) of pork shoulder butt that contains about 20 percent fat, or use 2 lbs. (910 g) of lean pork and ½ lb. (225 g) of back fat; cut the meat into ¾-inch (2 cm) cubes. Refrigerate the meat, and put the meat grinder in the refrigerator. If the sausage stuffer will be used, refrigerate it as well.

SEASONINGS AND OTHER INGREDIENTS

2½ tsp. (12.5 ml) salt
1 tsp. (5 ml) poultry seasoning—packed in the spoon
1 tsp. (5 ml) sage, rubbed—packed in the spoon
½ tsp. (2.5 ml) oregano or marjoram

½ tsp. (2.5 ml) black pepper

½ tsp. (2.5 ml) red pepper

¼ cup (60 ml) water

½ cup (120 ml) powdered skim milk

MIXING AND STUFFING

1. Grind the pork with a medium plate, and refrigerate it for 30 minutes.
2. Mix the seasoning, powdered skim milk, and water in a 5-quart (5 liter) mixing bowl. Refrigerate this seasoning mixture for about 15 minutes.
3. Blend the meat and the seasoning well by kneading for about three minutes. Shape the mixture into ⅜-inch (10 mm) thick patties, and wrap them in plastic food wrap. Alternatively, stuff the sausage into sheep or hog casings.
4. Refrigerate the sausage that will be eaten within the next two days, and freeze the remainder.

Please see Chapter 6 for cooking suggestions.

CHAPTER 9

Cured Sausage

NOTE: *Cured sausage contains a sausage curing powder (Cure #1) such as Prague Powder #1, Modern Cure, or Instacure #1. It may be cold smoked, hot smoked, or cooked by any method.*

The sausages in this chapter have been arranged in alphabetical order.

Alsatian French Sausage

Alsace is a region in northeastern France between the Rhine River and the Vosges Mountains. This area is the home of Alsatian Sausage.

In Chapter 8, there is another sausage, *French Country Sausage*, which also uses the special French blend of seasoning called *quatre épices*. The French use this blend of four spices to season various dishes. It can be purchased ready-mixed, or it can be blended in your own kitchen; please see Appendix 1 for blending instructions and additional information.

THE CASING

Natural casings are best for this sausage. If 24 to 26 mm (1 in. to 1¹⁄₁₆ in.) sheep casing is to be used, prepare about 14 feet (420 cm) of casing. If small-diameter hog casing will be used, prepare 7 feet (210 cm). Rinse the casing, and refrigerate it in water overnight. Rinse again, and soak in warm water a few minutes before using.

MEAT FOR 2½ LBS. (1,150 G) OF SAUSAGE

Prepare 2½ lbs. (1,150 g) of pork shoulder butt that contains about 20 percent fat. Cut the pork shoulder into ¾-inch (2 cm) cubes. Refrigerate the meat, and put the meat grinder and sausage stuffer in the refrigerator while the meat is being prepared.

SEASONINGS AND OTHER INGREDIENTS
2 tsp. (10 ml) salt
½ tsp. (2.5 ml) Cure #1
¾ tsp. (3.75 ml) black pepper
½ tsp. (2.5 ml) *quatre épices*
⅛ tsp. (0.625 ml) ground ginger
1 Tbsp. (15 ml) light corn syrup
2 Tbsp. (30 ml) cold water

MIXING AND STUFFING
1. Grind the pork with a fine plate, and refrigerate it for 30 minutes.
2. Mix the seasoning, corn syrup, and water in a 5-quart (5 liter) mixing bowl. Refrigerate this seasoning mixture for about 15 minutes.
3. Blend the meat and the seasoning well by kneading for about three minutes. Stuff the sausage into sheep or hog casings.
4. Refrigerate the sausage that will be eaten within the next two days, and freeze the remainder.

This sausage is not smoked. Please see Chapter 6 for sautéing or poaching suggestions.

Andouille
Several varieties of andouille are made in France, but most of us associate this sausage with Cajun cooking. The Cajuns, too, make many varieties of this hot, spicy, and well-seasoned sausage. Some kinds are to be eaten just as they are, and other kinds are used primarily as an ingredient for boiled beans or other dishes. The andouille produced by this recipe works well for either purpose.

In spite of the convoluted French spelling, the pronunciation of *andouille* is very easy: *an' dewy.*

CASINGS
Hog casing, or the more tender sheep casings, may be used. If you wish to use the small hog casing, 7 feet (210 cm) will be required; if sheep casing will be

used, prepare 14 feet (420 cm). As usual, rinse the casing, and refrigerate it overnight in water. Rinse again, and soak in warm water for a few minutes before using.

THE MEAT FOR 2½ LBS. (1,150 G) OF ANDOUILLE

Prepare 2½ lbs. (1,150 g) of fatty pork shoulder; cut into ¾-inch (2 cm) cubes and refrigerate. While this meat is being prepared, chill the grinder and sausage stuffer in the refrigerator.

SEASONINGS AND OTHER INGREDIENTS

2 tsp. (10 ml) salt
½ tsp. (2.5 ml) Cure #1
1 Tbsp. (15 ml) paprika
1 Tbsp. (15 ml) onion granules
2 tsp. (10 ml) cayenne
1 tsp. (5 ml) black pepper, ground
1 tsp. (5 ml) garlic granules
1 tsp. (5 ml) thyme
½ tsp. (2.5 ml) mace
½ tsp. (2.5 ml) mustard powder—packed in the spoon
½ tsp. (2.5 ml) whole mustard seeds
⅛ tsp. (0.625 ml) allspice
⅛ tsp. (0.625 ml) cloves (powdered)
1 Tbsp. (15 ml) light corn syrup
½ cup (120 ml) finely powdered skim milk
¼ cup (60 ml) cold water

MIXING AND STUFFING

1. Grind the chilled meat with a ³⁄₁₆-inch (4.8 mm) or smaller plate. Refrigerate the ground meat for about 30 minutes.
2. While the meat is chilling, mix all of the remaining ingredients thoroughly in a large mixing bowl. Refrigerate this mixture for about 15 minutes.
3. Add the chilled ground meat to the seasoning mixture, and knead until it is well mixed and uniform. This will require about three minutes. Chill this meat and seasoning mixture again while the sausage stuffer and casings are being prepared.
4. Stuff the sausage into the hog or sheep casing, and twist the sausage rope into 6-inch (15 cm) links. Refrigerate the links overnight to permit the

seasoning to be absorbed by the meat. Use an uncovered container (or cover with paper towels) so the casings will dry.

Usually, this variety of andouille is hot smoked. If you wish to smoke the links, please see Chapter 7 for suggestions and directions. If you wish to omit smoking, please go directly to the cooking suggestions in Chapter 6.

Berliner Sausage

This German snack sausage is cured and seasoned very simply with salt, pepper, a little garlic, and minced raw onion. In this recipe, the traditional 20 percent veal has been replaced with chicken or turkey thighs.

CASING

Any size of fibrous casing may be used. A large casing such as a 4-inch (10.16 cm) one is most common, but a 2½-inch (6.35 cm) casing is easier and faster to process, so it is recommended. For 2½ lbs. (1,150 g) of sausage, two of these casings—12 inches (30 cm) long—will be required. Prepare the casings by soaking in lukewarm water for 30 minutes. Be sure to put warm water inside the casings.

MEAT

Prepare 1½ lbs. (680 g) of pork butt, ½ lb. (225 g) of beef chuck, and ½ lb. (225 g) of either boned chicken thighs or boned turkey thighs. Cut the meat into ¾-inch (2 cm) cubes. The total fat content should be about 20 to 25 percent of the meat. (Beef heart or venison may be substituted for some of the beef chuck.) Refrigerate the meat for 30 minutes. While the meat is being prepared, chill the meat grinder and stuffer.

Grind the meat with a ³⁄₁₆-inch (4.8 mm) plate. Chill the meat again while the seasoning and other ingredients are being prepared.

THE SEASONING AND OTHER INGREDIENTS

2¼ tsp. (11.25 ml) salt
½ tsp. (2.5 ml) Cure #1
½ tsp. (2.5 ml) white pepper, finely ground
¼ tsp. (1.25 ml) garlic granules
¼ cup (60 ml) finely minced onion

½ cup (120 ml) powdered skim milk
¼ cup (60 ml) cold water
1 Tbsp. (15 ml) light corn syrup

MIXING AND STUFFING

1. While the ground meat is chilling, mix the seasoning and other ingredients in a large bowl until the slurry is uniform.
2. Add the meat to the seasoning mixture. Blend by kneading until it is uniform. This will require about three minutes.
3. Stuff the sausage into fibrous casings. Insert the cable probe of an electronic thermometer in the open end of one of the chubs, and close the casing around the probe with butcher's twine.
4. Refrigerate the sausage chubs overnight to blend the seasoning and curing powder with the meat.
5. The next morning, the chubs may be smoked. (Cold smoking followed by hot smoking is traditional.) Please see Chapter 7 for smoking details and suggestions. If the sausage will not be smoked, steaming or poaching is recommended. Cooking by steaming or poaching is explained in Chapter 6.

Bierwurst

In spite of the name, bierwurst does not have beer as an ingredient. It got its name because it goes well with beer. It is sliced and eaten cold as a snack sausage or luncheon meat. Bierwurst is a hot smoked sausage, but smoking is not essential.

A few hours before this sausage is made, it is best to soak the minced garlic in the rum and water. This will help to distribute the garlic flavor better.

CASING

Bierwurst is traditionally stuffed in large beef bungs or small beef bladders, but 2½-inch (6.35 cm) fibrous casings, or large hog casings, are easier and faster to process, so they are recommended. For 2½ lbs. (1,150 g) of sausage, two fibrous casings—each 12 inches (30 cm) long—will be required. Prepare the fibrous casings by soaking in lukewarm water for about 30 minutes. Be sure to put warm water inside the casings. If large hog casing will be used, it should be prepared a day in advance.

MEAT
Prepare the meats listed below. Cut the meat into ¾-inch (2 cm) cubes. The total fat content should be about 25 percent of the meat. While the meat is being prepared, chill the meat grinder and stuffer.

- 1½ lbs. (680 g) pork shoulder butt
- ½ lb. (225 g) beef chuck
- ¼ lb. (115 g) bacon
- ¼ lb. (115 g) beef heart

Refrigerate the meat for at least 30 minutes, and then grind the meat with a ³⁄₁₆-inch (4.8 mm) plate—or use a plate with smaller holes, if available. Chill the meat again while the seasoning and other ingredients are being prepared.

THE SEASONING
2 tsp. (10 ml) salt
2 tsp. (10 ml) garlic, minced and packed in the spoon (about 4 cloves)
1½ tsp. (7.5 ml) sugar
½ tsp. (2.5 ml) Cure #1
¾ tsp. (3.75 ml) black pepper, ground
¾ tsp. (3.75 ml) MSG (optional)
¼ tsp. (1.25 ml) cardamom seed, ground
¼ tsp. (1.25 ml) nutmeg
¼ cup (60 ml) powdered skim milk
¼ cup (60 ml) cold water
2 Tbsp. (30 ml) white rum

MIXING AND STUFFING
1. While the ground meat is chilling, mix all the seasoning ingredients, powdered milk, water, and rum in a large bowl until the slurry is uniform.
2. Add the meat to the seasoning mixture. Blend by kneading until it is uniform. This will require about three minutes.
3. Stuff the sausage into casings. Insert the cable probe of an electronic thermometer in the open end of one of the sausages, and close the casing around the probe with butcher's twine.
4. Refrigerate the stuffed sausage overnight so the seasoning and curing powder will blend with the meat.

The next morning, the sausage may be smoked. Please see Chapter 7 for smoking instructions and suggestions. If it will be smoked, hot smoking is recommended, but cold smoking and steam cooking will also yield good results. If the sausage will not be smoked, steaming or poaching is recommended. Cooking by steaming or poaching is explained in Chapter 6.

Chinese Cha Shu Sausage

This exotically seasoned, piquant Chinese sausage is very good for seasoning stir-fried dishes. The seasoning of this sausage is similar to some varieties of Chinese style barbecued pork served as an appetizer in Chinese restaurants. This sausage, too, can be sliced thinly and served with hot mustard and toasted sesame seeds. The special character of this variety results from the use of *five-spice powder*—a special Chinese spice blend with a unique aroma. In Chapter 8, there is a similar recipe for a Chinese *cha shu* sausage, but it is not cured and does not use five-spice powder (see *Chinese-Style BBQ Pork Sausage*).

Nowadays, many Chinese culinary ingredients are available in the ethnic sections of well-stocked grocery stores. But, if you can't find what you need, try an Asian grocer or use the Internet. The Chinese light soy sauce is milder than the common soy sauce, but regular soy sauce can be used for this sausage. The five-spice powder must be Chinese style; there is a European five-spice powder, but that is not the same. A certain American company manufactures many Chinese culinary ingredients, including five-spice powder, under the brand name of *Sun Luck*. This brand is sometimes available in common grocery stores. For additional information on five-spice powder, please see Appendix 1.

Some people love the unique and distinctive aroma of five-spice powder, and others cannot tolerate it. Consequently, you might wish to reduce the amount from ½ tsp. (2.5 ml) to ¼ tsp. (1.25 ml) for the first batch of this sausage.

CASINGS

Sheep casings are definitely preferable, but small-diameter hog casings may be used. However, please keep in mind that the required drying time increases as the diameter of the casing increases. If you wish to use the small hog casing, rinse 7 feet (210 cm) of casing, and refrigerate it overnight in a cup of water. If 24 to 26 mm (1 in. to 1¹⁄₁₆ in.) sheep casing is to be used, prepare about 14 feet (420 cm). Rinse the casing again, and soak it in warm water for a few minutes before using.

THE MEAT FOR 2½ LBS. (1,150 G) OF CHA SHU SAUSAGE

Prepare 2½ lbs. (1,150 g) of pork butt. Cut the meat into ¾-inch (2 cm) cubes and refrigerate.

SEASONINGS AND OTHER INGREDIENTS FOR MARINADE

⅓ cup (80 ml) honey

¼ cup (60 ml) sherry

¼ cup (60 ml) sugar

3 Tbsp. (45 ml) Chinese light soy sauce

1 Tbsp. (15 ml) hoisin sauce

1 Tbsp. (15 ml) ginger root, grated OR 1 tsp. (5 ml) ginger powder

2 tsp. (10 ml) sesame (seed) oil

1½ tsp. (7.5 ml) salt

½ tsp. (2.5 ml) Cure #1

½ tsp. (2.5 ml) 5-spice powder (vary this amount to suit taste)

¼ tsp. (1.25 ml) white pepper

2 cloves garlic, minced

MIXING, CURING, GRINDING, AND STUFFING

1. *Day 1, morning*: In a large plastic food container with a lid, mix the season-ing and other ingredients for the marinade. Add the cubes of pork and stir well. Refrigerate. Shake the container, or stir the pork from time to time to redistribute the marinade and to recoat the pork cubes.

2. *Day 2*: Shake the container of marinating pork (or stir) two or three times.

3. *Day 3, morning*: Drain the pork, and discard the marinade. Rinse the pork briefly, and drain in a colander for at least one hour in the refrigerator. Chill the grinder and stuffer in the refrigerator.

4. Grind the meat with a coarse plate, and refrigerate it for about 30 minutes while the sausage stuffer and casings are being prepared.

5. Stuff the sausage into the casings, and twist into 6-inch (15 cm) links. Cut every other twist so that each link is joined to another link to form a pair.

6. Dry the stuffed sausage for one or two hours in front of an electric fan—until the surface is dry to the touch and the fingertips slide smoothly on the cas-ing. Remove the sausages to a smoker preheated to 140° F (60° C), and open the smoker vents fully. (Do not smoke the sausage; use the smoker for drying only.) If possible, hang each pair on a rod. If they must be placed in baskets, ensure that there is adequate space between the links to facilitate drying.

7. Raise the smoker temperature to 175° F (79° C) slowly—over the period of one hour or so—and continue cooking without smoke until the internal temperature of the thickest link reaches 160° F (71° C). Remove the links from the smoker, place them in front of an electric fan for one hour, and then refrigerate them—uncovered—until they are well chilled.

8. Hang the sausage pairs on a rod in the refrigerator and allow them to dry for three days. When the drying is finished, wrap them in plastic food wrap, put them in a plastic bag, and freeze the links for future use as a seasoning ingredient for other dishes.

Chinese-Style Mushroom Sausage

Chinese sausages tend to be highly seasoned, and they are often sliced thinly, minced, or julienned for seasoning stir-fried and steamed dishes. This sausage is a milder, somewhat westernized version of the true Chinese mushroom sausage, so it is a better match for the American and European palate.

A few ingredients have no good substitutes, and a few are unlikely to be found in a common grocery store. Hopefully, there is an Asian grocer in your town. If not, these ingredients can be found on the Internet.

The Chinese light soy sauce is milder than common soy sauce, but regular soy sauce can be substituted. The black mushrooms (*shiitake*) in the recipe are actually Japanese mushrooms, and dried *shiitake* are easy to buy in Asian food stores. However, if these dried mushrooms can't be found, use about ¼ pound (115 g) of fresh button mushrooms, or fresh *shiitake* mushrooms. (Recently, fresh *shiitake* can be found in common grocery stores.) Sesame (seed) oil should be available in the ethnic food section of a well-stocked supermarket.

CASINGS

Sheep casings are definitely preferable, but small-diameter hog casings may be used. However, please keep in mind that the required drying time increases as the diameter of the casing increases. If you wish to use the small hog casing, rinse 7 feet (210 cm), and refrigerate it overnight in a little water. If 24 to 26 mm (1 in. to 1¹⁄₁₆ in.) sheep casing is to be used, prepare about 14 feet (420 cm). Rinse the casing again, and soak it in warm water for a few minutes before using.

THE MEAT FOR 2½ LBS. (1,150 G) OF MUSHROOM SAUSAGE

Prepare 2½ lbs. (1,150 g) of pork butt. Cut the meat into ¾-inch (2 cm) cubes and refrigerate. While this meat is being prepared, chill the grinder and sausage stuffer in the refrigerator.

SEASONINGS AND OTHER INGREDIENTS

1 oz. (28 g) black mushrooms (*shiitake*), dried
1 to 2 cups (240 to 480 ml) water for soaking (rehydrating) mushrooms

3 Tbsp. (45 ml) Chinese light soy sauce
½ tsp. (2.5 ml) Cure #1
2 Tbsp. (30 ml) sherry
1 Tbsp. (15 ml) onion granules
1 Tbsp. (15 ml) sesame (seed) oil
1 Tbsp. (15 ml) sugar
1 Tbsp. (15 ml) ginger, powdered
1 tsp. (5 ml) garlic granules
1 tsp. (5 ml) salt
¾ tsp. (3.75 ml) white pepper
¼ tsp. (1.25 ml) liquid smoke (optional)
¼ cup (60 ml) cold water

MIXING AND STUFFING

1. Rehydrate the dried black mushrooms by putting them in a bowl of water for about 30 minutes. (If fresh mushrooms are used, omit this step.)

2. Grind the pork with a coarse plate. Refrigerate the ground meat for about 30 minutes.

3. Remove and discard the hard stems from the black mushrooms, chop the mushrooms finely, and put them in a large mixing bowl. While the ground meat is chilling, add all the rest of the ingredients to the same mixing bowl. Stir until well blended. Refrigerate this mixture for about 15 minutes.

4. Add the chilled ground meat to the seasoning mixture, and knead until it is well mixed and uniform. This will require about three minutes. Chill this meat and seasoning mixture again while the sausage stuffer and casings are being prepared.

5. Stuff the sausage into the casings, and twist into 6-inch (15 cm) links. Cut every other twist so that each link is joined to another link to form a pair. (Later on, each pair will be optionally hung to dry over a rod in the smoker and a rod in the refrigerator.) Refrigerate the links overnight to permit the seasoning to be absorbed by the meat. (It is not necessary to hang them at this time.) Use an uncovered container, but cover the sausage with a paper towel.

6. The next morning, dry the stuffed sausage for one or two hours in front of an electric fan until the surface is dry to the touch and the fingertips slide smoothly on the casing. Remove the sausages to a smoker preheated to 140° F (60° C) and open the smoker vents fully. If possible, hang each pair on a rod. If they must be placed in baskets, ensure that there is adequate space between the links to facilitate drying.

7. Raise the smoker temperature to 175° F (79° C) slowly—over the period of one hour or so—and continue cooking without smoke until the internal temperature of the thickest link reaches 160° F (71° C). Remove the links from the smoker, place them in front of an electric fan for one hour, and then refrigerate them—uncovered—until they are well chilled.

8. Hang the sausage pairs on a rod in the refrigerator and allow them to dry for three days. (If they can't be hung, place them on paper towels.) When the drying is finished, wrap them in plastic food wrap, put them in a plastic bag, and freeze the links for future use as a seasoning ingredient.

Cotto Salami

Cotto salami is one of the best-known lunchmeat sausages in the United States. The origin of this sausage is Italy. In Italian, it is called *salame cotto*, which means *cooked salami*. Each region of Italy has its own variation of seasoning ingredients, but beef and pork are invariably used.

Cotto salami is usually smoked—and smoking is recommended—but if it will not be smoked, the optional liquid smoke will impart a similar smoked aroma. If the recommended amount of liquid smoke is exceeded, it may produce an unpleasant taste.

CASING

Any size of fibrous casing may be used. A large casing such as a 4-inch (10.16 cm) one is most common, but a 2½-inch (6.35 cm) casing is easier and faster to process, so it is recommended. For 2½ lbs. (1,150 g) of sausage, two of these casings—each 12 inches (30 cm) long—will be required. Prepare the casings by soaking in lukewarm water for 30 minutes. Be sure to flood the inside of the casings with warm water.

MEAT

Prepare 1½ lbs. (680 g) of beef chuck and 1 lb. (450 g) of pork butt; cut the meat into ¾-inch (2 cm) cubes. The total fat content should be about 20 to 25 percent of the meat. (Beef heart or wild game may be substituted for some of the beef chuck.) Refrigerate the meat for 30 minutes. While the meat is being prepared, chill the meat grinder and stuffer.

Grind the meat with a ³⁄₁₆-inch (4.8 mm) plate—or use a plate with smaller holes, if available. Chill the meat again while the seasoning and other ingredients are being prepared.

THE SEASONING

2 tsp. (10 ml) salt
½ tsp. (2.5 ml) Cure #1
2 tsp. (10 ml) black peppercorns, cracked
1½ tsp. (7.5 ml) black pepper, ground
1 tsp. (5 ml) garlic granules
½ tsp. (2.5 ml) caraway seed, ground
⅛ tsp. (0.625 ml) ginger powder
⅛ tsp. (0.625 ml) allspice
⅛ tsp. (0.625 ml) nutmeg
½ cup (120 ml) powdered skim milk
¼ cup (60 ml) red wine
¼ tsp. (1.25 ml) Wright's liquid smoke (optional)
2 Tbsp. (30 ml) light corn syrup

MIXING AND STUFFING

1. Mix the seasoning, red wine, corn syrup, powdered milk, and the optional liquid smoke in a large bowl until the ingredients are uniformly distributed. Refrigerate for 15 minutes.

2. Add the meat to the seasoning mixture. Blend by kneading until it is uniformly mixed. This will require about three minutes. Chill this sausage paste for about 30 minutes.

3. Stuff the sausage into fibrous casings. Insert the cable probe of an electronic thermometer in the open end of one of the sausages, and close the casing around the probe with butcher's twine.

4. Refrigerate the sausage chubs overnight so the seasoning and curing powder will blend with the meat.

5. The next morning, the sausage chubs may be smoked. Please see Chapter 7 for smoking suggestions. If they will be smoked, cold smoking followed by steam cooking is recommended. If the sausage will not be smoked, steaming or poaching is recommended. Cooking by steaming or poaching is explained in Chapter 6.

Cured Bratwurst

Most recipes for bratwurst are for fresh bratwurst, but some people like the cured variety, and others like it both cured and smoked. The formulation below is very similar to the fresh bratwurst in Chapter 9, except Cure #1 (curing powder) has been added, and nutmeg has been replaced by marjoram. (Marjoram is used instead of nutmeg or mace in many bratwurst formulas.) If this sausage is served between two halves of a roll and garnished with horseradish mustard, chopped onions, and dill pickle sticks, it will be a memorable treat. Don't forget the cold beer!

CASINGS

Rinse 7 feet (210 cm) of small-diameter hog casing, and refrigerate it overnight in a little water. Rinse again in warm water before using.

THE MEAT FOR 2½ LBS. (1,150 G) OF SAUSAGE

Prepare the meats listed below; cut into ¾-inch (2 cm) cubes and refrigerate. While this meat is being prepared, chill the grinder and sausage stuffer in the refrigerator.

- 1½ lbs. (680 g) of lean pork and ½ lb. (225 g) of back fat—or 2 lbs. (910 g) of fatty pork shoulder.
- ½ lb. (225 g) of lean veal (beef, chicken thighs, or turkey thighs may be substituted).

SEASONINGS AND OTHER INGREDIENTS

2 tsp. (10 ml) salt
½ tsp. (2.5 ml) Cure #1
1 tsp. (5 ml) white pepper
1 tsp. (5 ml) ground mustard—packed in the spoon
1 tsp. (5 ml) marjoram
½ tsp. (2.5 ml) garlic granules
½ tsp. (2.5 ml) sage—packed in the spoon
½ cup (120 ml) finely powdered skim milk
¼ cup (60 ml) water
1 Tbsp. (15 ml) light corn syrup
2 eggs

MIXING AND STUFFING

1. Grind the meats together with a ³⁄₁₆-inch (4.8 mm) or smaller plate. Refrigerate the ground meat for about 30 minutes.
2. Mix the seasoning, powdered skim milk, eggs, corn syrup, and water together in a large mixing bowl. Refrigerate this seasoning mixture for about 15 minutes.

3. Add the chilled ground meat to the seasoning mixture, and knead until it is thoroughly mixed and uniform. This will require about three minutes. Chill this meat and seasoning mixture again while the sausage stuffer and hog casings are being prepared.
4. Stuff the sausage into the hog casings, and twist into 6-inch (15 cm) links. Refrigerate the links overnight to permit the seasoning to be absorbed by the meat. Cover the links with paper towels.
5. Sausages that will not be eaten within two days should be wrapped in plastic food wrap individually, placed in a plastic bag, and frozen.
6. If you wish to smoke the links, please see Chapter 7 for suggestions and directions. If you wish to omit smoking, please see the cooking suggestions in Chapter 6.

Deviled Ham

Recipes for homemade deviled ham appeared in homestead cookbooks in the 18th century. Making deviled ham was a way of using the scraps of ham left after a whole ham was carved. The scraps of ham were chopped or ground, mixed with seasoning and other ingredients, and spread on bread, biscuits, or crackers.

In 1822, an Englishman named William Underwood set up a small company that initially processed and sold mustard. Soon, other condiments packed in glass jars were added to the list of products. After 1836, Mr. Underwood's company made a fortune selling various foods packed in tin plated cans. In about 1864, William Underwood's sons developed the famous canned deviled ham by blending ground ham with special seasonings and canning it. They printed the now familiar trademark drawing of a red devil on the can label in 1870. Today, the same brand of canned deviled ham is still sold in grocery stores.

For me, and for many others of my generation, deviled ham sandwiches were regular fare in the lunch boxes we took to school. Deviled ham is nostalgia in a can. For some reason, kids love deviled ham sandwiches and deviled ham spread on crackers.

Making the deviled ham from ham scraps, as they did in the old days, is very easy, especially if a meat grinder is available. However, with just a little more effort, we can cure cubes of pork and change them into ham. These cubes of homemade ham provide the main ingredient required for deviled ham, and we need not wait until we have scraps of ham on hand.

The basic plan for making deviled ham from scratch is as follows:

- Regular Boston butt (shoulder butt), or other pork that is commonly used to make sausage, will be cut into cubes and cured for five days. This pork should contain about 15 percent fat. At the end of five days, these cubes of fresh pork will have been changed to cubes of cured ham.
- These cubes of cured ham will be rinsed, drained, and finely ground.
- Seasoning will be added, and the deviled ham will be steamed or baked. It can be stored in the refrigerator or freezer for future use.

THE MEAT FOR 2½ LBS. (1,150 G) OF HAM CUBES

Prepare 2½ lbs. (1,150 g) of pork containing about 15 percent fat. Cut this pork into ¾-inch (2 cm) cubes. Refrigerate these cubes until they are well chilled.

CURING INGREDIENTS FOR 2½ LBS. (1,150 G) OF HAM CUBES

1 Tbsp. (15 ml) salt
1 Tbsp. (15 ml) brown sugar—packed in the spoon
½ tsp. (2.5 ml) Cure #1
½ tsp. (2.5 ml) onion granules
½ tsp. (2.5 ml) garlic powder
½ tsp. (2.5 ml) white pepper
¼ tsp. (1.25 ml) allspice
2 Tbsp. (30 ml) cold water to make a slurry

CURING THE HAM CUBES

1. *Day 1*: Measure the cure ingredients into a plastic food container that is large enough to allow the cubes to be stirred easily. (The container should have a tight-fitting lid.) Add enough cold water to make a slurry. Place the pork cubes in the container and stir the cubes vigorously to ensure that all surfaces of each cube are coated with the seasoned cure. Push the cubes down in the curing container so that they are packed together tightly. Cover and refrigerate.
2. *Days 2 and 3*: Each day, stir the cubes thoroughly at least one time in order to recoat each of the cubes with cure. Push the cubes down to re-pack tightly.
3. *Day 4*: The curing is finished. Remove the cubes from the plastic container, place them in a colander, and spray with cold water thoroughly to remove all curing compound from the surfaces of the cubes. Drain well in the colander, and then place the cubes atop a paper towel with newspaper underneath. Refrigerate the cubes while they are on the paper. While the deviled ham seasoning is being prepared, chill the meat grinder.

DEVILED HAM SEASONINGS AND OTHER INGREDIENTS

2 Tbsp. (30 ml) flour
1 tsp. (5 ml) Worcestershire sauce
1½ tsp. (7.5 ml) white pepper
½ tsp. (2.5 ml) allspice
½ tsp. (2.5 ml) mustard powder
½ tsp. (2.5 ml) paprika
¼ tsp. (1.25 ml) cayenne
¼ cup cold water

MIXING

1. Grind the cured ham cubes with the smallest plate available—the smaller the better. Refrigerate for about 30 minutes.
2. Measure the seasoning and other ingredients into a large stainless steel mixing bowl. Add cold water to make a slurry. Stir until the mixture is uniform. Refrigerate for about 15 minutes.
3. Add the chilled ground meat to the chilled seasoning mixture, and knead until it is well mixed and uniform. This will require about three minutes. Place the deviled ham paste in the freezer, and stir the meat every 10 minutes or so. The goal is to chill this sausage paste in the freezer until most of it is crunchy, but not frozen hard.
4. When the sausage mixture has become crunchy, grind it again with the smallest plate available. (This second grinding is optional. The second grinding will cause the particle size to become smaller.)
5. Place the deviled ham paste in a Pyrex, ceramic, or non-reactive baking dish, and cover with a lid or aluminum foil.
6. Steam at 212° F (100° C), or bake at 220° F (104° C) for 3 hours. Place the "loaf" on a wire grate to drain the rendered fat. Discard the fat. Let the loaf cool to almost room temperature. Divide the loaf into about four parts, wrap each part with plastic food wrap, place in a plastic bag, and freeze or refrigerate.

Deviled ham can be used as a sandwich spread, veggie dip, or as a topping for hors d'oeuvres. When time comes to use the deviled ham, thaw it in the refrigerator, add one or more of the following (or anything else that appeals to you), and blend the mixture by using a food processor. There are also numerous recipes on the Internet for using deviled ham.

- Mayonnaise
- Minced dill pickles
- Sweet pickle relish
- Minced onions or minced green onions
- Finely chopped celery
- Sour cream
- Chopped black olives

Duckwurst

A little over ten years ago, while living in Japan, a retired Japanese radio announcer who was a good friend of mine used to give freshly harvested wild duck to me, and I would cure it, smoke it, and share the smoked duck with him. Duck hunting was one of his hobbies. The cure that I used for the smoked duck was one that I developed especially for wild waterfowl.

This sausage formula is based on that cure for smoked wild duck. It makes a spicy and aromatic duck sausage, and it works well with either wild or domesticated duck or geese.

Duckwurst is clearly gourmet fare, and is best served in a way that suggests that it is on a higher level than a common sausage. For example, after stuffing, smoking, and cooking, I recommend removal of the hog casings before slicing. Thin slices that are not more than the diameter of a fifty-cent piece look very attractive on delicate, whole-grain crackers.

Save the duck carcass. At the end of the sausage recipe, "Duck Sausage," in Chapter 8, there are simple instructions on how to use the carcass to make delicious duck soup.

THE CASINGS

If you wish to use small hog casing, rinse 7 feet (210 cm), and refrigerate it overnight in a little water. Rinse the casing again, and soak it in warm water for a few minutes before using.

THE MEAT

Domesticated ducks sold at grocery stores are commonly pumped with a salt solution before freezing. If such ducks are used to make sausage, the sausage will be too salty. Ducks that have not been pumped are available, but you might have to search for them.

Prepare 2½ lbs. (1,150 g) of duck meat; the skin and fat should not exceed about 25 percent of the total meat. Cube the meat, and refrigerate it for at least 30 minutes. While the meat is being prepared, chill the meat grinder and stuffer.

Mince the meat with the smallest plate available. It would be best to mince the meat two times; mincing twice provides a finely textured sausage. Chill the meat between each grinding. After the grinding is finished, chill the meat for about 30 minutes.

SEASONINGS AND OTHER INGREDIENTS
2 tsp. (10 ml) salt
½ tsp. (2.5 ml) Cure #1
1 tsp. (5 ml) poultry seasoning—packed in the spoon
1 tsp. (5 ml) onion granules
½ tsp. (2.5 ml) paprika
½ tsp. (2.5 ml) sage—packed in the spoon
½ tsp. (2.5 ml) marjoram
½ tsp. (2.5 ml) white pepper
¼ tsp. (1.25 ml) thyme
¼ tsp. (1.25 ml) garlic granules
⅛ tsp. (0.625 ml) bay leaf powder
1 Tbsp. (15 ml) light corn syrup
2 Tbsp. (30 ml) cold water

MIXING AND STUFFING
1. Mix the seasonings and other ingredients well in a large mixing bowl, chill the mixture for about 15 minutes, and then add the meat and blend well. Knead for about three minutes.
2. Stuff the sausage.
3. To ensure migration and blending of the curing agent and seasonings, let the sausage rest overnight in the refrigerator.
4. Cold smoking followed by hot smoking or steaming is recommended— please see Chapter 7 for instruction details. Please see Chapter 6 for suggestions if the sausage will be cooked without smoking.

German Bologna
The commercially produced bologna luncheon meat sold here in the United States is, in my opinion, almost inedible. However, this homemade bologna is

delicious. The taste, texture, and appearance are completely different from that offered in supermarkets. Furthermore, we can be sure that this product does not contain any mystery meat such as pig snouts or cow navels.

The sausage in this formula is not emulsified. If you prefer emulsified bologna like the kind sold in the supermarket, please read HOW TO EMULSIFY SAUSAGE in Chapter 10 and follow the emulsification instructions given for either Beef Bologna or Bologna in that chapter.

THE CASINGS

Soak fibrous casings in water for 30 minutes before using. Make sure that there is a liberal amount of water inside the casings. If you are using 2½-inch (6.4 cm) diameter casings that are about 12 inches (30 cm) long, two of them will be required.

THE MEAT

Prepare 1½ lbs. (680 g) of beef chuck and 1 lb. (450 g) of pork butt, and cut the meat into cubes. Refrigerate for about 30 minutes. Refrigerate the grinder and the stuffer while the meat is being prepared.

Grind the meat with a ³⁄₁₆-inch (4.8 mm) plate—use a plate with smaller holes, if available. Pass the meat through the grinder twice if you want it to be particularly fine. Chill the meat thoroughly while the seasoning is being prepared.

THE SEASONING AND OTHER INGREDIENTS

2 tsp. (10 ml) salt
½ tsp. (2.5 ml) Cure #1
1 tsp. (5 ml) black pepper, finely ground
½ tsp. (2.5 ml) mustard, ground—packed in the spoon
½ tsp. (2.5 ml) celery seed, ground
½ tsp. (2.5 ml) garlic powder
¼ tsp. (1.25 ml) coriander—packed in the spoon
¼ tsp. (1.25 ml) nutmeg
1 Tbsp. (15 ml) light corn syrup
¼ cup (60 ml) water
½ cup (120 ml) powdered skim milk

MIXING AND STUFFING

1. While the ground meat is being chilled, mix all the seasoning ingredients thoroughly in a large bowl, including the water and powdered milk. Refrigerate for at least 15 minutes.

2. Add the ground meat to the seasoning mixture. Blend by kneading until it is uniformly mixed. This will require about three minutes.

3. Stuff the sausage into casings. Insert the cable probe of an electronic thermometer in the open end of one of the sausages, and close the casing around the probe with butcher's twine.

4. Refrigerate the stuffed sausage overnight so the seasoning and curing powder will blend with the meat.

The next morning, the sausage may be smoked. Please see Chapter 7 for smoking instructions and suggestions. Cold smoking and steam cooking are recommended. If the sausage will not be smoked, steaming or poaching is recommended. Cooking by steaming or poaching is explained in Chapter 6.

Hot and Spicy Ham—Coppa Style

Sometimes there is a fuzzy line between sausage and cured meat, and this recipe is a good example. This product is made of pieces of seasoned and cured pork that are stuffed into a fibrous casing; stuffing the meat into a casing seems to make it a sausage. However, the meat is not chopped into tiny pieces—it is cut into hunks that, on the average, have a volume of about 1½ cubic inches (3.8 cubic centimeters). Considering this, *Hot and Spicy Ham* could be called cured ham that is stuffed into casings. (A similar product, *Krakowska,* is presented later in this chapter.)

The inspiration for this product came from an Italian sausage called *coppa.* Coppa is similar to *Hot and Spicy Ham* because both are cured hunks of pork that are seasoned in a similar way and stuffed into casings. Coppa, however, is dry cured using a lot of salt, and it is not cooked before it is eaten. Hot and Spicy Ham is gently cured with just the right amount of salt for good taste. It is lightly smoked, and is fully cooked for health and safety.

MEAT FOR 2½ LBS. (1,150 G) OF HAM

Prepare 2½ lbs. (1,150 g) of *lean* pork. (Usually meat for sausage making should be about 25 percent fat, but this is an exception.) These hunks of lean pork can be any shape, but uniform curing is easier to accomplish if the hunks are not more than about ¾ inch (2 cm) thick. The easiest way to accomplish the cutting is to slice the pork into ¾-inch (2 cm) slabs, and then to cut the slabs into any shape that measures something like 1 to 1½ inches (2.5 to 4 cm). Any lean pork may be used. For example, the cubes may be cut from pork sirloin, pork loin, uncured ham (hind leg), or even from the lean parts of pork butt. Refrigerate these cubes until they are well chilled. Keep the meat chilled while the seasoning and other ingredients are being prepared.

THE SEASONING, CURE, AND OTHER INGREDIENTS
1 Tbsp. (15 ml) salt
1 Tbsp. (15 ml) brown sugar—packed in the spoon
½ tsp. (2.5 ml) Cure #1
1 Tbsp. (15 ml) paprika
1 Tbsp. (15 ml) black pepper, ground
1½ tsp. (7.5 ml) coriander, ground—packed in the spoon
1 tsp. (5 ml) cayenne
1 tsp. (5 ml) garlic, minced
½ tsp. (2.5 ml) allspice
½ tsp. (2.5 ml) mace
¼ cup (60 ml) red wine

MIXING, CURING, AND STUFFING
1. *Day 1*: While the pork hunks are being chilled, mix the seasoning and other ingredients in a food container with a tight-fitting lid. Stir the mixture until it is uniform. The container should be large enough to hold all the meat cubes, and large enough to permit them to be stirred easily.
2. Add the pork hunks to the seasoning mixture and stir well. All surfaces of the cubes must be coated with the seasoning cure. Push the cubes down in the curing container so that they are packed together tightly.
3. *Days 2, 3, and 4*: Each day, stir the cubes thoroughly at least once in order to recoat each of the cubes with cure. Push the cubes down to repack tightly.
4. *Day 5*: The curing is finished. Remove the cubes from the plastic container, place them in a colander, and spray with cold water while thoroughly agitating them. (This is to remove all curing compound and excess seasoning from the surfaces of the cubes.) Drain well in the colander, and then place the cubes atop a paper towel with newspaper underneath. Refrigerate the cubes while they are on the paper, and prepare to finish making and stuffing the sausage.

CASING AND STUFFING
Any size of fibrous casing may be used, but you likely have 2½-inch (6.35 cm) casings on hand, and these work well. For 2½ lbs. (1,150 g) of sausage, two of

these casings—each 12 inches (30 cm) long—will be required. Prepare the casings by soaking in lukewarm water for 30 minutes. Be sure to flood the inside of the casing with warm water.

1. Stuff the cured ham hunks into fibrous casings *by hand*. Insert the cable probe of an electronic thermometer in the open end of one of the sausages, and close the casing around the probe with butcher's twine.
2. Refrigerate the sausage chubs overnight.

The next morning, the chubs may be smoked. Please see Chapter 7 for smoking suggestions. If they will be smoked, cold smoking and steam cooking is recommended. If the sausage will not be smoked, steaming or poaching is recommended. Cooking by steaming or poaching is explained in Chapter 6.

Käsewurst (Cheese Sausage)

Variations of Käsewurst (Cheese Sausage) appear in Germany, Austria, and Switzerland. Some of the formulations resemble cured Bratwurst with the addition of cheese cubes. This formulation is similar to that made in Switzerland, and it uses the famous Emmenthaler cheese of Switzerland, which most people in the United States call Swiss cheese.

The melted cheese goes well with the ham-like taste of this cured sausage, so this wurst has many devotees.

Half a pound (225 g) of cheese is added to the normal amount of meat, so this formulation will result in 3 lbs. (1,360 g) of sausage.

CASING

Prepare 9 feet (270 cm) of hog casing; rinse thoroughly. Soak in water, in the refrigerator, overnight. Rinse again, and soak in warm water for a few minutes before using.

MEAT AND CHEESE

Cut ½ lb. (225 g) of Emmenthaler cheese (or Swiss cheese) into ¼-inch (6 mm) cubes. Place the cheese in the refrigerator until the sausage paste has been prepared.

Prepare 2½ lbs. (1,150 g) of pork butt; cut the meat into ¾-inch (2 cm) cubes. Refrigerate the meat for at least 30 minutes. While the meat is being prepared, refrigerate the meat grinder and stuffer.

Grind the meat with a coarse plate—about a ¼-inch (6.35 mm) plate. Return the ground meat to the refrigerator while the seasoning and other ingredients are being prepared.

THE SEASONING AND OTHER INGREDIENTS
2 tsp. (10 ml) salt
½ tsp. (2.5 ml) Cure #1
1 tsp. (5 ml) black pepper, finely ground
½ tsp. (2.5 ml) granulated garlic
½ tsp. (2.5 ml) oregano
¼ tsp. (1.25 ml) thyme
6 Tbsp. (90 ml) fresh milk
½ cup (120 ml) powdered skim milk

MIXING AND STUFFING
1. Mix the seasoning, milk, and powdered milk in a 5-quart (5 liter) mixing bowl. Refrigerate this seasoning mixture for about 15 minutes.
2. Blend the meat and the seasoning well by kneading for about three minutes.
3. Sprinkle the cheese cubes on the sausage paste, and knead again until the cubes appear to be evenly distributed in the paste.
4. Stuff the sausage in hog casings, and twist the sausage rope into links.
5. Refrigerate overnight.

Steaming or poaching, followed by grilling or frying, is suggested. Please see the cooking suggestions in Chapter 6.

Krakowska
This "sausage" is similar to the *Hot and Spicy Ham* presented earlier in this chapter. Krakowska, too, is a ham-in-a-casing sausage; it is named after the city Krakow in southern Poland. The fact that the meat hunks are stuffed in a casing seems to be the only reason it is called a sausage. In the case of Krakowska, the lean pork is cured and changed to ham within the casing, but the pork for the other product earlier in this chapter is cured outside of the casing. The seasoning, also, is very different for the two products. But if you like ham, you are certain to like one of them, and you will probably like both. Krakowska, by the way, is pronounced *krah-KOV-skah*.

A good point to keep in mind about these products is that they are very low in fat. Therefore, they are much lower in cholesterol than conventional sausage. Consequently, they may be among the few varieties of sausage edible by a person on a low cholesterol diet.

MEAT FOR 2½ LBS. (1,150 G) OF KRAKOWSKA

Prepare 2½ lbs. (1,150 g) of *lean* pork. (Usually meat for sausage making should be about 25 percent fat, but Krakowska is an exception.) The pieces of lean pork can be any shape, but the thickness of each piece should not exceed ½ inch (13 mm). The easiest way to accomplish this is to cut the large hunks of meat into ½-inch (13 mm) slabs, and then cut the slabs into smaller pieces. (Pieces thicker than about ½ inch, or 13 mm, would require a longer curing time, which is undesirable.)

Traditionally, the well-trimmed hind leg of the pig is used (well-trimmed, fresh, uncured ham), but any lean pork will do. For example, the ½-inch (13 mm) thick pieces may be cut from pork sirloin, pork loin, or even from the lean parts of pork butt. (I usually use pork sirloin because it is lean, economical, boneless, and similar to fresh ham.) Refrigerate these hunks until they are well chilled. Keep the meat chilled while the seasoning and other ingredients are being prepared. Stuffing the sausage by hand is recommended, but if the stuffer will be used to stuff these large meat chunks, refrigerate the stuffer while the meat is being prepared.

THE SEASONING, CURE, AND OTHER INGREDIENTS

2¼ tsp. (11.25 ml) salt
½ tsp. (2.5 ml) Cure #1
1½ tsp. (7.5 ml) mustard powder—packed in the spoon
1 tsp. (5 ml) garlic granules
¼ tsp. (1.25 ml) white pepper, finely ground
¼ tsp. (1.25 ml) coriander, ground—packed in the spoon
¼ tsp. (1.25 ml) marjoram
¼ tsp. (1.25 ml) allspice
1 Tbsp. (15 ml) light corn syrup
2 Tbsp. (30 ml) cold water

CASING

Any size of fibrous casing may be used, but you likely have 2½-inch (6.35 cm) casings on hand, and these work well. For 2½ lbs. (1,150 g) of sausage, two of these casings—each 12 inches (30 cm) long—will be required. Prepare the casings by soaking in warm water for 30 minutes. Be sure to flood the inside of the casing with warm water.

DAY 1: MIXING AND STUFFING

1. Mix the seasoning, corn syrup, and water in a large mixing bowl, and stir the ingredients until the mixture is uniform. Refrigerate the slurry until it is well chilled.
2. Add the pork hunks to the seasoning mixture and stir well. All surfaces of the cubes must be coated with the seasoning cure.
3. Stuff the ham hunks into fibrous casings by hand, or use a large stuffing horn. *Make sure that all of the leftover curing slurry is divided equally and put into the two casings.* Insert the cable probe of an electronic thermometer in the open end of one of the sausages, and close the casing around the probe with butcher's twine. Refrigerate again until Day 3, morning. During this curing period, the chunks of pork will become chunks of cured, raw ham.

DAY 3, MORNING: SMOKING (OPTIONAL) AND COOKING

On the morning of the third day, the sausage chubs may be optionally smoked. (Either cold smoking for several hours and then steam cooking, or cold smoking followed by hot smoking until the meat is fully cooked is recommended.) Please see Chapter 7 for smoking suggestions. If the sausage will not be smoked, steaming or poaching is recommended. Cooking by steaming or poaching is explained in Chapter 6.

Linguisa (Portuguese)

This well-seasoned and flavorful sausage is a Portuguese classic. It is particularly popular in Hawaii where there are many people of Portuguese descent. This sausage contains vinegar. If you have never used vinegar in sausage, you might consider reducing the vinegar in the first batch; some people love it, and others can't stand it.

THE CASINGS

Prepare 7 feet (210 cm) of hog casing; rinse thoroughly. Soak the casing in a little water, and refrigerate overnight. Rinse again before using.

THE MEAT

Prepare 2 lbs. (910g) of lean pork and ½ lb. (225 g) of back fat—or 2½ lbs. (1,150 g) of pork shoulder. Cut into ¾-inch (2 cm) cubes, and chill this meat for at least 30 minutes. While this meat is being prepared, chill the grinder and sausage stuffer. Grind with a medium plate.

THE SEASONING

2 tsp. (10 ml) salt
½ tsp. (2.5 ml) Cure #1
1 Tbsp. (15 ml) paprika
1 tsp. (5 ml) black pepper
½ tsp. (2.5 ml) marjoram
½ tsp. (2.5 ml) oregano
¼ tsp. (1.25 ml) coriander—packed in the spoon
2 cloves garlic, minced
2 Tbsp. (30 ml) apple cider vinegar or wine vinegar
2 Tbsp. (30 ml) water
½ cup (120 ml) powdered skim milk

MIXING AND STUFFING

1. Mix the seasonings, vinegar, water, and skim milk in a large stainless steel mixing bowl until they are thoroughly blended and the powdered milk has dissolved. Refrigerate this mixture for at least 15 minutes.
2. Blend the meat and the seasoning well by kneading for about three minutes.
3. Stuff the sausage in hog casings, and twist the sausage rope into links. For linguisa, links about 10 inches (25 cm) long are traditional.
4. Refrigerate overnight to allow Cure #1 and the seasonings to penetrate the meat. Do not cover, or cover with paper towels only.
5. Linguisa is sometimes smoked. If you wish to smoke the linguisa, please see Chapter 7 for suggestions and directions. If you wish to omit smoking, please see the cooking suggestions in Chapter 6.

Mashelle's Hotlinks

Mashelle Cromis, a friend, asked me if I could make a sausage similar to her favorite brand of sausage: Fletcher's Louisiana Hotlinks. I accepted the challenge. A branch of a Canadian company that produces ham, bacon, and sausage for the Pacific Northwest makes Fletcher products. A few grocery stores in this area sell them.

I bought and tasted the Fletcher's Louisiana Hotlinks. The Fletcher product is cured, and it seems to be like a mild version of a sausage called Texas hotlinks. There is an uncured hot sausage made in Louisiana called chaurice—sometimes called Louisiana hotlinks—but the Fletcher product is not the same.

I created a first-test formulation to imitate the Fletcher's Louisiana Hotlinks. I prepared, cooked, and tasted the sausage myself. I also gave some of the links to Mashelle so that she could serve them as she usually serves the store-bought product. I then tinkered with the formulation to make it a little closer to the Fletcher product. This testing, tasting, and tinkering was done several times, and the result is below. Mashelle believes that I met the challenge; the taste is not exactly the same, but the sausage is just as good, and the homemade version has a milder and more pleasant salt content.

CASINGS

The Fletcher product is stuffed in a collagen casing that is about the same diameter as a hot dog. It is dyed bright red. To imitate that casing, I used sheep casing and dyed it red by putting about a teaspoon (5 ml) of red food color in the water used to soak it overnight. About 14 feet (420 cm) of casing is required. Rinse the casing well. Add the food color (optional) to a small about of water, and soak it in the refrigerator overnight. Rinse again, and soak in warm water for a few minutes before using.

The red food color effectively dyed the casing and made an interesting visual impact. However, using the dyed casing was messy because the red color was transferred to the hands and to everything it touched—though it was easily washed off. If this dyeing of the casing and the resulting visual impact is desirable, you may wish to buy the red food color at a restaurant supply grocery store. A 16 fluid oz.- (2 cups or 475 ml) bottle purchased at a restaurant supply store is much more economical than using the tiny bottles of food color sold at a common grocery store.

THE MEAT FOR 2½ LBS. (1,150 G) OF MASHELLE'S HOTLINKS

Prepare 2½ lbs. (1,150 g) of pork shoulder. Cut into ¾-inch (2 cm) cubes and refrigerate. While this meat is being prepared, chill the grinder and sausage stuffer in the refrigerator.

SEASONINGS AND OTHER INGREDIENTS

2 tsp. (10 ml) salt

½ tsp. (2.5 ml) Cure #1

4 tsp. (20 ml) black pepper, ground

1 Tbsp. (15 ml) paprika

2 tsp. (10 ml) crushed red pepper

2 tsp. (10 ml) cayenne

1 tsp. (5 ml) thyme

½ tsp. (2.5 ml) granulated garlic

½ tsp. (2.5 ml) coriander—packed in the spoon

½ tsp. (2.5 ml) mustard powder—packed in the spoon

¼ tsp. (1.25 ml) powdered bay leaf

¼ tsp. (1.25 ml) powdered anise

¼ tsp. (1.25 ml) MSG (optional)

1 Tbsp. (15 ml) light corn syrup

½ cup (120 ml) finely powdered skim milk

¼ cup (60 ml) cold water

¼ cup (60 ml) cold red wine

MIXING AND STUFFING

1. Grind the chilled pork with a ³⁄₁₆-inch (4.8 mm) plate. Refrigerate the ground meat for about 30 minutes.

2. While the meat is chilling, mix all of the remaining ingredients thoroughly in a large mixing bowl. Refrigerate this mixture for about 15 minutes.

3. Add the chilled ground meat to the seasoning mixture, and knead until it is well mixed and uniform. This will require about three minutes. Chill this meat and seasoning mixture again while the sausage stuffer and casings are being prepared.

4. Stuff the sausage into the casing, and twist the sausage rope into links. Refrigerate the links overnight to permit the seasoning to be absorbed by the meat. Use an uncovered container (or cover with paper towels) so the casings will dry.

5. If you wish to smoke the hotlinks, please see Chapter 7 for suggestions and directions. If you wish to omit smoking, please go directly to the cooking suggestions in Chapter 6.

Mettwurst

All of the famous sausages have many variations, and Mettwurst is no exception. Most recipes give instructions for a cured mettwurst that is not cooked; it is smoked at about 100° F (38° C) for 12 hours or so. Of course, when the sausage is finished it is still raw meat—very red and very raw. This raw, ground meat is spread on crusty bread or crackers and eaten. To this, I say no, thank you—I prefer cooked sausage.

The following recipe will be for a cured and fully cooked mettwurst, made of beef and pork, stuffed in a fibrous casing, and intended to be eaten as snack or lunchmeat sausage. It is a tasty, safe, healthy, and appetizing sausage.

THE CASINGS

Soak fibrous casings in warm water for 30 minutes before using. Make sure that there is a liberal amount of water inside the casings. If you are using 2½-inch (6.4 cm) diameter casings that are about 12 inches (30 cm) long, two of them will be required.

THE MEAT

Prepare 1½ lbs. (680 g) of beef chuck and 1 lb. (450 g) of pork butt. Cut the meat into cubes. Refrigerate for about 30 minutes. Refrigerate the grinder and the stuffer while the meat is being prepared.

Grind the meat with a ³⁄₁₆-inch (4.8 mm) plate. Chill the meat thoroughly while the seasoning is being prepared.

THE SEASONING

2 tsp. (10 ml) salt
½ tsp. (2.5 ml) Cure #1
½ tsp. (2.5 ml) white pepper, finely ground
½ tsp. (2.5 ml) allspice
½ tsp. (2.5 ml) whole mustard seed
¼ tsp. (1.25 ml) marjoram
¼ tsp. (1.25 ml) coriander—packed in the spoon
¼ tsp. (1.25 ml) nutmeg
¼ tsp. (1.25 ml) ginger powder
¼ tsp. (1.25 ml) celery seed, ground
1 Tbsp. (15 ml) light corn syrup
¼ cup (60 ml) water
½ cup (120 ml) powdered skim milk

MIXING AND STUFFING

1. Mix all the seasoning ingredients thoroughly in a large bowl, including the corn syrup, water, and powdered milk.
2. Add the meat to the seasoning mixture. Blend by kneading until it is uniform. This will require about three minutes.
3. Stuff the sausage into fibrous casings. Insert the cable probe of an electronic thermometer in the open end of one of the sausages, and close the casing around the probe with butcher's twine.
4. Refrigerate the stuffed sausage overnight so the seasoning and curing powder will blend with the meat.

The next morning, the sausage may be smoked. Please see Chapter 7 for smoking instructions and suggestions. Cold smoking and steam cooking is recommended. If the sausage will not be smoked, steaming or poaching is recommended. Cooking by steaming or poaching is explained in Chapter 6.

Minced-Ham Lunchmeat

Many kinds of lunchmeats are actually sausages. A product variously called *chopped ham*, *minced ham,* or *pressed ham* is one such product, and it is widely sold in grocery stores. The commercially produced product looks good, but the taste of salt overrides all other flavors. If you make the product described below, it is likely that you will no longer be satisfied with the commercial product. The following minced ham will look similar to the commercial product, but it will have a delicious ham flavor that is lacking in minced-ham lunchmeat offered by the large meat processors.

THE CASINGS

Fibrous casings about 2½ inches (6.4 cm) in diameter are used for this sausage. Two casings that are about 12 inches (30 cm) long each will be required. Soak the casings in water for 30 minutes before stuffing. Be sure to flood the inside of the casing with warm water. If this product will not be smoked, it may be processed in a loaf pan instead of fibrous casings—please see *Sausage Loaf (Lunchmeat Loaf)* in Chapter 6.

THE MEAT

Use 2½ lbs. (1,150 g) of pork butt. Roughly separate the lean meat from the fat. Mince the lean meat with a ¼-inch (6.4 mm) plate, and mince the fat with a

³⁄₁₆-inch (4.8 mm) plate. The fat should be partially frozen before it is ground. Combine the lean meat and the fat. Refrigerate the meat while the curing mixture is being prepared.

SEASONINGS AND OTHER INGREDIENTS
2 tsp. (10 ml) salt
½ tsp. (2.5 ml) Cure #1
½ tsp. (2.5 ml) white pepper
½ tsp. (2.5 ml) onion powder
½ tsp. (2.5 ml) garlic powder
4 tsp. (20 ml) maple syrup OR 1 Tbsp. (15 ml) honey
¼ cup (60 ml) water
½ cup (120 ml) powdered skim milk

MIXING AND STUFFING
1. Mix all the seasoning ingredients thoroughly in a large bowl, including the water and powdered milk.
2. Add the meat to the seasoning mixture. Blend by kneading until it is uniform. This will require about three minutes.
3. Stuff the sausage into casings. Insert the cable probe of an electronic thermometer in the open end of one of the sausages, and close the casing around the probe with butcher's twine.
4. Refrigerate the stuffed sausage overnight so the seasoning and curing powder will blend with the meat.

The next morning, the sausage may be smoked. Please see Chapter 7 for smoking instructions and suggestions. Cold smoking and steam cooking is recommended. If the sausage will not be smoked, steaming or poaching is recommended. Cooking by steaming or poaching is explained in Chapter 6.

Old-Fashioned Frankfurter
The commercially produced frankfurter that we know today is made of emulsified meat. It is the most popular sausage in the United States and in several other countries. The frankfurter is also called wiener, frank, or hot dog. (Please see Chapter 10 for information about emulsified sausage.)

Many people believe that the original frankfurter was made in Frankfurt, Germany, though not all experts agree on this. However, no matter where it originated, it was not made with emulsified meat; meat emulsifiers did not exist at that time. It is with this fact in mind that the words *old-fashioned* are used to name this product; the product below will be much more like the original frankfurters than the ones sold in grocery stores today.

CASING
Prepare 7 feet (210 cm) of hog casing; rinse thoroughly. Refrigerate the casing overnight in a little water. Rinse again, and soak in warm water before using.

MEAT
Prepare 1½ lbs. (680 g) of pork butt and 1 lb. (450 g) of beef chuck; cut the meat into ¾-inch (2 cm) cubes. Refrigerate the meat for 30 minutes. While the meat is being prepared, refrigerate the meat grinder and stuffer.

Grind the meat with a ³⁄₁₆-inch (4.8 mm) plate—or use a plate with smaller holes, if available. Chill the meat again for about 30 minutes, and then grind it one more time if you want the meat ground finer. Return the ground meat to the refrigerator while the seasoning and other ingredients are being prepared.

THE SEASONING AND OTHER INGREDIENTS
2 tsp. (10 ml) salt
½ tsp. (2.5 ml) Cure #1
1½ tsp. (7.5 ml) coriander, ground—packed in the spoon
1 tsp. (5 ml) onion powder
1 tsp. (5 ml) black pepper, finely ground
½ tsp. (2.5 ml) mustard, ground—packed in the spoon
¼ tsp. (1.25 ml) garlic powder
¼ tsp. (1.25 ml) marjoram
¼ tsp. (1.25 ml) mace
1 egg, large, well beaten
⅓ cup (80 ml) water
½ cup (120 ml) powdered skim milk

MIXING AND STUFFING
1. Mix all the seasoning ingredients (including the egg, water, and powdered skim milk) in a 5-quart (5 liter) mixing bowl. Refrigerate this seasoning mixture for about 15 minutes.
2. Blend the meat and the seasoning well by kneading for about three minutes.
3. Stuff the sausage in hog casings, and twist the sausage rope into links.

4. Refrigerate the links overnight in an uncovered container.
5. If you wish to smoke the franks, please see Chapter 7 for suggestions and directions. (Frankfurters are traditionally smoked.) If you wish to omit smoking, please see the cooking suggestions in Chapter 6.

Old-Fashioned Loaf

When I was young, this product could be found in all the large grocery stores, but I have not seen it in recent years. It was not as popular as pressed ham, for example, but it was a good lunchmeat if the processor made it with quality ingredients.

Old-fashioned loaf may be processed in a bread loaf pan and steamed—please see *Sausage Loaf (Lunchmeat Loaf)* in Chapter 6. If fibrous casings are preferred, the instructions are given below.

The sausage in this formula is not emulsified. If you prefer emulsified old-fashioned loaf, please read HOW TO EMULSIFY SAUSAGE in Chapter 10 and follow the emulsification instructions given for either Beef Bologna or Bologna in that chapter.

Old-fashioned loaf is not smoked.

CASING

The 2½-inch (6.4 cm) fibrous casings work well for this sausage. For 2½ lbs. (1,150 g) of sausage, two fibrous casings—each 12 inches (30 cm) long—will be required. Prepare the fibrous casings by soaking them in lukewarm water for about 30 minutes. Be sure to put water inside the casings.

THE MEAT

Prepare 1¾ lbs. (800 g) of pork butt and ¾ lbs. (350 g) of beef chuck. Refrigerate. While the meat is being prepared, chill the meat grinder and stuffer.

Cut the meat into ¾-inch (2 cm) cubes, and refrigerate it for at least 30 minutes. Grind with a ³⁄₁₆-inch (4.8 mm) or smaller plate.

SEASONINGS

2¼ tsp. (11.25 ml) salt
½ tsp. (2.5 ml) Cure #1
1 Tbsp. (15 ml) onion powder
¾ tsp. (3.75 ml) white pepper
½ tsp. (2.5 ml) ground celery seed
½ tsp. (2.5 ml) ground coriander—packed in the spoon

2 Tbsp. (30 ml) light corn syrup
¼ cup (60 ml) ice water
½ cup (120 ml) powdered skim milk

MIXING AND STUFFING

1. Mix all the seasoning ingredients thoroughly in a large bowl, including the water and powdered milk.
2. Add the meat to the seasoning mixture. Blend by kneading until it is uniform. This will require about three minutes.
3. Stuff the sausage into casings. Insert the cable probe of an electronic thermometer in the open end of one of the sausages, and close the casing around the probe with butcher's twine.
4. Refrigerate the stuffed sausage overnight so the seasoning and curing powder will blend with the meat.

Cooking by steaming or poaching is explained in Chapter 6.

Parmesan Cheese Sausage

This is a tasty and unusual variety of Italian sausage. The copious Parmesan cheese and wine make the difference. If a stronger cheese flavor is desired, Romano cheese may be used in place of all or part of the Parmesan.

CASINGS

Hog casing is recommended. Rinse 7 feet (210 cm), and refrigerate it overnight in a little water. Rinse again, and soak in warm water for a few minutes before using.

THE MEAT FOR 2½ LBS. (1,150 G) OF SAUSAGE LINKS

Prepare 1½ lbs. (680 g) of pork shoulder and 1 lb. (450 g) of beef chuck. Cut into ¾-inch (2 cm) cubes and refrigerate. While this meat is being prepared, chill the grinder and sausage stuffer in the refrigerator.

SEASONINGS AND OTHER INGREDIENTS

1½ tsp. (7.5 ml) salt
½ tsp. (2.5 ml) Cure #1
1 Tbsp. (15 ml) parsley, dried
1 tsp. (5 ml) fennel seed, coarse ground or powder

2 tsp. (10 ml) whole mustard seed

2 tsp. (10 ml) brown sugar—packed in the spoon

1 tsp. (5 ml) black pepper, ground

1 tsp. (5 ml) red pepper flakes

½ tsp. (2.5 ml) granulated garlic

½ tsp. (2.5 ml) oregano

½ tsp. (2.5 ml) basil, dried and crushed

¼ tsp. (1.25 ml) powdered bay leaf

½ cup (120 ml) finely powdered skim milk

½ cup (120 ml) parmesan cheese, grated

⅓ cup (80 ml) cold red wine

¼ cup (60 ml) cold water

MIXING AND STUFFING

1. Grind the chilled meat with a ¼-inch (6.35 mm) coarse plate. Refrigerate the ground meat for about 30 minutes.

2. While the meat is chilling, mix all the remaining ingredients thoroughly in a large mixing bowl. Refrigerate this mixture for about 15 minutes.

3. Add the chilled ground meat to the seasoning mixture, and knead until it is well mixed and uniform. This will require about three minutes. Chill this meat and seasoning mixture again while the sausage stuffer and casings are being prepared.

4. Stuff the sausage into the casing, and twist the sausage rope into links. Refrigerate the links overnight to permit the seasoning to be absorbed by the meat. Use an uncovered container (or cover with paper towels) so the casings will dry on the surface.

5. If you wish to smoke the links, please see Chapter 7 for suggestions and directions. If you wish to omit smoking, please go directly to the cooking suggestions in Chapter 6.

Pastrami Sausage

After successfully making many kinds of tasty luncheon meats, I realized that I had never made a luncheon meat sausage with 100 percent beef. I have never heard of a product called *pastrami sausage*, but I thought that a beef-based product that is seasoned like pastrami would be very good; I was correct. The kinds of spices used in this sausage are the same as those I use when I cure solid-muscle beef to make regular smoked pastrami.

The instructions below assume that you will use a fibrous casing. However, it may be processed in a loaf pan instead—see *Sausage Loaf (Lunchmeat Loaf)* in Chapter 6.

CASING

The 2½-inch (6.35 cm) fibrous casings are ideal for this sausage. For 2½ lbs. (1,150 g) of sausage, two fibrous casings—each 12 inches (30 cm) long—will be required. Prepare the fibrous casings by soaking in lukewarm water for about 30 minutes. Be sure to put warm water inside the casings.

MEAT

Use 2½ lbs. (1,150 g) of fatty ground chuck. You could also use 2 lbs. (900 g) of lean beef and ½ lb. (225 g) of pork fat if you have only lean beef on hand.

Another option for the raw material would be venison, bear, elk, or moose. Wild game meat that has been trimmed of all fat and mixed with an equal amount of fatty pork or beef would make an excellent product.

Trim the meats, and cut into ¾-inch (2 cm) cubes. Refrigerate the meat for at least 30 minutes. While the meat is being prepared, chill the meat grinder and stuffer.

Grind the meat with a ³⁄₁₆-inch (4.8 mm) plate, or use a plate with smaller holes, if available. Chill the meat again while the seasoning and other ingredients are being prepared.

THE SEASONING

2 tsp. (10 ml) salt
2 tsp. (10 ml) light corn syrup
2 tsp. (10 ml) black peppercorns, cracked
½ tsp. (2.5 ml) Cure #1
½ tsp. (2.5 ml) onion powder
½ tsp. (2.5 ml) garlic powder
¼ tsp. (1.25 ml) cayenne
¼ tsp. (1.25 ml) paprika
¼ tsp. (1.25 ml) oregano
⅛ tsp. (0.625 ml) allspice
⅛ tsp. (0.625 ml) ginger powder
¼ cup (60 ml) water
½ cup (120 ml) powdered skim milk

MIXING AND STUFFING

1. Mix all the seasoning ingredients thoroughly in a large bowl, including the water and powdered milk.
2. Add the meat to the seasoning mixture. Blend by kneading until it is uniform. This will require about three minutes.
3. Stuff the sausage into casings. Insert the cable probe of an electronic thermometer in the open end of one of the sausages, and close the casing around the probe with butcher's twine.
4. Refrigerate the stuffed sausage overnight so the seasoning and curing powder will blend with the meat.

The next morning, the sausage may be smoked. Please see Chapter 7 for smoking instructions and suggestions. Cold smoking and steam cooking is recommended. If the sausage will not be smoked, steaming or poaching is recommended. Cooking by steaming or poaching is explained in Chapter 6.

Polish Lemon Sausage

This is a mildly seasoned snack sausage with a hint of tartness.

CASING

Any size of fibrous casing may be used. A large casing such as a 4-inch (10.16 cm) one is most common, but a 2½-inch (6.35 cm) casing is easier and faster to process, so it is recommended. For 2½ lbs. (1,150 g) of sausage, two of these casings—each 12 inches (30 cm) long—will be required. Soak them in lukewarm water for about 30 minutes. Be sure to put warm water inside the casings.

MEAT

Prepare 2 lbs. (910 g) of pork butt and ½ lb. (225 g) of beef chuck; cut the meat into ¾-inch (2 cm) cubes. The total fat content should be about 20 to 25 percent of the meat. Refrigerate the meat for 30 minutes. While the meat is being prepared, chill the meat grinder and stuffer.

Grind the meat with a 3⁄16-inch (4.8 mm) plate, or use a plate with smaller holes, if available. Chill the meat again while the seasoning and other ingredients are being prepared.

THE SEASONING

2 tsp. (10 ml) salt

½ tsp. (2.5 ml) Cure #1

¾ tsp. (3.75 ml) black pepper, ground

½ tsp. (2.5 ml) lemon zest (grated lemon peel)—packed in the spoon

¼ tsp. (1.25 ml) nutmeg

1 Tbsp. (15 ml) lemon juice

1 Tbsp. (15 ml) cold water

2 Tbsp. (30 ml) light corn syrup

MIXING AND STUFFING

1. Mix the seasoning and liquids in a large bowl until the ingredients are uniform. Refrigerate for 15 minutes.
2. Add the meat to the seasoning mixture. Blend by kneading until it is uniform. This will require about three minutes. Chill this sausage paste for about 30 minutes.
3. Stuff the sausage into fibrous casings. Insert the cable probe of an electronic thermometer in the open end of one of the sausages, and close the casing around the probe with butcher's twine.
4. Refrigerate the sausage chubs overnight so the seasoning and curing powder will blend with the meat.

The next morning, the chubs may be smoked. Please see Chapter 7 for smoking suggestions. If they will be smoked, hot smoking is recommended. If the sausage will not be smoked, steaming or poaching is recommended. Cooking by steaming or poaching is explained in Chapter 6.

Ring Bologna

Bologna is one of the most popular sausages in the United States, but because it is processed in a large casing and sliced for use as a lunchmeat, probably most people do not consider it a sausage. This product will look exactly like a sausage because it is stuffed in relatively small hog casings and tied in a ring, as is Polish kielbasa. Try it either hot or cold.

This sausage can be emulsified easily, if you wish. Study the processing instructions for *Bologna* in Chapter 10, and emulsify this product in the same way *Bologna* is emulsified.

Sausage rings. Ring bologna, kielbasa, and krautwurst are examples of three kinds of sausage that are traditionally tied into rings.

CASINGS

Either small or medium hog casing may be used. If you wish to use the small casing, rinse 7 feet (210 cm) of casing, and refrigerate it overnight in a cup of water. Rinse again, and soak in warm water a few minutes before using.

THE MEAT FOR 2½ LBS. (1,150 G) OF RING BOLOGNA

Prepare the meats listed below; cut into ¾-inch (2 cm) cubes and refrigerate. While this meat is being prepared, chill the grinder and sausage stuffer in the refrigerator.

- 1½ lbs. (680 g) of lean pork and ½ lb. (225 g) of back fat—or 2 lbs. (910 g) of fatty pork shoulder
- ½ lb. (225 g) of beef heart, or lean wild game

SEASONINGS AND OTHER INGREDIENTS

2 tsp. (10 ml) salt
½ tsp. (2.5 ml) Cure #1
1 tsp. (5 ml) mustard powder—packed in the spoon
1 tsp. (5 ml) white pepper
½ tsp. (2.5 ml) allspice
½ tsp. (2.5 ml) marjoram
2 cloves garlic, well minced
½ cup (120 ml) finely powdered skim milk
¼ cup (60 ml) cold water

MIXING AND STUFFING

1. Grind the chilled meats together with a ³⁄₁₆-inch (4.8 mm) or smaller plate. Refrigerate the ground meat for about 30 minutes.

2. Grind the meat one more time to make the meat particles even smaller. Refrigerate the ground meat again for 30 minutes.

3. While the meat is chilling, mix all the remaining ingredients thoroughly in a large mixing bowl. Refrigerate this mixture for about 15 minutes.

4. Add the chilled ground meat to the seasoning mixture, and knead until it is well mixed and uniform. This will require about three minutes. Chill this meat and seasoning mixture again while the sausage stuffer and hog casings are being prepared.

5. Stuff the sausage into the hog casing, and twist the sausage rope into four long links. Use string to close the end of each link securely, and then cut the casing between the ends to separate the links. Tie the ends of each link together to form four rings. Refrigerate the rings overnight to permit the seasoning to be absorbed by the meat. Use an uncovered container (or cover with paper towels) so the casings will dry.

6. If you wish to smoke the ring bologna, please see Chapter 7 for suggestions and directions. (Ring bologna is traditionally smoked.) If you wish to omit smoking, please see the cooking suggestions in Chapter 6.

Savory Polish Sausage

This sausage is more robustly flavored than most Polish sausages.

CASING

Prepare 7 feet (210 cm) of hog casing; rinse thoroughly. Refrigerate in a small amount of water overnight. Rinse again, and soak in warm water a few minutes before using.

MEAT

Prepare 2½ lbs. (1,150 g) of pork butt; cut it into ¾-inch (2 cm) cubes. Refrigerate the meat for 30 minutes. While the meat is being prepared, refrigerate the meat grinder and stuffer.

Grind the meat with a ³⁄₁₆-inch (4.8 mm) or larger plate. Chill the meat again while the seasoning and other ingredients are being prepared.

THE SEASONING

2 tsp. (10 ml) salt
½ tsp. (2.5 ml) Cure #1
2 Tbsp. (30 ml) brown sugar—packed in the spoon
1½ tsp. (7.5 ml) black pepper, finely ground
1 tsp. (5 ml) mustard, ground—packed in the spoon
1 tsp. (5 ml) garlic granules
1 tsp. (5 ml) MSG (optional)
½ tsp. (2.5 ml) summer savory
½ tsp. (2.5 ml) coriander—packed in the spoon
¼ tsp. (1.25 ml) mace
½ cup (120 ml) powdered skim milk
¼ cup (60 ml) water

MIXING AND STUFFING

1. Mix the seasoning, powdered skim milk, and water in a 5-quart (5 liter) mixing bowl. Refrigerate this mixture for at least 15 minutes.
2. Blend the meat and the seasoning well by kneading for about three minutes.
3. Stuff the sausage in hog casings, and twist the sausage rope into links.
4. Refrigerate overnight, uncovered (or covered with paper towels).
5. If you wish to smoke the sausage, please see Chapter 7 for suggestions and directions. If you wish to omit smoking, please see the cooking suggestions in Chapter 6.

Smoked Kielbasa

When I was living in Chicago in the 1970s, I frequently enjoyed eating kielbasa at the many sausage stands in the city. Chicago has a very large population of Polish Americans. In fact, several people told me that the population of Polish Americans in Chicago is greater than the population of Poles in Warsaw, the capital of Poland. The large population of Poles in this country has doubtlessly contributed to the popularity of their sausage.

In Polish, *kielbasa* means *sausage,* and there are many recipes for products called *kielbasa.* The use of cardamom and ground mustard seed makes this recipe interesting.

CASING
Prepare 7 feet (210 cm) of hog casing; rinse thoroughly. Refrigerate the casing overnight in a cup of water. Rinse again before using.

MEAT
Prepare 2½ lbs. (1,150 g) of pork butt; cut it into ¾-inch (2 cm) cubes. Refrigerate the meat for 30 minutes. While the meat is being prepared, refrigerate the meat grinder and stuffer.

Grind the meat with a ³⁄₁₆-inch (4.8 mm) plate. Chill the meat again while the seasoning and other ingredients are being prepared.

THE SEASONING AND OTHER INGREDIENTS
2 tsp. (10 ml) salt
½ tsp. (2.5 ml) Cure #1
1 tsp. (5 ml) mustard, ground—packed in the spoon
1 tsp. (5 ml) garlic granules
½ tsp. (2.5 ml) white pepper, finely ground
½ tsp. (2.5 ml) marjoram
½ tsp. (2.5 ml) cardamom
½ cup (120 ml) powdered skim milk
¼ cup (60 ml) water
2 Tbsp. (30 ml) light corn syrup

MIXING AND STUFFING
1. Mix the seasoning, powdered skim milk, corn syrup, and water in a 5-quart (5 liter) mixing bowl. Refrigerate this mixture for at least 15 minutes.
2. Blend the meat and the seasoning well by kneading for about three minutes.
3. Stuff the sausage in hog casings, and twist the sausage rope into links, or tie the sausage into rings. (Rings are traditional for this sausage. See photo of sausage rings in this chapter, *Ring Bologna*.)
4. Refrigerate overnight, uncovered (or cover with paper towels).
5. If you wish to smoke the kielbasa, please see Chapter 7 for suggestions and directions. (This variety of kielbasa is traditionally smoked.) If you wish to omit smoking, please see the cooking suggestions in Chapter 6.

Smoked Loukanika (Greek)
Fresh loukanika appeared in Chapter 8. The formulation of this cured and smoked version is a little different.

CASINGS

Hog casings are recommended. If you intend to use small-diameter hog casing, rinse 7½ feet (210 cm) of the casing, and refrigerate it overnight in a little water. Rinse again in warm water before using.

THE MEAT FOR 2½ LBS. (1,150 G) OF SAUSAGE

Prepare the meats listed below; cut into ¾-inch (2 cm) cubes and refrigerate. While this meat is being prepared, chill the grinder and sausage stuffer in the refrigerator.

- 1½ lbs. (680 g) of lean pork and ½ lb. (225 g) of back fat—or 2 lbs. (910 g) of fatty pork shoulder
- ½ lb. (225 g) of lean lamb

NOTE: This sausage is also made with beef instead of lamb, and it is often made with 100 percent pork, as well.

SEASONINGS AND OTHER INGREDIENTS

2 tsp. (10 ml) salt
½ tsp. (2.5 ml) Cure #1
1 Tbsp. (15 ml) olive oil
1 tsp. (5 ml) thyme
1 tsp. (5 ml) marjoram
½ tsp. (2.5 ml) black pepper
½ tsp. (2.5 ml) ground allspice
½ tsp. (2.5 ml) coriander—packed in the spoon
½ tsp. (2.5 ml) oregano
2 cloves garlic, finely minced
¼ cup (60 ml) red wine
½ cup (120 ml) finely powdered skim milk
½ cup (120 ml) minced onion
grated orange peel from one orange (orange zest)

MIXING AND STUFFING

1. Grind the meats together with a medium-size plate. Refrigerate the ground meat for about 30 minutes.
2. Mix the seasoning, powdered skim milk, and water in a large mixing bowl. Refrigerate this seasoning mixture for about 15 minutes.

3. Add the chilled ground meat to the seasoning mixture, and knead until it is thoroughly mixed and uniform. This will require about three minutes. Chill this meat and seasoning mixture again while the sausage stuffer and hog casings are being prepared.

4. Stuff the sausage into the hog casings, and twist into 6-inch (15 cm) links. Refrigerate the links overnight to permit the seasoning to be absorbed by the meat. Cover the container with a paper towel.

5. If you wish to hot smoke or cold smoke the links, please see Chapter 7 for suggestions and directions. (These cured loukanika are traditionally smoked for a short time.) If you wish to omit smoking, please see the cooking suggestions in Chapter 6.

Spicy French Sausage

Savory is not among the common spices used in sausage, but the other spices used in Spicy French Sausage are quite common. Most of the spices are used generously, making it a flavorful product. It tastes much like spicy cured ham.

THE CASING

Patties or natural casings are best for this sausage. If 24 to 26 mm (1 in. to $1\frac{1}{16}$ in.) sheep casing is to be used, prepare about 14 feet (420 cm) of casing. If small-diameter hog casing will be used, prepare 7 feet (210 cm). Rinse the casing, and refrigerate it in water overnight. Rinse again, and soak in warm water a few minutes before using.

MEAT FOR 2½ LBS. (1,150 G) OF SAUSAGE

Prepare $1\frac{3}{4}$ lbs. (800 g) of pork shoulder butt that contains about 20 percent fat, and ¾ lb. (340 g) bacon. Cut the pork shoulder into ¾-inch (2 cm) cubes, and cut the bacon into squares. Refrigerate the meat, and put the meat grinder in the refrigerator. If the sausage stuffer will be used, refrigerate it, as well.

SEASONINGS AND OTHER INGREDIENTS

2 tsp. (10 ml) salt
½ tsp. (2.5 ml) Cure #1
1 tsp. (5 ml) black pepper
¾ tsp. (3.75 ml) thyme
½ tsp. (2.5 ml) summer savory
½ tsp. (2.5 ml) oregano or marjoram
¼ tsp. (1.25 ml) ground coriander—packed in the spoon

⅛ tsp. (0.625 ml) bay leaf, ground
¼ cup (60 ml) red wine
¼ cup (60 ml) powdered skim milk

MIXING AND STUFFING

1. Grind the pork and bacon together with a fine plate, and refrigerate it for 30 minutes.
2. Mix the seasoning, wine, and powdered milk in a 5-quart (5 liter) mixing bowl. Refrigerate this seasoning mixture for about 15 minutes.
3. Blend the meat and the seasoning well by kneading for about three minutes. Shape the mixture into ⅜-inch (10 mm) thick patties, and wrap them in plastic food wrap. Alternatively, stuff the sausage into sheep or hog casings.
4. Refrigerate the sausage that will be eaten within the next two days, and freeze the remainder.

This sausage can be smoked. If it will be smoked, please see Chapter 7. If it will be cooked without smoking, please see Chapter 6.

Texas Hotlinks

This hot, spicy, complex, and flavorful sausage is great for grilling, and it is popular with beer drinkers. Because this is a well-seasoned sausage, and because this sausage contains beef, it is an excellent candidate for conversion to a wild game sausage. Replace the ¾ pound of beef with wild game trimmed of all fat, and use 1¾ pounds (800 g) of extra fatty pork shoulder. Even as much as 50 percent wild game would make an excellent sausage.

CASINGS

Either small or medium hog casing may be used. If you wish to use the small casing, rinse 7 feet (210 cm), and refrigerate it overnight in water. Rinse again, and soak in warm water for a few minutes before using.

THE MEAT FOR 2½ LBS. (1,150 G) OF TEXAS HOTLINKS

Prepare the meats listed below; cut into ¾-inch (2 cm) cubes, and refrigerate. While this meat is being prepared, chill the grinder and sausage stuffer in the refrigerator.

- 1¾ lbs. (800 g) of fatty pork shoulder
- ¾ lb. (340 g) of beef chuck

SEASONINGS AND OTHER INGREDIENTS

2 tsp. (10 ml) salt

½ tsp. (2.5 ml) Cure #1

2 tsp. (10 ml) black pepper, ground

2 tsp. (10 ml) paprika

2 tsp. (10 ml) crushed red pepper

1 tsp. (5 ml) cayenne

1 tsp. (5 ml) granulated garlic

¾ tsp. (3.75 ml) thyme

½ tsp. (2.5 ml) coriander—packed in the spoon

½ tsp. (2.5 ml) mustard powder—packed in the spoon

½ tsp. (2.5 ml) allspice

½ tsp. (2.5 ml) MSG (optional)

¼ tsp. (1.25 ml) powdered bay leaf

¼ tsp. (1.25 ml) whole mustard seeds

¼ tsp. (1.25 ml) powdered anise

1 Tbsp. (15 ml) light corn syrup

½ cup (120 ml) finely powdered skim milk

½ cup (120 ml) cold beer or cold water

MIXING AND STUFFING

1. Grind the chilled meats together with a ³⁄₁₆-inch (4.8 mm) plate. Refrigerate the ground meat for about 30 minutes.
2. While the meat is chilling, mix all of the remaining ingredients thoroughly in a large mixing bowl. The cold beer—or cold water—will make a slurry or a thin paste with the various seasonings and ingredients. Refrigerate this mixture for about 15 minutes.
3. Add the chilled ground meat to the seasoning mixture, and knead until it is well mixed and uniform. This will require about three minutes. Chill this meat and seasoning mixture again while the sausage stuffer and hog casings are being prepared.
4. Stuff the sausage into the hog casing, and twist the sausage rope into links. Refrigerate the links overnight to permit the seasoning to be absorbed by the meat. Use an uncovered container (or cover with paper towels) so the casings will dry.
5. If you wish to smoke the hotlinks, please see Chapter 7 for suggestions and directions. If you wish to omit smoking, please go directly to the cooking suggestions in Chapter 6.

Turkey Kielbasa

Turkey is certainly not traditional meat for making kielbasa, and I have never heard of kielbasa with poultry seasoning in the formula, but this sausage tastes good, nevertheless.

CASING

Prepare 7 feet (210 cm) of hog casing; rinse thoroughly. Refrigerate the casing in water overnight. Rinse again, and soak in warm water before using.

MEAT

Prepare 2½ lbs. (1,150 g) of dark fowl meat (turkey thighs, chicken thighs or waterfowl), and cube the meat. Be sure to use the skin and a reasonable amount of fat. Refrigerate the meat for 30 minutes. While the meat is being prepared, refrigerate the meat grinder and stuffer.

Grind the meat with a ³⁄₁₆-inch (4.8 mm) plate. Chill the meat again while the seasoning and other ingredients are being prepared.

THE SEASONING AND OTHER INGREDIENTS

2 tsp. (10 ml) salt
½ tsp. (2.5 ml) Cure #1
1 Tbsp. (15 ml) onion granules
1 tsp. (5 ml) white pepper, finely ground
1 tsp. (5 ml) poultry seasoning
1 tsp. (5 ml) paprika
½ tsp. (2.5 ml) garlic granules
½ tsp. (2.5 ml) marjoram
½ tsp. (2.5 ml) ground coriander—packed in the spoon
½ tsp. (2.5 ml) ginger powder
½ tsp. (2.5 ml) dried parsley
¼ tsp. (1.25 ml) cayenne
⅛ tsp. (0.625 ml) allspice
1 Tbsp. (15 ml) light corn syrup
½ cup (120 ml) powdered skim milk
¼ cup (60 ml) water

MIXING AND STUFFING

1. Mix the seasoning, corn syrup, powdered milk, and water in a 5-quart (5 liter) mixing bowl. Refrigerate this mixture for at least 15 minutes.

2. Blend the meat and the seasoning well by kneading for about three minutes.
3. Stuff the sausage into hog casings, and twist the sausage rope into links.
4. Refrigerate overnight, uncovered (or covered with paper towels).
5. If you wish to smoke the kielbasa, please see Chapter 7 for suggestions and directions. If you wish to omit smoking, please see the cooking suggestions in Chapter 6.

Turkey or Waterfowl Cotto Salami

Cotto salami (cooked salami) is usually made with beef and pork, but very good tasting cotto salami can also be made with the dark meat of turkey or chicken. All of the meat on ducks or geese is dark, so any part of these birds—wild or domesticated—may be used.

Cotto salami is usually smoked—and smoking is recommended—but if it will not be smoked, the optional liquid smoke will impart a similar smoked aroma.

CASING

Any size of fibrous casing may be used. A large casing such as a 4-inch (10.16 cm) one is most common, but a 2½-inch (6.35 cm) casing is easier and faster to process, so it is recommended. For 2½ lbs. (1,150 g) of sausage, two of these casings—12 inches (30 cm) long—will be required. Prepare the casings by soaking in lukewarm water for about 30 minutes. Be sure to put some warm water inside the casings.

MEAT

Prepare 2½ lbs. (1,150 g) of chicken or turkey; use the dark meat only. Be sure to use the skin and available fat. Alternatively, wild or domesticated waterfowl may be used, but make sure that the fat does not exceed 25 percent of the total meat. Cube the meat, and refrigerate it for at least 30 minutes. While the meat is being prepared, chill the meat grinder and stuffer, too.

Grind the meat with a ³⁄₁₆-inch (4.8 mm) plate. Chill the meat again while the seasoning and other ingredients are being prepared.

THE SEASONING AND OTHER INGREDIENTS

2¼ tsp. (11.25 ml) salt
½ tsp. (2.5 ml) Cure #1
2 tsp. (10 ml) black peppercorns, cracked

1 tsp. (5 ml) white pepper, ground

½ tsp. (2.5 ml) garlic granules

½ tsp. (2.5 ml) coriander, ground—packed in the spoon

¼ tsp. (1.25 ml) Wright's liquid smoke (optional)

⅛ tsp. (0.625 ml) ginger powder—packed in the spoon

⅛ tsp. (0.625 ml) allspice

½ cup (120 ml) powdered skim milk

3 Tbsp. (45 ml) water

1 Tbsp. (15 ml) light corn syrup

1 Tbsp. (15 ml) red wine

MIXING AND STUFFING

1. Mix the seasoning and other ingredients—except for the meat—in a large bowl until the mixture is uniform.

2. Add the meat to the seasoning mixture. Blend by kneading until it is uniform. This will require about three minutes.

3. Stuff the sausage into fibrous casings. Insert the cable probe of an electronic thermometer in the open end of one of the sausages, and close the casing around the probe with butcher's twine.

4. Refrigerate the stuffed sausage chubs overnight so that the seasoning and curing powder will blend with the meat.

5. The next morning, the sausage chubs may be smoked. Please see Chapter 7 for smoking suggestions. If they will be smoked, cold smoking and steam cooking is recommended. If the sausage will not be smoked, steaming or poaching is recommended. Cooking by steaming or poaching is explained in Chapter 6.

Venison Sausage

The word venison usually referrers to deer meat, but the meat of other herbivorous wild game animals such as elk, moose, antelope, and caribou is also called venison. The following recipe is good for all varieties of venison.

This sausage may be stuffed into natural casings, cooked, and eaten on a bun as one would eat bratwurst. It may also be stuffed into fibrous casings, cooked, chilled, and eaten cold as a luncheon meat. If you have no casings, make it into patties.

The amount of any seasoning, *except Cure #1*, may be increased or decreased to suit your taste.

CASING

Prepare 7 feet (210 cm) of hog casing; rinse thoroughly. Refrigerate the casing overnight in about one cup of water. Rinse again, and soak in warm water before using. If 24 to 26 mm (1 in. to 1¹⁄₁₆ in.) sheep casing is to be used, prepare about 14 feet (420 cm) of casing. If fibrous casing will be used, two 2½-inch (6.4 cm) casings, each 12 inches (30 cm) long, will be required. Fibrous casings must be prepared for use by soaking them in warm water 30 minutes before stuffing. Be sure to flood the inside of the casings with warm water.

MEAT

Prepare 1½ lbs. (680 g) of lean venison; remove all fat and sinew. Also, prepare ½ lb. (225 g) of lean pork and ½ lb. (225 g) of pork fat. Cut the meat into ¾-inch (2 cm) cubes. Refrigerate the meat for 30 minutes. While the meat is being prepared, refrigerate the meat grinder and stuffer.

Grind the meat with a ³⁄₁₆-inch (4.8 mm) plate; chill the meat again for about 30 minutes. Return the ground meat to the refrigerator while the seasoning and other ingredients are being prepared.

THE SEASONING

2 tsp. (10 ml) salt
½ tsp. (2.5 ml) Cure #1
1 Tbsp. (15 ml) brown sugar—packed in the spoon
1½ tsp. (7.5 ml) onion powder
1 tsp. (5 ml) paprika
1 tsp. (5 ml) black pepper, finely ground
½ tsp. (2.5 ml) cayenne
½ tsp. (2.5 ml) sage
½ tsp. (2.5 ml) thyme
¼ tsp. (1.25 ml) garlic powder
¼ tsp. (1.25 ml) nutmeg
¼ tsp. (1.25 ml) allspice
¼ cup (60 ml) of your favorite wine—white or red
½ cup (120 ml) powdered skim milk

MIXING AND STUFFING

1. Mix all the seasoning ingredients, the wine, and the powdered milk in a 5-quart (5 liter) mixing bowl. Refrigerate this seasoning mixture for at least 15 minutes.

2. Blend the meat and the seasoning well by kneading for about three minutes.
3. Stuff the sausage in casings. If natural casings have been used, twist the sausage rope into links.
4. Refrigerate overnight to allow the meat to absorb the flavoring.

If you wish to smoke the stuffed venison sausage, please see Chapter 7 for suggestions and directions. If you wish to omit smoking, please see the cooking suggestions in Chapter 6.

Vienna Sausage

You may have heard of Vienna sausage. If you live in the United States or Canada, you may have sampled the tiny Vienna sausages that are sold in a small can. Many of the ingredients in the formula below are the same as those in the canned variety, but the finished product will be different. You should not expect the same taste and texture as the canned variety, but you should expect that it will be something that is very good to eat.

Near the end of Chapter 10 there is a sausage called Wienerwurst. Wienerwurst is another name for Vienna sausage. If you want to make an emulsified version that will have a bite texture similar to the canned Vienna sausage, try the Wienerwurst.

Vienna sausage is a cured sausage, but it is not normally smoked. However, it does have Cure #1 in the formula, so it can be smoked, if you wish.

THE CASINGS

Prepare 7 feet (210 cm) of hog casings or 14 feet (420 cm) of sheep casing. Rinse the casing, and soak it in water overnight. Rinse it again, and soak in warm water for 30 minutes before stuffing.

THE MEAT

- 1½ lbs. (680 g) fatty pork
- ½ lb. (225 g) lean beef
- ½ lb. (225 g) lean veal (traditional) OR chicken (dark meat)

While the meat is being weighed, trimmed, and cubed, refrigerate the meat grinder and stuffer.

Mince the meats with a ³⁄₁₆-inch (4.8 mm) or smaller plate. It would be best to mince the meats two times; mincing twice provides a finely textured sausage. Chill the meat between each grinding. Blend the pork, beef, and veal (or chicken) and refrigerate.

OTHER INGREDIENTS AND SEASONINGS

4 tsp. (20 ml) onions, finely minced
1 Tbsp. (15 ml) flour
2 tsp. (10 ml) salt
1 tsp. (5 ml) coriander—packed in the spoon
¾ tsp. (3.75 ml) paprika
¾ tsp. (3.75 ml) sugar
½ tsp. (2.5 ml) Cure #1
¼ tsp. (1.25 ml) cayenne
⅛ tsp. (0.625 ml) mace powder
¼ cup (60 ml) cold water
½ cup (120 ml) skim milk powder

MIXING AND STUFFING

1. Mix the seasonings, water, and powdered milk in a large mixing bowl, and refrigerate for 15 minutes. Add the meat and knead the mixture for about three minutes. Refrigerate this sausage paste for at least 30 minutes.
2. Stuff the sausage.
3. To ensure migration of the curing agent and seasonings into the ground meat, let the sausage rest overnight in the refrigerator.

Cooking by steaming or poaching is suggested. Please see Chapter 6 for suggestions.

CHAPTER 10

Emulsified Sausage

We cannot emulsify a sausage mixture as efficiently as commercial producers can, but we can imitate the process surprisingly well and produce almost the same result. To accomplish this, however, a powerful food processor is required. It need not be a professional-grade food processor, but a sturdy and powerful machine for home use is required. The 7-cup (680 ml) Cuisinart food processor I use does the job; it is an old model DLC-7 rated at 560 watts. With this food processor, I am able to process 1¼ pounds (570 g) at a time. If sausage is to be emulsified at home, a food processor equivalent to this machine will be required. Emulsifying meat puts a lot of strain on a processor, and the motor might be damaged if the appliance is underpowered.

I strongly recommend that you try to emulsify sausage at least once. It is not as difficult as it may seem, and the results are nothing short of dramatic. It may not change the taste, but the bite texture and appearance will give the sausage a special appeal—and making emulsified sausage will do a lot for your image as a sausage maker. However, a good food processor is a considerable investment, so—if you have doubts—it would be wise to borrow a suitable processor from a friend or relative until you are sure that this is something you wish to do.

A 2½-pound (1,150 g) recipe of sausage is divided into two parts for processing. When the sausage is being emulsified, about ½ cup (120 ml) of crushed ice is added to each of the two 1¼ pound (570 g) loads. This ice not only lowers the temperature of the sausage paste and makes it more fluid, but it increases the volume of the paste as well. The air that is whipped into the sausage paste also increases the volume. Finally, the volume is increased by interior garnishes such as olives and pistachio nuts. Consequently, if natural casing is used, a greater length of casing than normal will be required for emulsified sausage.

In addition, if synthetic fibrous casing is used, more volume capacity than usual will be required because of the increase in volume mentioned above. Normally, for non-emulsified sausage, *two* of the foot-long (30 cm), 2½-inch (6.4 cm) diameter casings will hold 2½ lbs. (1,150 g) of sausage. However, when sausage is emulsified and stuffed into synthetic casings, *three* of these casings will be required. The three fibrous casings will not be full, but two casings will not hold all the paste. Obviously, another option would be to use two 3-inch (7.62 mm) diameter casings, each 12 inches (30 mm) long.

Note: The sausages in this chapter have been arranged in alphabetical order. Most of the sausages are cured sausages, but there are fresh sausages as well.

The emulsification process is the same for every sausage in this chapter, and that process is explained immediately below:

How to Emulsify Sausage

Keeping the temperature of the sausage paste at less than 60° F (15.6° C) while emulsifying it is the most important point to keep in mind. This might seem difficult, but I have emulsified sausage many, many times, and I have never failed to achieve a good emulsification before the critical temperature of 60° F (15.6° C) is reached. If the ground meat is chilled in the freezer to the point of being slightly crunchy, and the specified amount of ice is added, there will be no problem.

1. Follow the instructions for the sausage you wish to make. At the appropriate point, the instructions will direct you to follow these processing directions (*HOW TO EMULSIFY SAUSAGE*).

2. Add the chilled ground meat to the seasoning and other ingredients, and knead this mixture until it is uniform. This will require about three minutes. Place this sausage paste in the freezer, and stir the paste about every 10 minutes while the food processor is being set up. The goal is to chill this sausage paste in the freezer until most of it is crunchy, but not frozen hard.

3. Prepare at least 1 cup (240 ml) of crushed ice by processing about 10 large ice cubes in the food processor. It is better to have a little extra rather than not enough. Refrigerate.

4. When the sausage mixture has become crunchy, divide it in half. Put half in the food processor with ½ cup (120 ml) of crushed ice, and refrigerate

the remaining half of the paste and the remaining crushed ice. Process the sausage paste in the food processor for 30 seconds, and then measure the temperature with an instant-read thermometer. If the temperature is under 40° F (4.4° C), process it another 30 seconds. Continue to process the sausage paste 30 seconds at a time until 40° F (4.4° C) is reached.

5. When the temperature of the paste reaches 40° F (4.4° C), process it again for 15 seconds, if necessary. Continue to process 15 seconds (or less) at a time until 55° F (12.8° C) is reached—*or until the paste is emulsified*. Do not exceed 60° F (15.6° C); if this temperature is exceeded, the emulsion will probably *break*, meaning that the fat will liquefy and separate from the emulsion. Refrigerate the emulsified sausage paste. *Note: Do not overprocess the sausage paste. When it is obvious that emulsification has been accomplished, the processing should be stopped, even if the temperature of the paste is below 40° F (4.4° C). (Emulsified sausage paste will have a swirled appearance like soft ice cream, and the surface will be glossy.)*

6. Repeat steps 4 and 5 for the remaining half of the sausage paste. Refrigerate.

7. Return to the original sausage recipe for instructions and suggestions regarding stuffing, smoking, and cooking.

Beef Bologna (Baloney)

Beef bologna is a popular variation of the version made with beef and pork. The bite texture will be similar because both are emulsified. The darker color of a 100 percent beef sausage, and the differences in seasoning, will provide a different appearance and taste.

Our sausage will be made with quality ingredients, and it will taste better than the commercial offerings. The texture will be remarkably similar to the commercially produced products, but it will have a milder and more pleasant flavor.

CASINGS

If 2½-inch (6.4 cm) diameter fibrous casings are used, three 12-inch (30 cm) casings will be required. Fibrous casings must be soaked in water 30 minutes before stuffing. Be sure to fill the casing with warm water.

THE MEAT FOR 2½ LBS. (1,150 G) OF BEEF BOLOGNA

Prepare 2½ lbs. (1,150 g) of beef chuck. (Lean wild game and beef suet may be substituted for some of the beef.) Cut the beef chuck into ¾-inch (2 cm) cubes.

Refrigerate the meat until it is well chilled. While this meat is being prepared, chill the grinder and sausage stuffer in the refrigerator.

SEASONINGS AND OTHER INGREDIENTS

2¼ tsp. (11.25 ml) salt
½ tsp. (2.5 ml) Cure #1
1½ tsp. (7.5 ml) paprika
1 tsp. (5 ml) onion granules
¾ tsp. (3.75 ml) white pepper, ground
½ tsp. (2.5 ml) mustard, ground—packed in the spoon
½ tsp. (2.5 ml) garlic powder
½ tsp. (2.5 ml) coriander—packed in the spoon
½ tsp. (2.5 ml) marjoram
¼ tsp. (1.25 ml) nutmeg
¼ tsp. (1.25 ml) allspice
¼ tsp. (1.25 ml) MSG (optional)
1 Tbsp. (15 ml) light corn syrup
¼ cup (60 ml) cold tap water
½ cup (120 ml) finely powdered skim milk

MIXING AND STUFFING

1. Grind the beef chuck with a ³⁄₁₆-inch (4.8 mm) or smaller plate—the smaller the better. Refrigerate for about 30 minutes.

2. Measure the seasoning and other ingredients—except for the meat—into a large stainless steel mixing bowl. Stir until the mixture is uniform; it will be a thin paste. Refrigerate for about 15 minutes.

3. Follow the instructions in *HOW TO EMULSIFY SAUSAGE* near the beginning of this chapter.

4. Stuff the emulsified sausage into the prepared fibrous casings. If an electronic thermometer will be used when the sausage is cooked, insert the cable probe into one of the chubs. Close the ends of the chubs with twine. Refrigerate overnight (or for at least a few hours) to permit the seasoning to be absorbed by the meat. Use an uncovered container with a paper towel placed over the chubs.

5. If the bologna will be smoked, please see Chapter 7. (Cold smoking followed by steaming is recommended.) If it will be cooked without smoking, please see Chapter 6.

Bologna (Baloney)

Common, commercially produced bologna tastes awful, but it is popular nevertheless. The two major reasons for its popularity, I believe, are the low price and the emulsified texture. People like the emulsified texture, and because the product is emulsified, any meat deemed fit for human consumption can be used; this keeps the price low, and the emulsification makes it impossible for the consumer to identify the meat. Nowadays, even poultry is an ingredient in bologna lunchmeats, and parts of the bird that you and I would discard are emulsified and used. The texture of our sausage will be remarkably similar to the commercially produced bologna, but our product will be made with quality ingredients, and it will taste much better.

CASINGS

If 2½-inch (6.4 cm) diameter fibrous casings are used, three 12-inch (30 cm) casings will be required. Fibrous casings must be soaked in water for 30 minutes before stuffing. Be sure to fill the casings with warm water.

THE MEAT FOR 2½ LBS. (1,150 G) OF BOLOGNA

Prepare 1 lb. (450 g) of pork shoulder butt, and 1½ lbs. (680 g) of beef chuck. (Lean wild game and extra pork fat may be substituted for the beef.) Cut the pork butt and beef chuck into ¾-inch (2 cm) cubes. Refrigerate these two meats until they are well chilled. While this meat is being prepared, chill the grinder and sausage stuffer in the refrigerator.

SEASONINGS AND OTHER INGREDIENTS

2¼ tsp. (11.25 ml) salt
½ tsp. (2.5 ml) Cure #1
1½ tsp. (7.5 ml) paprika
1 tsp. (5 ml) onion granules
½ tsp. (2.5 ml) white pepper, ground
½ tsp. (2.5 ml) mustard, ground—packed in the spoon
½ tsp. (2.5 ml) coriander—packed in the spoon
½ tsp. (2.5 ml) marjoram
¼ tsp. (1.25 ml) nutmeg
¼ tsp. (1.25 ml) allspice
1 Tbsp. (15 ml) light corn syrup
¼ cup (60 ml) cold tap water
½ cup (120 ml) finely powdered skim milk

MIXING AND STUFFING

1. Grind the pork butt and the beef chuck with a ³⁄₁₆-inch (4.8 mm) or smaller plate—the smaller the better. Refrigerate for about 30 minutes.
2. Measure the seasoning, water, and powdered milk into a large stainless steel mixing bowl. Stir until the mixture is uniform. It will be a thin paste. Refrigerate for about 15 minutes.
3. Follow the instructions in *HOW TO EMULSIFY SAUSAGE* near the beginning of this chapter.
4. Stuff the emulsified sausage into the prepared fibrous casings. If an electronic thermometer will be used when the sausage is cooked, insert the cable probe into one of the chubs. Close the ends of the chubs with twine. Refrigerate overnight (or for at least a few hours) to permit the seasoning to be absorbed by the meat. Use an uncovered container with a paper towel placed over the chubs.
5. If the bologna will be smoked, please see Chapter 7. (Cold smoking followed by steaming is recommended.) If it will be cooked without smoking, please see Chapter 6.

Braunschweiger

I like the taste of liver, and I have liked Braunschweiger since I was a kid. The fact that I could not buy it in Japan is one of the reasons I began to study the craft of making sausage. Braunschweiger is cured and usually smoked, but smoking may be omitted.

This sausage is traditionally made with pork liver, but calf, beef, or poultry liver may be used instead. Pork liver has the strongest taste and is therefore not as popular as other kinds of liver; it is seldom seen in common grocery stores. If you want to buy pork liver, look for it in ethnic grocery stores. Beef liver is milder than pork, but stronger tasting than calf. Poultry liver is the mildest-tasting liver, and chicken liver is reasonably priced and easy to buy. Depending on my mood at the time, I use beef or pork liver to make Braunschweiger.

CASINGS

If 2½-inch (6.4 cm) diameter fibrous casings are used, three 12-inch (30 cm) casings will be required. Fibrous casings must be soaked in water for 30 minutes before stuffing. Be sure to fill the casings with warm water.

THE MEAT FOR 2½ LBS. (1,150 G) OF BRAUNSCHWEIGER

Prepare 1 lb. (450 g) of pork shoulder butt, ½ lb. (225 g) of bacon, and 1 lb. (450 g) of liver. Cut the pork butt into ¾-inch (2 cm) cubes, and cut the bacon into squares. Refrigerate these two meats until they are well chilled. If large livers are being used, cut the liver into pieces that will fit into the hopper of the meat grinder. Refrigerate the liver in a separate dish from the pork and bacon. While this meat is being prepared, chill the grinder and sausage stuffer in the refrigerator.

SEASONINGS AND OTHER INGREDIENTS

2¼ tsp. (11.25 ml) salt
½ tsp. (2.5 ml) Cure #1
2 tsp. (10 ml) onion granules
¾ tsp. (3.75 ml) white pepper, ground
½ tsp. (2.5 ml) marjoram or oregano
¼ tsp. (1.25 ml) mustard, ground—packed in the spoon
¼ tsp. (1.25 ml) allspice
¼ tsp. (1.25 ml) ginger powder
¼ tsp. (1.25 ml) nutmeg
¼ tsp. (1.25 ml) coriander—packed in the spoon
1 Tbsp. (15 ml) light corn syrup
¼ cup (60 ml) cold tap water
½ cup (120 ml) finely powdered skim milk

MIXING AND STUFFING

1. Grind the liver, bacon, and pork butt. Use a ³⁄₁₆-inch (4.8 mm) or smaller plate—the smaller the better. It is best to grind the soft liver first; the bacon second, and the harder pork last. (The harder pork cubes will help push the softer meats through the grinder.) Refrigerate the ground meat mixture for about 30 minutes.

2. Measure all of the seasonings, water, and powdered milk into a large mixing bowl, and mix thoroughly. Refrigerate for at least 15 minutes.

3. Follow the instructions in *HOW TO EMULSIFY SAUSAGE* near the beginning of this chapter.

4. Stuff the emulsified sausage into the prepared fibrous casings. If an electronic thermometer will be used when the sausage is cooked, insert the cable probe into one of the chubs. Close the ends of the chubs with twine.

Refrigerate overnight (or at least a few hours) to permit the seasoning to be absorbed by the meat. Use an uncovered container with a paper towel placed over the chubs.

5. If the Braunschweiger will be smoked, please see Chapter 7. (Cold smoking followed by steaming is recommended.) If it will be cooked without smoking, please see Chapter 6.

Cervelas de Strasbourg

Strasbourg is the name of a city in northeast France, and this sausage is a variation of the Swiss *Cervelat* sausage, the next sausage presented in this book. In spite of the facts that the names are similar and they are considered variations of one another, the respective seasonings and meat are considerably different. (*Cervelas* is the modern French spelling of *cervelat*—these words are the same.)

A distinctive feature of cervelas de Strasbourg is the tiny cubes of pork fat that are used as an interior garnish. Pork fat cubes measuring only ⅛ inch (3 mm) are mixed with the emulsified red meat. This interior garnish has a visual impact and a unique bite texture, too.

CASINGS

Small, natural casing is best for this French sausage. If 24 to 26 mm (1 in. to 1¹⁄₁₆ in.) sheep casing is to be used, prepare about 18 feet (480 cm). If small-diameter hog casing will be used, prepare 8½ feet (255 cm). Rinse the casing, and refrigerate it in water overnight. Rinse again, and soak in warm water a few minutes before using.

THE MEAT FOR 2½ LBS. (1,150 G) OF CERVELAS

Prepare 1¾ lbs. (800 g) of marbled pork shoulder and ¾ lb. (340 g) of pork fat, preferably back fat. Cut the pork shoulder—*not the pork fat*—into ¾-inch (2 cm) cubes and refrigerate. While the pork shoulder is being prepared, chill the grinder and sausage stuffer in the refrigerator.

Cut the pork fat into tiny ⅛-inch (3 mm) cubes, and blanch these cubes in boiling water for three minutes. Place them a wire mesh strainer and rinse in cold water. Drain them on a paper towel that has been placed on several layers of newspaper. Refrigerate these cubes in a small bowl (separately from the pork shoulder). Blanching of the tiny pork cubes helps to prevent them from sticking together in clumps.

SEASONINGS AND OTHER INGREDIENTS
2 tsp. (10 ml) salt
½ tsp. (2.5 ml) Cure #1
1½ tsp. (7.5 ml) white pepper, ground
¾ tsp. (3.75 ml) garlic granules
¼ tsp. (1.25 ml) nutmeg
¼ tsp. (1.25 ml) cayenne
⅛ tsp. (0.625 ml) cumin
1 Tbsp. (15 ml) finely powdered milk
¼ cup (60 ml) cold water

MIXING AND STUFFING
1. Grind the pork shoulder—*not the tiny cubes of pork fat*—with a ³⁄₁₆-inch (4.8 mm) or smaller plate—the smaller the better. Refrigerate for about 30 minutes. (The tiny pork fat cubes will be added to the sausage paste after emulsification has been finished.)
2. Measure the seasoning, water, and powdered milk into a large stainless steel mixing bowl. Stir until the mixture is uniform. It will be a thin paste. Refrigerate.
3. Follow the instructions in *HOW TO EMULSIFY SAUSAGE* near the beginning of this chapter.
4. Sprinkle the tiny cubes of pork fat on the emulsified sausage paste, and knead until they are mixed uniformly with the paste.
5. Stuff the emulsified sausage into the prepared casings, and twist the links. Refrigerate the links overnight (or at least a few hours) to permit the seasoning to be absorbed by the meat. Use an uncovered container with a paper towel placed over the sausage.

Traditionally, this sausage is not smoked, but it can be smoked if desired. If the cervelas will be smoked, please see Chapter 7. If it will be cooked without smoking, please see Chapter 6. It is most often poached, but it can be cooked by any method.

Cervelat
Cervelat is especially popular in Switzerland. The German speaking Swiss call it *cervelat*, the French speaking Swiss call it *cervelas*, and the Italian speakers call it *cervelato*. The original formulation specified pork brains as part of the meat,

and all of these words are derived from the Latin word *cerebrum*—brains (via the Milanese dialect). Basel, Switzerland was the birthplace of the original contemporary recipe. It is traditionally emulsified, stuffed into Swiss cow casings, and lightly smoked. Cooking is most often accomplished by poaching, but it may also be steamed, grilled, or fried. The per capita consumption of cervelat in Switzerland is estimated to be 25 links per year, and it is often referred to as the country's national sausage.

There are many formulations for this sausage, but pork brains are no longer used. Some call for 100 percent pork, while others specify some combination of pork, beef, bacon, and pork rind. This recipe employs pork, beef, and bacon.

Pistachio nuts are a common interior garnish, but they are optional. These nuts make a very interesting addition to the sausage and they have a crunchy and pleasing bite texture when the sausage is very fresh, but they become soggy after the links are a couple of days old. Personally, I prefer this sausage without the addition of the nuts.

CASINGS
Beef casing is traditional, but hog casing works well. If small-diameter hog casing will be used, prepare 8½ feet (255 cm). Rinse the casing, and refrigerate it overnight in water. Rinse again, and soak in warm water a few minutes before using.

THE MEAT FOR 2½ LBS. (1,150 G) OF CERVELAT
Prepare 1¼ lbs. (570 g) of pork shoulder, ¾ lb. (340 g) beef chuck, and ½ lb. (225 g) of bacon. Cut the pork and beef into ¾-inch (2 cm) cubes. Cut the bacon into large squares. Refrigerate these meats until they are well chilled. While this meat is being prepared, chill the grinder and sausage stuffer in the refrigerator.

SEASONINGS AND OTHER INGREDIENTS
1¾ tsp. (8.75 ml) salt
½ tsp. (2.5 ml) Cure #1
1½ tsp. (7.5 ml) white pepper, ground
¾ tsp. (3.75 ml) garlic granules
¼ tsp. (1.25 ml) coriander—packed in the spoon
¼ tsp. (1.25 ml) nutmeg
¼ tsp. (1.25 ml) thyme

1 Tbsp. (15 ml) light corn syrup
2 Tbsp. (30 ml) sherry
2 Tbsp. (30 ml) cold tap water
½ cup (120 ml) pistachio nuts, optional (see instruction No. 2, below)
½ cup (120 ml) finely powdered skim milk

MIXING AND STUFFING

1. Grind the three kinds of meat with a ³⁄₁₆-inch (4.8 mm) or smaller plate—the smaller the better. Refrigerate for about 30 minutes.
2. Measure the seasoning and other ingredients—*except the pistachio nuts and ground meat*—into a large stainless steel mixing bowl. Stir until the mixture is uniform; it will be a thin paste. Refrigerate. (The optional pistachio nuts will be added to the emulsified sausage.)
3. Follow the instructions in *HOW TO EMULSIFY SAUSAGE* near the beginning of this chapter.
4. Sprinkle the optional pistachio nuts on the emulsified sausage paste, and knead until they are mixed uniformly.
5. Stuff the emulsified sausage into the prepared casings, and twist the links. Refrigerate the links overnight (or for at least a few hours) to permit the seasoning to be absorbed by the meat. Use an uncovered container with a paper towel placed over the sausage.

If the cervelat will be smoked, please see Chapter 7. (Cold smoking for an hour or two is traditional.) If it will be cooked without smoking, please see Chapter 6. It is most often grilled or poached, but it can be cooked by any method.

Chicken Wieners

Chicken is commonly used in sausages nowadays, particularly in wieners. In most cases, however, it is mixed with pork or beef, or a combination of these two meats. This wienie is made from 100 percent chicken, but you may add other meats if you like; fatty pork, for example, would make the wieners juicier.

Commercially produced sausage use what is called "mechanically separated chicken." This means that a machine is used to strip the meat from the chicken bones. When a machine is used for this, the machine does not discriminate between the good meat and the poor quality skin and pinfeathers that you and I would discard. Without question, homemade sausages using home-ground chicken flesh are higher quality than those offered by the commercial processors.

CASINGS

If 24 to 26 mm (1 in. to 1¹⁄₁₆ in.) sheep casing is to be used (recommended), pre-pare about 16 feet (480 cm). If small-diameter hog casing will be used, prepare 8½ feet (255 cm). Rinse the casing, and refrigerate it in water overnight. Rinse again, and soak in warm water a few minutes before using.

THE MEAT FOR 2½ LBS. (1,150 G) OF CHICKEN WIENERS

Prepare 2½ lbs. (1,150 g) of boned chicken thighs (retain and use the skin and the fat). Cut the thighs into small hunks. Refrigerate the meat until it is well chilled. While this meat is being prepared, chill the grinder and sausage stuffer in the refrigerator.

SEASONINGS AND OTHER INGREDIENTS

2¼ tsp. (11.25 ml) salt
½ tsp. (2.5 ml) Cure #1
2 tsp. (10 ml) paprika
1 tsp. (5 ml) mustard, ground—packed in the spoon
1 tsp. (5 ml) onion granules
1 tsp. (5 ml) coriander—packed in the spoon
½ tsp. (2.5 ml) garlic granules
½ tsp. (2.5 ml) marjoram
¼ tsp. (1.25 ml) white pepper, ground
¼ tsp. (1.25 ml) mace
1 large egg, well beaten
2 Tbsp. (30 ml) light corn syrup
5 Tbsp (75 ml) cold tap water
½ cup (120 ml) finely powdered skim milk

MIXING AND STUFFING

1. Grind the chicken with a ³⁄₁₆-inch (4.8 mm) or smaller plate—the smaller the better. Refrigerate for about 30 minutes.
2. Measure the seasoning and other ingredients—including the egg, corn syr-up, water, and powdered milk—into a large stainless steel mixing bowl. Stir until the mixture is uniform; it will be a slurry or a thin paste. Refrigerate.
3. Follow the instructions in *HOW TO EMULSIFY SAUSAGE* near the begin-ning of this chapter.
4. Stuff the emulsified sausage into the prepared casings, and twist the links. Refrigerate the links overnight (or at least a few hours) to permit the sea-

soning to be absorbed by the meat. Use an uncovered container with a paper towel placed over the sausage.

If the wieners will be smoked, please see Chapter 7. (If they will be smoked, cold smoking is recommended.) If they will be cooked without smoking, please see Chapter 6.

Greek Gyro

When our family lived in Chicago in the 1970s, we often went to one of the numerous gyro restaurants for a delicious gyro. What is a gyro? It could be called a Greek sandwich. It is thinly sliced roasted meat piled on pita bread, garnished with chopped onions, chopped tomatoes, shredded lettuce, and a little crumbled feta cheese. A dressing made of yogurt and shredded cucumber is drizzled on top of these fillers. The round, thin, pita bread is folded over the filling—much like one would fold a flour tortilla.

The word *gyro* comes from the Greek work *gyros*, which means *to turn*. (The meat is turned as it is roasted.) I have heard the word *gyro* pronounced in many different ways, but one of the common pronunciations is "yē rō."

The two things that make this sandwich-like creation so decadently delicious are the exotically seasoned roasted meat and the yogurt sauce. We left Chicago in 1980, and I have not been able to find a gyro equal to the Chicago gyro. The ones I have had in Portland, Oregon, and even the ones I had in Detroit, Michigan, pale in comparison.

The yogurt dressing is easy to make, and various recipes for it can be found on the Internet. However, the meat filler is difficult to duplicate because recipes that produce roasted meat equal to the taste of that used in the Chicago gyro could not be found. The gyro loaf recipe below is my creation. The taste and texture are close to what I tasted in Chicago.

In Chicago, the professionals use a special roaster having upright panels that partially surround the cylindrical-shaped mass of meat. The mass of seasoned meat rotates vertically—not horizontally, as in a common rotisserie—and the radiant heat inside the hot walls of the roaster cooks the meat. The chef slices off the meat a little at a time when a gyro is to be prepared.

In this recipe, the gyro meat is cooked as a loaf. Custom meat processors here in the United States prepare and cook large gyro loaves in a similar way and sell them—cooked, presliced, and frozen—to small Greek restaurants that want to offer gyros on the menu, but do not wish to invest in the special roaster.

Instructions for preparing the cucumber-flavored yogurt sauce, and suggestions for preparing and serving the gyros, are below the instructions for making and cooking the meat.

THE MEAT FOR 2½ LBS. (1,150 G) OF GYRO LOAF

A combination of lamb and beef is usually used for the gyro loaf. But, in the United States, it seems that some people use only beef, others use only lamb, and yet others use various combinations of beef, pork, and lamb. About 50 percent pork and 50 percent beef is suggested to start, and then you may wish to use the more expensive lamb after some experience with the formulation and processing has been acquired. If lamb is used, you might wish to use lean lamb, and use the more pleasant tasting beef fat to replace the lamb fat. The total fat content of the meat should be about 20 to 25 percent.

Prepare 1¼ lbs. (570 g) of pork shoulder butt (or lamb), and 1¼ lbs. (570 g) of beef chuck. Cut the pork butt and beef chuck into ¾-inch (2 cm) cubes. Refrigerate these two meats until they are well chilled. While this meat is being prepared, chill the grinder in the refrigerator.

SEASONINGS AND OTHER INGREDIENTS

2½ tsp. (12.5 ml) salt
1 Tbsp. (15 ml) lemon juice
1 tsp. (5 ml) crushed dry mint
1 tsp. (5 ml) marjoram
½ tsp. (2.5 ml) granulated onion
½ tsp. (2.5 ml) rosemary
½ tsp. (2.5 ml) black pepper, ground
½ tsp. (2.5 ml) coriander—packed in the spoon
¼ tsp. (1.25 ml) summer savory
¼ tsp. (1.25 ml) thyme
¼ tsp. (1.25 ml) garlic granules
1 egg, well beaten
¼ cup (60 ml) cold tap water
¼ cup (60 ml) powdered milk

MIXING AND STUFFING

1. Grind the pork butt and the beef chuck with a ³⁄₁₆-inch (4.8 mm) or smaller plate—the smaller the better. Refrigerate for about 30 minutes.

2. Measure the seasoning, water, and powdered milk into a large stainless steel mixing bowl, and add the egg. Stir until the mixture is uniform; it will be a thin paste. Refrigerate for about 15 minutes.

3. Follow the instructions in HOW TO EMULSIFY SAUSAGE near the beginning of this chapter.

4. Grease the inside of a loaf pan with margarine, butter, or shortening. Pack the emulsified gyro paste into the pan. (A loaf pan measuring about 8¾ × 5 × 3 inches works well. Metric measurements are 22 × 13 × 8 cm.) Refrigerate the sausage loaf while the steamer is being prepared.

5. Insert the cable probe of an electronic thermometer into the center of the loaf. Cover the loaf pan and the thermometer probe with aluminum foil. Steam the loaf at about 175° F (79° C) until the internal temperature is 160° F (71° C).

6. Remove the loaf from the pan. Cool at room temperature for about 15 minutes. Cover with paper towels and refrigerate. The next morning the loaf may be sliced and wrapped. Freeze the portion that will not be used within a few days.

TZATZIKI SAUCE

This sauce is spooned onto the gyro after the sliced meat, chopped tomatoes, sliced onions, and shredded lettuce are put on the pita bread.

1 lb. (450 g) plain yogurt
1 medium cucumber, peeled, seeded, and shredded
1 Tbsp. (15 ml) olive oil
2 tsp. (10 ml) white wine vinegar
¼ tsp. (1.25 ml) garlic granules
¼ tsp. (1.25 ml) salt

1. The best tzatziki sauce is made from yogurt with reduced water content. This is not difficult to do, but it is a little messy. Suspend a tea towel (a dishtowel) over a bowl by using whatever method you can improvise: clothespins, a large rubber band, paper clamps, etc. Spoon the yogurt onto the towel. Allow the water from the yogurt to drain through the tea towel into the bowl for 2 hours while it is in the refrigerator.

2. Remove as much moisture from the shredded cucumber as possible by placing it on paper towels atop several layers of newspaper, or by putting the shredded cucumber in a tea towel and squeezing it.

3. Discard the liquids from the yogurt and the cucumber. Combine the yogurt, cucumber, and all the other tzatziki ingredients in a small mixing bowl, and mix well. It may be refrigerated in an airtight container for up to a week.

SERVING GYROS

A generous quantity of cold, sliced gyro meat is piled on a piece of cold pita bread. This is put on a plate and heated in the microwave oven for about 40 seconds.

Next, the chopped tomatoes, sliced sweet onions, crumbled feta cheese, and shredded lettuce are put on the meat. Finally, the meat and vegetables are drenched in tzatziki sauce, and the pita bread is folded over—similar to the way a flour tortilla is folded. Enjoy!

Ham Sausage Supreme

Ham Sausage Supreme is one of those sausages that most everyone likes. As far as seasoning ingredients are concerned, it is one of the simplest sausages in this book. Pork is naturally flavorful, and pork made into ham needs only a few ingredients to complement that flavor.

This sausage is not difficult to make, but the processing time is long because five days of waiting patiently are required to cure the chunks of ham that will be embedded in the sausage paste.

The basic plan for making this sausage is as follows:

• Half of the meat will be lean pork; it will be cut into large cubes and cured for five days. At the end of five days, these cubes of fresh pork will have been changed to cubes of raw ham.
• The remaining pork will be ground, seasoned like ham, and made into emulsified sausage paste.
• The cubes of ham will be mixed with the emulsified paste, stuffed into fibrous casings, smoked (optional), and cooked.

THE MEAT FOR 1¼ LBS. (570 G) OF HAM CUBES

Prepare 1¼ lbs. (570 g) of lean pork. Cut this pork into 1-inch (2.5 cm) "cubes." (These small hunks of pork can be any shape, but the volume should be one cubic inch, more or less.) Any lean pork may be used. The cubes may be cut from pork sirloin, pork loin, or even from the lean parts of pork butt, for example. Refrigerate these cubes until they are well chilled.

CURE INGREDIENTS FOR 1¼ LBS. (570 G) HAM CUBES

1½ tsp. (7.5 ml) salt

1½ tsp. (7.5 ml) brown sugar—packed in the spoon

¼ tsp. (1.25 ml) Cure #1

½ tsp. (2.5 ml) onion granules

½ tsp. (2.5 ml) white pepper

¼ tsp. (1.25 ml) garlic powder

¼ tsp. (1.25 ml) allspice

cold water to make a slurry

CURING THE HAM CUBES

1. *Day 1*: Measure the cure ingredients into a plastic container that is large enough to allow the cubes to be stirred easily. (The container should have a tight-fitting lid.) Add enough cold water to make a slurry. Place the pork cubes in the container, and stir the cubes vigorously to ensure that all surfaces of each cube are coated with the seasoning cure. Push the cubes down in the curing container so that they are packed together tightly. Cover and refrigerate.

2. *Days 2, 3, and 4*: Each day, stir the cubes thoroughly at least once in order to recoat each of the cubes with curing mixture. Again, push the cubes down in the curing container so that they are packed together tightly.

3. *Day 5*: The curing is finished. Remove the cubes from the plastic container, place them in a colander, and spray with cold water while thoroughly agitating them. (This is to remove all curing compound and excess seasoning from the surfaces of the cubes.) Drain well in the colander, and then place the cubes atop a paper towel with several layers of newspaper underneath. Refrigerate the cubes while they are on the paper, and prepare to finish mixing and stuffing the sausage.

CASINGS

If 2½-inch (6.4 cm) diameter fibrous casings are used, three 12-inch (30 cm) casings will be required. Fibrous casings must be soaked in water for 30 minutes before stuffing. Be sure to fill the casings with warm water.

THE MEAT FOR 1¼ LBS. (570 G) OF SAUSAGE PASTE

Prepare 1¼ lbs. (570 g) of regular pork butt that has about 25 percent fat. Cut this pork into ¾-inch (2 cm) cubes. Refrigerate these cubes until they are well chilled. Chill the meat grinder and the sausage stuffer in the refrigerator while this meat is being prepared.

SAUSAGE PASTE SEASONINGS AND OTHER INGREDIENTS

¾ tsp. (3.75 ml) salt

¼ tsp. (1.25 ml) Cure #1

1 tsp. (5 ml) brown sugar—packed in the spoon

½ tsp. (2.5 ml) onion granules

½ tsp. (2.5 ml) white pepper

¼ tsp. (1.25 ml) garlic powder

¼ tsp. (1.25 ml) allspice

4 tsp. (20 ml) cold water

MIXING AND STUFFING

Note: Half of the sausage filler is emulsified and half is not. Because of this, and in order to avoid confusion, instructions are given in more detail than are given for other emulsified sausages.

1. Grind the pork butt with a ³⁄₁₆-inch (4.8 mm) or smaller plate—the smaller the better. Refrigerate for about 30 minutes. *Important:* Do not grind the previously cured ham hunks.

2. Measure the seasoning into a large stainless steel mixing bowl. Add the cold water to make a thin paste. Stir until the mixture is uniform. Refrigerate for about 15 minutes.

3. Add the chilled ground meat to the chilled seasoning mixture, and knead until it is well mixed. This will require about three minutes. Place the sausage paste in the freezer, and stir the meat about every 10 minutes while the food processor is being set up and Step 4 is being accomplished. The goal is to chill this sausage paste in the freezer until most of it is crunchy, but not frozen hard.

4. Prepare at least ½ cup (120 ml) of crushed ice by processing about five large ice cubes in the food processor. It is better to have a little extra rather than not enough. Refrigerate.

5. When the sausage mixture has become crunchy, put it in the food processor with ½ cup (120 ml) of crushed ice. Process the sausage paste in the food processor for 30 seconds, and then measure the temperature with an instant-read thermometer. If the temperature is under 40° F (4.4° C), process it another 30 seconds. Continue to process 30 seconds at a time until 40° F (4.4° C) is reached.

6. When the temperature reaches 40° F (4.4° C), process it again for 15 seconds, if necessary. Continue to process 15 seconds (or less) at a time until 55° F (12.8° C) is reached or until the paste is emulsified. Do not exceed

60° F (15.6° C); if this temperature is exceeded, the emulsion will probably *break*—the fat will liquefy and separate from the emulsion. Refrigerate. *Note: Do not over-process the sausage. When it is obvious that emulsification has been accomplished, the processing should be stopped, even if the temperature of the paste is below 40° F (4.4° C).*

7. Remove the previously prepared ham hunks from the refrigerator, and fold them into the emulsified sausage paste so that the cubes are coated with the paste and are uniformly distributed.

8. Stuff the emulsified sausage and ham cube mixture into the prepared fibrous casings. If an electronic thermometer will be used when the sausage is cooked, insert the cable probe into one of the chubs. Close the ends of the chubs with twine. Refrigerate overnight (or for at least a few hours) to permit the seasoning to be absorbed by the meat. Use an uncovered container with a paper towel placed over the chubs.

9. If the ham sausage will be smoked, please see Chapter 7. (Cold smoking followed by steaming is recommended.) If it will be cooked without smoking, please see Chapter 6.

Knockwurst

In German, the spelling is *knackwurst*, and *knacken* means "crackle." Probably it was given that name because of the sound it makes when someone bites into it. It is usually stuffed in large size hog casings and twisted into short links. Knockwurst is often, but not always, emulsified. It is steamed, poached, or hot smoked—never fried. The German version of this sausage uses about 60 percent veal and 40 percent pork. This version uses 30 percent turkey, 30 percent beef, and 40 percent pork. Knockwurst (or *knackwurst*) is most often used as an ingredient when preparing other dishes; it goes very well with braised cabbage or sauerkraut.

CASINGS
Hog casing is recommended. If small-diameter hog casing will be used, prepare 8½ feet (255 cm). Rinse the casing, and refrigerate it overnight in water. Rinse again, and soak in warm water a few minutes before using.

THE MEAT FOR 2½ LBS. (1,150 G) OF KNOCKWURST
Prepare ¾ lb. (340 g) of boned turkey thighs (the skin and fat may be included), 1 lb. (450 g) of pork shoulder butt, and ¾ lb. (340 g) of beef chuck. Cut the

meat into ¾-inch (2 cm) cubes. Refrigerate this meat until it is well chilled. While the meat is being prepared, chill the grinder and sausage stuffer in the refrigerator.

SEASONINGS AND OTHER INGREDIENTS
2 tsp. (10 ml) salt
½ tsp. (2.5 ml) Cure #1
1 Tbsp. (15 ml) white pepper, ground
1½ tsp. (7.5 ml) paprika
¾ tsp. (3.75) mace
¼ tsp. (1.25 ml) coriander—packed in the spoon
¼ tsp. (1.25 ml) garlic granules
⅛ tsp. (0.625 ml) allspice
2 Tbsp. (30 ml) light corn syrup
¼ cup (60 ml) cold tap water
½ cup (120 ml) finely powdered skim milk

MIXING AND STUFFING
1. Grind the three kinds of meat with a ³⁄₁₆-inch (4.8 mm) or smaller plate—the smaller the better. Refrigerate for about 30 minutes.
2. Measure the seasoning, water, and powdered milk into a large stainless steel mixing bowl. Stir until the mixture is uniform; it will be a thin paste. Refrigerate.
3. Follow the instructions in *HOW TO EMULSIFY SAUSAGE* near the beginning of this chapter.
4. Stuff the emulsified sausage into the prepared casings, and twist into short links. Refrigerate the links overnight (or for at least a few hours) to permit the seasoning to be absorbed by the meat. Use an uncovered container with a paper towel placed over the sausage.

If the knockwurst will be smoked, please see Chapter 7. (Cold smoking followed by steaming is recommended.) If it will be cooked without smoking, please see Chapter 6. It should be steamed or poached—it should not be sautéed.

Leberkäse
Leber is German for *liver*, and *käse* means *cheese*; but true leberkäse contains neither. Leberkäse was first made in the 1700s and, undoubtedly, there was a

good reason for calling it "liver cheese" at that time. The American headcheese is made from the meat attached to the head of a pig, but it, too, contains no cheese. Nevertheless, this American sausage concoction somehow acquired the name "headcheese." The etymology of sausage names is interesting, but this book is about sausage making, so we'll get on with the job of explaining how to make this most unusual German sausage with the ill-fitting name: *leberkäse*.

Many people have facetiously described sausage making as the art of making many flavors of meat loaf. The making of leberkäse is not far from this description; leberkäse is, undeniably, a type of cured and emulsified sausage, but it is cooked as a meatloaf.

Leberkäse should be served as the main course for dinner, but leftovers make great snacks and sandwiches. If you have some leftover, try a German *strammer max*: Toast a slice of rye or whole wheat bread, place a thick slice of leberkäse (heated in the microwave) on it, and top it with a fried egg and a garnish of fried onions.

THE MEAT FOR 2½ LBS. (1,150 G) OF LEBERKÄSE

Prepare 1¼ lbs. (570 g) of pork shoulder butt and 1¼ lbs. (570 g) of beef chuck. (Lean wild game and extra pork fat may be substituted for the beef.) Cut the pork butt and beef chuck into ¾-inch (2 cm) cubes. Refrigerate these two meats until they are well chilled. While this meat is being prepared, chill the grinder in the refrigerator.

SEASONINGS AND OTHER INGREDIENTS

2 tsp. (10 ml) salt
1 tsp. (5 ml) lemon juice
½ tsp. (2.5 ml) Cure #1
½ tsp. (2.5 ml) onion granules
½ tsp. (2.5 ml) white pepper, ground
½ tsp. (2.5 ml) sugar
¼ tsp. (1.25 ml) garlic granules
¼ tsp. (1.25 ml) ginger powder
¼ tsp. (1.25 ml) coriander—packed in the spoon
⅛ tsp. (0.625 ml) nutmeg
⅛ tsp. (0.625 ml) allspice
¼ cup (60 ml) cold tap water
½ cup (120 ml) finely powdered skim milk

MIXING AND STUFFING

1. Grind the pork butt and the beef chuck with a ³⁄₁₆-inch (4.8 mm) or smaller plate—the smaller the better. Refrigerate for about 30 minutes.
2. Measure the seasoning, water, and powdered milk into a large stainless steel mixing bowl. Stir until the mixture is uniform; it will be a thin paste. Refrigerate for about 15 minutes.
3. Follow the instructions in *HOW TO EMULSIFY SAUSAGE* near the beginning of this chapter.
4. Grease a bread loaf pan with margarine, butter, or shortening. Put the emulsified sausage paste in the loaf pan, and shape the mass into a loaf by using a rubber bowl scraper dipped in water. Cover the loaf with plastic food wrap, and refrigerate it overnight (or for at least a few hours) to permit the seasoning to be absorbed by the meat. (If necessary, this emulsified sausage paste may be frozen for up to two months either before or after it is put in the loaf pan.)
5. Preheat the oven to 300° F (150° C). Remove the plastic food wrap, and bake about 1½ to 2 hours until the internal temperature is a little below 160° F (71° C). (The cooking time will vary with the thickness of the loaf.) Remove the loaf from the oven, and let the loaf rest a few minutes (the internal temperature will continue to climb). Slice and serve.

Liverwurst

This is one of the most popular German sausages, but only liver lovers appreciate it. Next to Braunschweiger, it is my favorite liver sausage. A sandwich made with slices of either one of these liver sausages, together with a slice of sweet white onion, is a popular way to eat them.

This sausage is traditionally made with pork liver, but calf, beef, wild game, or poultry liver may be used. Pork liver has the strongest taste of any kind of liver and, because of that, it is not popular and is difficult to locate; try ethnic grocery stores if you want to buy pork liver. Beef liver is milder than pork, but stronger tasting than calf. Poultry liver is the mildest tasting liver. Usually, I use pork or beef liver.

CASINGS

If 2½-inch (6.4 cm) diameter fibrous casings are used, three 12-inch (30 cm) casings will be required. Fibrous casings must be soaked in water for 30 minutes before stuffing. Be sure to fill the casings with warm water.

Liverwurst is traditionally made with about 60 percent fatty pork and 40 percent liver. Some of this pork can be replaced with lean venison or venison heart, together with pork fat.

THE MEAT FOR 2½ LBS. (1,150 G) OF LIVERWURST

Prepare 1½ lbs. (680 g) of pork shoulder butt and 1 lb. (450 g) of liver. Cut the pork butt into ¾-inch (2 cm) cubes. If large livers are being used, cut the liver into pieces that will fit into the hopper of the meat grinder. Refrigerate the liver in a separate dish from the pork. While this meat is being prepared, chill the grinder and sausage stuffer in the refrigerator.

SEASONINGS AND OTHER INGREDIENTS

2¼ tsp. (11.25 ml) salt
½ tsp. (2.5 ml) Cure #1
1½ tsp. (7.5 ml) onion granules
1 tsp. (5 ml) paprika
¾ tsp. (3.75 ml) white pepper, ground
½ tsp. (2.5 ml) marjoram
¼ tsp. (1.25 ml) allspice
¼ tsp. (1.25 ml) ginger powder
¼ tsp. (1.25 ml) mace or nutmeg
¼ tsp. (1.25 ml) sage—packed in the spoon
¼ tsp. (1.25 ml) coriander—packed in the spoon
1 Tbsp. (15 ml) light corn syrup
¼ cup (60 ml) cold tap water
½ cup (120 ml) finely powdered skim milk

MIXING AND STUFFING

1. Grind the liver and the pork butt. Use a ³⁄₁₆-inch (4.8 mm) or smaller plate—the smaller the better. It is best to grind the soft liver first and the harder pork last. (The harder pork cubes will help push the softer liver through the grinder.) Refrigerate the ground meat mixture for about 30 minutes.
2. Measure all of the seasonings, water, and powdered milk into a large mixing bowl, and mix thoroughly. Refrigerate for at least 15 minutes.
3. Follow the instructions in *HOW TO EMULSIFY SAUSAGE* near the beginning of this chapter.
4. Stuff the emulsified sausage into the prepared fibrous casings. If an electronic thermometer will be used when the sausage is cooked, insert the

cable probe into one of the chubs. Close the ends of the chubs with twine. Refrigerate overnight (or for at least a few hours) to permit the seasoning to be absorbed by the meat.

Traditionally, liverwurst is not smoked. Steam cooking is recommended, but it can be poached. Please see Chapter 6 for detailed cooking information.

Mortadella

Bologna and mortadella are often said to be similar, and they are similar in many ways. Both are similarly seasoned, have a large diameter, are Italian in origin, are emulsified, and are made to be eaten cold. But there are differences, too. Mortadella is usually a pork sausage, but bologna is (or should be) a mixture of beef and pork. When bologna is sliced, it is a plain-looking pink sausage, but when mortadella is sliced, chunks of pork fatback and peppercorns are visible. If the mortadella contains olives and pistachios, these ingredients will also be visible in the slices. Mortadella is a mild but attractive sausage. The appeal to the eye competes with the appeal to the palate. In Italy, this sausage is often served as bite-size cubes, but it is also served thinly sliced.

CASINGS

Large casings are used for mortadella—3 to 4 inches (7.6 to 10 cm) in diameter, but the 2½-inch (6.4 cm) diameter fibrous casing used for other large sausages in this book will do the job. Three of these casings—each 12 inches (30 cm) long—will be required.

Fibrous casings must be soaked in water for 30 minutes before stuffing. Be sure to fill the casings with warm water.

THE MEAT FOR 2½ LBS. (1,150 G) OF MORTADELLA

Prepare 2¼ lbs. (1,020 g) of pork shoulder butt and ¼ lb. (115 g) of pork fatback. (Instead of pork fatback, medium-hard pork fat from any part of the pig will work.) Cut the pork butt into ¾-inch (2 cm) cubes, and cut the fatback into ¼- to ⅝-inch (about 1 cm) cubes. *Keep the fatback cubes in a small bowl, separate from the pork shoulder butt.* Refrigerate these two meats until they are well chilled. While this meat is being prepared, chill the grinder and sausage stuffer in the refrigerator.

SEASONINGS AND OTHER INGREDIENTS

2¼ tsp. (11.25 ml) salt

½ tsp. (2.5 ml) Cure #1

1 tsp. (5 ml) paprika

¾ tsp. (3.75 ml) white pepper, ground

¾ tsp. (3.75 ml) coriander—packed in the spoon

¼ tsp. (1.25 ml) nutmeg

¼ tsp. (1.25 ml) mace

¼ tsp. (1.25 ml) garlic granules

⅛ tsp. (0.625 ml) cinnamon

1 Tbsp. (15 ml) good tasting wine—red or white

1 Tbsp. (15 ml) light corn syrup

¼ cup (60 ml) cold tap water

½ cup (120 ml) finely powdered skim milk

1 tsp. (5 ml) whole or cracked black peppercorns

½ cup (120 ml) black olives, pitted and cut in half lengthwise (optional)

MIXING AND STUFFING

1. Grind the pork butt with a ³⁄₁₆-inch (4.8 mm) or smaller plate—the smaller the better. Refrigerate for about 30 minutes. (Leave the small cubes of back fat in the refrigerator for the time being.)

2. Add the peppercorns (or the cracked peppercorns) to the small bowl containing the cubes of back fat. Cut the pitted black olives in half lengthwise, and put them in the same small bowl with the small cubes of fatback and peppercorns. (The fatback, the olives, and the peppercorns—or cracked peppercorns—will be added to the emulsified sausage paste just before it is stuffed into the casings.)

3. Measure the seasoning and other ingredients (except for the meat, black olives, peppercorns, and fatback cubes) into a large stainless steel mixing bowl. Stir until the mixture is uniform; it will be a thin paste. Refrigerate.

4. Follow the instructions in *HOW TO EMULSIFY SAUSAGE* near the beginning of this chapter.

5. Sprinkle the cut olives, peppercorns, and fatback cubes on the emulsified sausage paste, and knead the mixture until these ingredients are mixed uniformly with the paste. Stuff this emulsified sausage into the prepared fibrous casings. If an electronic thermometer will be used when the sausage is cooked, insert the cable probe into one of the chubs. Close the ends of the chubs with twine. Refrigerate overnight (or at least a few hours) to permit

the seasoning to be absorbed by the meat. Use an uncovered container with a paper towel placed over the chubs.

6. If the mortadella will be smoked, please see Chapter 7. (Cold smoking followed by steaming is recommended.) If it will be cooked without smoking, please see Chapter 6.

Olive Loaf

Olive loaf was once one of the popular luncheon meats, but it is being pushed off the shelf by the fancy, thinly sliced ham, turkey, chicken, and beef lunchmeats. Depending on where you live and where you shop, you may be able to find it. It is a shame that many young people have never tasted it.

The main feature of this lunchmeat is the numerous green olives (stuffed with pimento) embedded in the loaf, so it is an acquired taste. People who do not like the sour-bitter taste of green olives will not like this product, but that unique taste is a treat for those of us who do.

Olive loaf may be processed in a bread loaf pan and steamed—please see *Sausage Loaf (Lunchmeat Loaf)* in Chapter 6. If fibrous casings are preferred, the instructions are given below.

Olive loaf is not smoked.

CASINGS

If the olive loaf will be processed in casings, the 2½-inch (6.4 cm) diameter fibrous casings used for other large sausages in this book will do the job. Three of these casings, each 12 inches (30 cm) long, will be required.

Fibrous casings must be soaked in water for 30 minutes before stuffing. Be sure to fill the casings with warm water.

THE MEAT FOR 2½ LBS. (1,150 G) OF OLIVE LOAF

Prepare 1 lb. (450 g) of beef chuck and 1½ lbs. (680 g) of pork shoulder butt. Cut the meat into ¾-inch (2 cm) cubes. Refrigerate the meat until it is well chilled. While this meat is being prepared, chill the grinder and sausage stuffer in the refrigerator.

SEASONINGS AND OTHER INGREDIENTS

2¼ tsp. (11.25 ml) salt
½ tsp. (2.5 ml) Cure #1
1 tsp. (5 ml) paprika

¾ tsp. (3.75 ml) white pepper, ground

¾ tsp. (3.75 ml) coriander—packed in the spoon

¼ tsp. (1.25 ml) nutmeg

¼ tsp. (1.25 ml) mace

¼ tsp. (1.25 ml) garlic granules

⅛ tsp. (0.625) celery seed, ground

1 Tbsp. (15 ml) good tasting white wine

1 Tbsp. (15 ml) light corn syrup

¼ cup (60 ml) cold tap water

½ cup (120 ml) finely powdered skim milk

1 cup (240 ml) green olives, whole, stuffed (see instruction No. 2, below)

MIXING AND STUFFING

1. Grind the meat with a ³⁄₁₆-inch (4.8 mm) or smaller plate—the smaller the better. Refrigerate for about 30 minutes.

2. Cut each olive into quarters, place the quarters in a small bowl, and refrigerate. Measure the seasoning and other ingredients (except for the meat and green olives) into a large stainless steel mixing bowl. Stir until the mixture is uniform; it will be a thin paste. Refrigerate until well chilled. (The olives will be added to the emulsified sausage paste just before it is stuffed into the casings or put into the loaf pan.)

3. Follow the instructions in *HOW TO EMULSIFY SAUSAGE* near the beginning of this chapter.

4. Sprinkle the green olives on the emulsified sausage paste, and knead until they are mixed uniformly. Stuff this emulsified sausage into the prepared fibrous casings. If an electronic thermometer will be used when the sausage is cooked, insert the cable probe into one of the chubs. Close the ends of the chubs with twine. Refrigerate overnight (or at least a few hours) to permit the seasoning to be absorbed by the meat. Use an uncovered container with a paper towel placed over the chubs.

5. If the sausage has been stuffed in fibrous casings, poaching or steaming is recommended. Please see Chapter 6.

Pickle and Pimento Loaf

Pickle and pimento loaf was a popular lunchmeat, but it is difficult to find nowadays. It is simple to make if the easy-to-master technique of emulsification has been learned. I am sure you will find that this homemade version is superior to the commercial product.

Pickle and pimento loaf may be processed in a bread loaf pan and steamed—please see *Sausage Loaf (Lunchmeat Loaf)* in Chapter 6. If fibrous casings are preferred, the instructions for using them are given below.

Pickle and pimento loaf is not smoked.

CASINGS

If the pickle and pimento loaf will be processed in a casing, the 2½-inch (6.4 cm) diameter fibrous casing used for other large sausages in this book will do the job. Three of these casings—each 12 inches (30 cm) long—will be required.

Fibrous casings must be soaked in water for 30 minutes before stuffing. Be sure to fill the casings with warm water.

THE MEAT FOR 2½ LBS. (1,150 G) OF PICKLE AND PIMENTO LOAF

Prepare 1 lb. (450 g) of pork shoulder butt and 1½ lbs. (680 g) of beef chuck. Cut the meat into ¾-inch (2 cm) cubes, and refrigerate them until they are well chilled. While this meat is being prepared, chill the grinder and sausage stuffer in the refrigerator.

SEASONINGS AND OTHER INGREDIENTS

2½ tsp. (12.5 ml) salt
½ tsp. (2.5 ml) Cure #1
¾ tsp. (3.75 ml) coriander—packed in the spoon
½ tsp. (2.5 ml) white pepper
¼ tsp. (1.25 ml) nutmeg
¼ tsp. (1.25 ml) garlic granules
¼ tsp. (1.25 ml) onion granules
¼ tsp. (1.25 ml) ginger powder
⅛ tsp. (0.625 ml) celery seed, ground
⅛ tsp. (0.625 ml) mace
⅓ cup (80 ml) copped sweet pickle (see instruction No. 2, below)
⅓ cup (80 ml) copped canned pimento (see instruction No. 2, below)
1 Tbsp. (15 ml) good tasting white wine
1 Tbsp. (15 ml) light corn syrup
⅓ cup (80 ml) cold tap water
½ cup (120 ml) finely powdered skim milk

MIXING AND STUFFING

1. Grind the meat with a $\frac{3}{16}$-inch (4.8 mm) or smaller plate—the smaller the better. Refrigerate for about 30 minutes.

2. Chop the sweet pickles and the canned pimento into pieces about $\frac{1}{8}$ to $\frac{1}{4}$ inch (3 to 6 mm). Place the chopped pickles and pimento on a paper towel with several layers of newspaper underneath. Refrigerate. (The paper towel and newspaper will absorb the excess moisture.) Measure the seasoning and other ingredients (except for the meat, chopped sweet pickles, and pimento) into a large stainless steel mixing bowl. Stir until the mixture is uniform; it will be a thin paste. Refrigerate until well chilled. (The pickles and pimento will be added to the emulsified sausage paste just before it is stuffed into the casings or put into the loaf pan.)

3. Follow the instructions in *HOW TO EMULSIFY SAUSAGE* near the beginning of this chapter.

4. Sprinkle the chopped sweet pickle and pimento mixture on the sausage paste, and knead until they are mixed uniformly. Stuff the emulsified sausage into the prepared fibrous casings. If an electronic thermometer will be used when the sausage is cooked, insert the cable probe into one of the chubs. Close the ends of the chubs with twine. Refrigerate overnight (or at least a few hours) to permit the seasoning to be absorbed by the emulsified meat. Use an uncovered container with a paper towel placed over the chubs.

If the sausage has been stuffed in fibrous casings, poaching or steaming is recommended. Please see Chapter 6.

Weisswurst

In German, *weisswurst* is written *weißwurst* and the translated meaning is *white sausage*. Unfortunately, the Americans have assigned the nicknames *white sausage* or *white wieners* to *bockwurst*, so it would be very confusing to use the translation of weisswurst.

Lemon zest does not appear in all versions of this sausage, so this can be considered optional, but it does lend an interesting touch to the formula.

CASINGS

Sheep casings, or small hog casings, are recommended. If 24 to 26 mm (1 in. to $1\frac{1}{16}$ in.) sheep casings are to be used, prepare about 16 feet (480 cm). If small-diameter hog casings will be used, prepare 8½ feet (255 cm). Rinse the casing, and refrigerate it in water overnight. Rinse again, and soak in warm water a few minutes before using.

THE MEAT FOR 2½ LBS. (1,150 G) OF WEISSWURST

Traditionally, weisswurst is made of 50 percent veal and 50 percent pork. However, because veal is so expensive and sometimes difficult to purchase, boned chicken or turkey thighs have been substituted, and pork has been made the predominant meat.

Prepare 1½ lbs. (680 g) of fatty pork shoulder butt and 1 lb. (450 g) of boned chicken or turkey thighs (retain and use the skin and the fat). Cut the pork butt and fowl into ¾-inch (2 cm) cubes. Refrigerate these two meats until they are well chilled. While this meat is being prepared, chill the grinder and sausage stuffer in the refrigerator.

SEASONINGS AND OTHER INGREDIENTS

2½ tsp. (12.5 ml) salt
¾ tsp. (3.75 ml) white pepper, ground
½ tsp. (2.5) parsley, dried
¼ tsp. (1.25 ml) onion granules
¼ tsp. (1.25 ml) mace
¼ tsp. (1.25 ml) celery seed powder
¼ tsp. (1.25 ml) ginger powder
1 Tbsp. (15 ml) light corn syrup
1 Tbsp. (15 ml) lemon zest (optional)
¼ cup (60 ml) fresh milk
½ cup (120 ml) finely powdered skim milk

MIXING AND STUFFING

1. Grind the pork butt and the poultry thighs with a ³⁄₁₆-inch (4.8 mm) or smaller plate—the smaller the better. Refrigerate for about 30 minutes.
2. Except for the meat, measure the seasoning and other ingredients into a large stainless steel mixing bowl. Stir until the mixture is uniform; it will be a thin paste. Refrigerate.
3. Follow the instructions in *HOW TO EMULSIFY SAUSAGE* near the beginning of this chapter.

4. Stuff the emulsified sausage into the prepared casings, and twist into 6-inch (15 cm) links. Refrigerate the links overnight (or at least a few hours) to permit the seasoning to be absorbed by the meat.

Please see Chapter 6 for cooking suggestions.

White Wieners

White wiener is a nickname that Americans have given to a sausage that the Germans call bockwurst. Depending on the area of the United States, they are also called white sausages, white hot dogs, and white hots.

In German, *bock* means *buck*—the male of various species of herbivorous animals such as deer or antelope. There is also a German beer called bock beer, and this beer is commonly drunk while eating bockwurst.

This is a mild and pleasant-tasting sausage, and the pale, almost white, color is the reason for the nicknames given to it by Americans. In recent times, some processors emulsify bockwurst, and this is the emulsified version. However, it is an uncured, fresh sausage, so it is never smoked. Botulism is a possibility if these sausages are smoked, or if they are cooked at low temperatures for a log time.

Instructions for making a non-emulsified version of this sausage are in Chapter 8 (*Bockwurst*).

CASINGS

Sheep casings or small hog casings are recommended. If 24 to 26 mm (1 in. to 1¹⁄₁₆ in.) sheep casing is to be used, prepare about 16 feet (480 cm). If small-diameter hog casing will be used, prepare 8½ feet (255 cm). Rinse the casing, and refrigerate it in water overnight. Rinse again, and soak in warm water a few minutes before using.

THE MEAT FOR 2½ LBS. (1,150 G) OF WHITE WIENERS

Traditionally, bockwurst is made of about 60 percent veal and 40 percent pork. However, because veal is so expensive and sometimes difficult to purchase, boned chicken or turkey thighs have been substituted, and pork has been made the predominant meat.

Prepare 1½ lbs. (680 g) of fatty pork shoulder butt, and 1 lb. (450 g) of boned chicken or turkey thighs (retain and use the skin and the fat). Cut the pork butt and fowl into ¾-inch (2 cm) cubes. Refrigerate these two meats until they are well chilled. While this meat is being prepared, chill the grinder and sausage stuffer in the refrigerator.

SEASONINGS AND OTHER INGREDIENTS

2½ tsp. (12.5 ml) salt
2 tsp. (10 ml) onion granules
1 tsp. (5 ml) parsley, dehydrated
¾ tsp. (3.75 ml) white pepper, ground
½ tsp. (2.5 ml) mace
¼ tsp. (1.25 ml) celery seed powder
¼ tsp. (1.25 ml) ginger powder
1 egg, beaten
2 green onions, finely chopped
1 Tbsp. (15 ml) light corn syrup
¼ cup (60 ml) fresh milk
½ cup (120 ml) finely powdered skim milk

MIXING AND STUFFING

1. Grind the pork butt and the poultry thighs with a ³⁄₁₆-inch (4.8 mm) or smaller plate—the smaller the better. Refrigerate for about 30 minutes.
2. Except for the meat, measure the seasoning and other ingredients into a large stainless steel mixing bowl. Add the egg and chopped green onions. Stir until the mixture is uniform; it will be a thin paste. Refrigerate.
3. Follow the instructions in *HOW TO EMULSIFY SAUSAGE* near the beginning of this chapter.
4. Stuff the emulsified sausage into the prepared casings, and twist into 6-inch (15 cm) links. Refrigerate the links overnight (or for at least a few hours) to permit the seasoning to be absorbed by the meat.

Because bockwurst is a fresh sausage, there is a danger of botulism if they are smoked. Please see Chapter 6 for cooking suggestions.

Wieners

All European countries, and all countries in other areas of the world that have a culture based on European culture, eat hot dogs. The word they use is usually not *hot dog*, *frankfurter*, or *wiener*, but it is the same sausage, nevertheless. The world consumes more wieners than any other sausage.

The most common type of wiener in the United States and in many other countries is the emulsified, skinless type. After the sausage paste is emulsified, it is stuffed in an inedible cellulose casing and then precooked. When the cooking takes place, the sausage paste forms its own skin-like coating just under the cellulose casing. This skin-like coating on the sausage is composed of coagulated protein. The commercial sausage processor removes the cellulose casing mechanically before it is packaged for retail sale. (If you look closely at a skinless wiener, you will see a faint slit mark that goes from one end of the wiener to the other. This is where a razor blade has cut through the cellulose casing to prepare for its removal.)

CASINGS

Cellulose casings can be used, but natural casings are more convenient. If 24 to 26 mm (1 in. to 1¹⁄₁₆ in.) sheep casing is to be used (recommended), prepare about 16 feet (480 cm). If small-diameter hog casing will be used, prepare 8½ feet (255 cm). Rinse the casing, and refrigerate it in water overnight. Rinse again, and soak in warm water a few minutes before using.

THE MEAT FOR 2½ LBS. (1,150 G) OF WIENERS

Prepare 1 lb. (450 g) of pork shoulder butt and 1½ lbs. (680 g) of beef chuck. Cut the pork butt and beef chuck into ¾-inch (2 cm) cubes. Refrigerate these two meats until they are well chilled. While this meat is being prepared, chill the grinder and sausage stuffer in the refrigerator.

SEASONINGS AND OTHER INGREDIENTS

2½ tsp. (12.5 ml) salt
½ tsp. (2.5 ml) Cure #1
2 tsp. (10 ml) paprika
1½ tsp. (7.5 ml) mustard, ground—packed in the spoon
1½ tsp. (7.5 ml) coriander—packed in the spoon
1 tsp. (5 ml) onion granules
½ tsp. (2.5 ml) garlic granules
½ tsp. (2.5 ml) white pepper, ground
½ tsp. (2.5 ml) marjoram
¼ tsp. (1.25 ml) mace
2 Tbsp. (30 ml) light corn syrup
6 Tbsp. (90 ml) cold tap water
½ cup (120 ml) finely powdered skim milk

MIXING AND STUFFING

1. Grind the pork butt and the beef chuck with a ³⁄₁₆-inch (4.8 mm) or smaller plate—the smaller the better. Refrigerate for about 30 minutes.
2. Measure the seasoning, water, and powdered milk into a large stainless steel mixing bowl. Stir until the mixture is uniform; it will be a thin paste. Refrigerate.
3. Follow the instructions in *HOW TO EMULSIFY SAUSAGE* near the beginning of this chapter.
4. Stuff the emulsified sausage into the prepared casings, and twist the links. Refrigerate the links overnight (or for at least a few hours) to permit the seasoning to be absorbed by the meat. Use an uncovered container with a paper towel placed over the sausage.
5. If the wieners will be smoked, please see Chapter 7. (Cold smoking is recommended.) If they will be cooked without smoking, please see Chapter 6.

Wienerwurst (Vienna Sausage)

The word *wiener* that is commonly used in American English to mean frankfurter, is a shortened version of the German *Wienerwurst*, which means Vienna sausage. (In the Austrian language, *Vienna* is spelled and pronounced *Wien.*) Many people believe that the frankfurter did not originate in Frankfurt, Germany; they claim that it originated in Vienna, Austria.

The formulation and instructions below are for making an emulsified version of Vienna sausage. In the United States, Vienna sausage is usually the canned, emulsified type. In Chapter 9, there is another Vienna sausage recipe (*Vienna Sausage*) for a version made with non-emulsified ground meat.

Beef, veal, and pork are the meats traditionally used to make this sausage. However, because veal is expensive and somewhat difficult to buy, I replaced the veal with boned turkey thighs or chicken thighs. The United States canned version of Vienna sausage also uses fowl instead of veal.

CASINGS

Sheep casing is recommended. If 24 to 26 mm (1 in. to 1¹⁄₁₆ in.) sheep casing is to be used, prepare about 16 feet (480 cm). If small-diameter hog casing will be used, prepare 8½ feet (255 cm). Rinse the casing, and refrigerate it overnight in water. Rinse again, and soak in warm water a few minutes before using.

THE MEAT FOR 2½ LBS. (1,150 G) OF WIENERWURST

Prepare 1 lb. (450 g) of boned turkey thighs or chicken thighs (the skin and fat should be included), 1 lb. (450 g) of beef chuck, and ½ lb. (225 g) of pork shoulder butt. Cut the all of the meat into ¾-inch (2 cm) cubes. Refrigerate these meats until they are well chilled. While this meat is being prepared, chill the grinder and sausage stuffer in the refrigerator.

SEASONINGS AND OTHER INGREDIENTS

2¼ tsp. (11.25 ml) salt
½ tsp. (2.5 ml) Cure #1
1 tsp. (5 ml) paprika
1 tsp. (5 ml) onion granules
½ tsp. (2.5 ml) coriander—packed in the spoon
½ tsp. (2.5 ml) white pepper, ground
¼ tsp. (1.25 ml) nutmeg
4 tsp. (20 ml) light corn syrup
⅓ cup (80 ml) cold tap water
2 Tbsp. (30 ml) all-purpose flour
½ cup (120 ml) finely powdered skim milk

MIXING AND STUFFING

1. Grind the three kinds of meat with a ³⁄₁₆-inch (4.8 mm) or smaller plate—the smaller the better. Refrigerate for about 30 minutes.
2. Measure the seasoning, water, flour, and powdered milk into a large stainless steel mixing bowl. Stir until the mixture is uniform; it will be a thin paste. Refrigerate.
3. Follow the instructions in *HOW TO EMULSIFY SAUSAGE* near the beginning of this chapter.
4. Stuff the emulsified sausage into the prepared casings, and twist the links. Refrigerate the links overnight (or at least a few hours) to permit the seasoning to be absorbed by the meat.
5. Wienerwurst is not smoked. It is excellent grilled, or the links can be precooked by steaming or poaching and then grilled—or they can be reheated by simmering for about 10 minutes. Please see Chapter 6 for cooking details.

CHAPTER 11

Fermented-Style Sausage

Nowadays, it is dangerous to make authentic dry cured, fermented sausages at home because *E. coli* O157 is becoming resistant to being killed by the lactic acid produced in the fermentation process. (This is explained in Chapter 4, *Health Matters,* in the section on *E. coli* O157.) Furthermore, this type of sausage is extremely difficult to make because the fermenting and drying process requires special rooms or enclosures with round-the-clock temperature and humidity control. Failure must be expected because it occurs as often as success. Finally, fermented sausages must be made with the difficult-to-buy *certified pork* because the sausage is never cooked and the meat is still raw when it is eaten.

In this chapter, we will make fermented-*style* sausages that look and taste similar to the classic dry cured and fermented sausages, but they are comparatively fast and easy to make, and they are fully cooked. To help accomplish this, we will use a commercial product called Fermento. Fermento is a flavoring made from dairy products, and it is manufactured expressly for this purpose. Fermento contains lactic acid. In true fermented sausages, lactic acid is produced during the long fermentation process, and this is what provides the characteristic tangy taste of these kinds of sausages.

Because we are adding Fermento to give it the tangy taste, we do not need to wait for weeks for the lactic acid to develop and for the sausage to dry; we can dry the sausage quickly. These sausages will not be fully dry cured; they will be *semi*dry-cured. Also, because we are drying them quickly and are not cultivating bacteria, we need not maintain certain temperature and humidity conditions favorable to the proliferation of the lactic-acid-producing bacteria.

In this book, there are recipes for salami, summer sausage, pepperoni, Thuringer, and the like. However, instead of requiring weeks to process, they can be processed in just a little more time than it takes to process the common frankfurter. And, because they are cooked, trichinosis and *E. coli* are not a concern.

For all sausages in this chapter, dry seasoning and other dry ingredients are mixed together first. Then wet ingredients are added, and mixing takes place again. There is a reason for mixing the dry ingredients first: The mixing of Fermento with the other dry ingredients helps prevent clumping of the Fermento when wet ingredients are added.

Most mail order companies in Appendix 5 that sell sausage-making supplies will offer Fermento.

Note: The sausages in this chapter have been arranged in alphabetical order.

Hot Sticks

Hot sticks are spicy, semi-dried snack sausages that are great with cold beer. They are usually consumed with gusto. Consequently, once the formulation is tweaked to suit your taste, you will probably want to double the formula and make 5 pounds at a time.

The instructions given below will result in a sausage weight loss of about 15 percent. If the drying proceeds until 20 to 25 percent of the sausage weight has been lost, they will be even less perishable, and the flavor will be more concentrated.

CASINGS

Sheep casings or small hog casings may be used, but sheep casings are best because the processing time is faster, and the casing will be tender. However, if you wish to use the small hog casing, rinse 7 feet (210 cm), and refrigerate it overnight in a little water. If 24 to 26 mm (1 in. to $1\frac{1}{16}$ in.) sheep casing is to be used, prepare about 14 feet (420 cm). Rinse the casing again, and soak it in warm water for a few minutes before using.

THE MEAT FOR 2½ LBS. (1,150 G) OF HOT STICKS

A mixture of about $1\frac{1}{2}$ lbs. (680 g) of pork shoulder butt and 1 lb. (450 g) of beef chuck is suggested. Some or all of the beef may be in the form of beef heart, or lean wild game can be used. The meat, no matter what kind is selected, should contain about 25 percent fat, and the total weight should be 2½ lbs. (1,150 g). Cut the meat into ¾-inch (2 cm) cubes and refrigerate. While this meat is being prepared, chill the grinder and sausage stuffer in the refrigerator.

SEASONINGS AND OTHER INGREDIENTS
Dry ingredients
1¾ tsp. (8.75 ml) salt
½ tsp. (2.5 ml) Cure #1
1 tsp (5 ml) crushed red pepper
½ tsp. (2.5 ml) cayenne
½ tsp. (2.5 ml) thyme
½ tsp. (2.5 ml) garlic granules
¼ tsp. (1.25 ml) allspice
¼ tsp. (1.25 ml) ground coriander—packed in the spoon
¼ tsp. (1.25 ml) whole mustard seed
¼ tsp. (1.25 ml) mustard powder
¼ tsp. (1.25 ml) MSG (optional)
¼ cup (60 ml) Fermento

Wet ingredients
1 Tbsp. (15 ml) light corn syrup
½ cup (120 ml) cold beer or cold water

MIXING AND STUFFING
1. Grind the meats together with a ³⁄₁₆-inch (4.8 mm) or smaller plate. Refrigerate the ground meat for about 30 minutes.
2. Mix all dry ingredients thoroughly in a large mixing bowl. Add liquid ingredients, and mix well again. Refrigerate this mixture for about 15 minutes.
3. Add the chilled ground meat to the seasoning mixture, and knead until it is well mixed and uniform. This will require about three minutes. Chill this meat and seasoning mixture again while the sausage stuffer and casings are being prepared.
4. Stuff the sausage into the casings, and twist into long links. Weigh one of the links, record the weight, and mark it with a colored string, or the like. This weight is called the *green weight*. Refrigerate the links overnight to permit the seasoning to be absorbed by the meat. Use an uncovered container, but cover the sausage with a paper towel.

5. The next morning, dry the stuffed sausage for one or two hours in front of an electric fan. The drying is finished when the surface is dry to the touch and the fingertips slide smoothly on the casing. Alternatively, dry the surface of the casings in a 140° F (60° C) smoker with no smoke, and with the chimney vents fully open.

6. Smoke at the lowest possible temperature for two to four hours. The temperature should be held below 120° F (50° C), if possible. From this point, until the smoking, cooking, and drying are finished, the chimney vents should remain fully open to encourage maximum drying of the sausage.

7. Raise the smoker temperature to between 170° F (77° C) and 175° F (79° C) slowly—over the period of one hour or so—and continue cooking, with or without smoke, until the internal temperature of the thickest link reaches 160° F (71° C). Weigh the link marked with the colored string to determine if this link has lost at least 15 percent of its green weight. If it has, the smoking and cooking are finished. Proceed to step 9. If not, go to step 8.

8. If the link marked with colored string has not lost at least 15 percent of its green weight, reduce the smoker temperature to between 160° F (71° C) and 165° F (74° C) and continue cooking. Check the loss of weight every hour or so. When 15 percent of the weight has been lost, proceed to step 9.

9. When the sausage has lost at least 15 percent of the green weight, remove the links from the smoker, and cool the sausage in front of an electric fan for one hour.

10. Refrigerate the sausages overnight, uncovered. The next morning, cut them to single-portion lengths, and then wrap them in plastic food wrap. Sausages that will not be eaten within a few days should be individually wrapped in plastic food wrap, placed in a plastic bag, and frozen.

Landjager-Style Sausage

Landjager is German and means *land hunter*. It is appropriately named because landjager sausage is often used as a trail food.

The classic landjager is made with raw meat, and it is never cooked; it is only cold smoked and semidried.

The instructions below describe how to make the cooked version of landjager sausage. When the cooked version is eaten, trichinosis and *E. coli* 0157 are not a concern.

This is a great snack sausage, and some people prefer it to jerky. You might notice that the salt in the formulation is a little less than that normally used for cured sausage. The flavor is concentrated when the sausage is dried, so less salt is required.

The instructions suggest that the links be dried until they have lost at least 15 percent of their original weight. If the drying proceeds until 20 or 25 percent of the weight has been lost, they will be even less perishable and the flavor will be more concentrated.

CASINGS
The size of casing used is a matter of personal taste. Any size of casing from a small-diameter sheep casing to a medium-diameter hog casing may be used. The drying time for the sausage stuffed in smaller diameter casing will be shorter, however. If you wish to use the small hog casing, rinse 7 feet (210 cm), and refrigerate it overnight in a little water. If 24 to 26 mm (1 in. to 1$\frac{1}{16}$ in.) sheep casing is to be used, prepare about 14 feet (420 cm). Rinse the casing again, and soak it in warm water for a few minutes before using.

THE MEAT FOR 2½ LBS. (1,150 G) OF LANDJAGER
Prepare 1½ lbs. (680 g) of beef chuck and 1 lb. (450 g) of pork shoulder butt. Cut the meat into ¾-inch (2 cm) cubes and refrigerate. While this meat is being prepared, chill the grinder and sausage stuffer in the refrigerator.

SEASONINGS AND OTHER INGREDIENTS
Dry ingredients
1¾ tsp. (8.75 ml) salt
½ tsp. (2.5 ml) Cure #1
1 tsp. (5 ml) ground black pepper
¼ tsp. (1.25 ml) garlic granules
¼ tsp. (1.25 ml) ground caraway seeds
¼ tsp. (1.25 ml) coriander—packed in the spoon
¼ tsp. (1.25 ml) cardamom
¼ cup (60 ml) Fermento

Wet ingredients
2 Tbsp. (30 ml) light corn syrup
⅓ cup (80 ml) cold water

MIXING AND STUFFING

1. Grind the meats together with a ³⁄₁₆-inch (4.8 mm) or smaller plate. Refrigerate the ground meat for about 30 minutes.
2. Mix all dry ingredients thoroughly in a large mixing bowl. Add the liquid ingredients, and mix well again. Refrigerate this mixture for about 15 minutes.
3. Add the chilled ground meat to the seasoning mixture, and knead until it is well mixed and uniform. This will require about three minutes. Chill this meat and seasoning mixture again while the sausage stuffer and sausage casings are being prepared.
4. Stuff the sausage into the casings, and twist into the size of links you prefer. Weigh one of the links, record the weight, and mark it with a colored string, or the like. This weight is called the *green weight*. Refrigerate the links overnight to permit the seasoning to be absorbed by the meat. Use an uncovered container, but cover the sausage with a paper towel.
5. The next morning, dry the stuffed sausage in front of an electric fan until the surface is dry to the touch. Alternatively, dry the surface of the casings in a 140° F (60° C) smoker with no smoke.
6. Smoke at the lowest possible temperature for at least two hours. Make sure that the smoke vents are fully open; this will facilitate the required drying of the sausage.
7. Raise the smoker temperature to between 170° F (77° C) and 175° F (79° C) slowly—over the period of one hour or so—and continue cooking, with or without smoke, until the internal temperature of the thickest link reaches 160° F (71° C). Weigh the link marked with the colored string to determine if this link has lost at least 15 percent of its green weight. If it has, the smoking and cooking are finished. Proceed to step 9. If not, go to step 8.
8. If the link marked with colored string has not lost at least 15 percent of its green weight, reduce the smoker temperature to between 160° F (71° C) and 165° F (74° C) and continue cooking. Check the loss of weight every hour or so. When 15 percent of the weight has been lost, proceed to step 9.
9. When the sausage has lost at least 15 percent of the green weight, remove the links from the smoker, and cool the sausage in front of an electric fan for one hour.
10. Refrigerate the sausages, uncovered, overnight. The next morning, cut them to single-portion lengths, and then wrap them in plastic food wrap. Sausages that will not be eaten within a few days should be individually wrapped in plastic food wrap, placed in a plastic bag, and frozen.

Pepperoni for Pizza

Pepperoni is the most popular meat topping for pizza; it is more popular than Italian sausage. With this homemade pepperoni, you can make your own pizza, or your can fortify a bake-at-home pizza that was originally made with not quite enough pepperoni to suit your taste.

CASINGS

Large-diameter hog casings will produce a diameter similar to commercially produced pepperoni, but small hog casings will make a daintier product. If you wish to use the small casing, rinse 7 feet (210 cm) of casing, and refrigerate it overnight in water. Rinse again, and soak in warm water for 30 minutes before using.

THE MEAT FOR 2½ LBS. (1,150 G) OF PEPPERONI

Prepare the meats listed below; cut into ¾-inch (2 cm) cubes and refrigerate. While this meat is being prepared, chill the grinder and sausage stuffer in the refrigerator.

- 1 lb. (450 g) of lean pork and ½ lb. (225 g) of back fat—or 1½ lbs. (680 g) of fatty pork shoulder
- 1 lb. (450 g) of lean beef

SEASONINGS AND OTHER INGREDIENTS

Dry ingredients
1¾ tsp. (8.75 ml) salt
½ tsp. (2.5 ml) Cure #1
1 Tbsp. (15 ml) paprika
1½ tsp. (7.5 ml) cayenne
½ tsp. (2.5 ml) garlic granules
¼ tsp. (1.25 ml) anise
¼ tsp. (1.25 ml) allspice
½ cup (120 ml) finely powdered skim milk
¼ cup (60 ml) Fermento

Wet ingredients
2 Tbsp. (30 ml) light corn syrup
¼ cup (60 ml) red wine
6 Tbsp. (90 ml) cold water

MIXING AND STUFFING

1. Grind the chilled meats together with a 3/16-inch (4.8 mm) or smaller plate. Refrigerate the ground meat for about 30 minutes.
2. Mix all dry ingredients thoroughly in a large mixing bowl. Add the liquid ingredients, and mix well again. Refrigerate this mixture for about 15 minutes.
3. Add the chilled ground meat to the seasoning mixture, and knead until it is well mixed and uniform. This will require about three minutes. Chill this meat and seasoning mixture again while the sausage stuffer and hog casings are being prepared.
4. Stuff the sausage into the hog casings, and twist into 10-inch (25 cm) links. Weigh one of the links, record the weight, and mark it with a colored string, or the like. This weight is called the *green weight*. Refrigerate the links overnight to permit the seasoning to be absorbed by the meat. Use an uncovered container, but cover the sausage with a paper towel.
5. The next morning, dry the stuffed sausage in front of an electric fan until the surface is dry to the touch. Alternatively, dry the surface of the casings in a 140° F (60° C) smoker with no smoke.
6. Smoke at the lowest possible temperature for at least two hours. Make sure that the smoke chimney damper is fully open.
7. Raise the smoker temperature to between 170° F (77° C) and 175° F (79° C) slowly—over the period of one hour or so—and continue cooking, with or without smoke, until the internal temperature of the thickest link reaches 160° F (71° C). Weigh the link marked with the colored string to determine if this link has lost at least 15 percent of its green weight. If it has, the smoking and cooking are finished. Proceed to step 9. If not, go to step 8.
8. If the link marked with colored string has not lost at least 15 percent of its green weight, reduce the smoker temperature to between 160° F (71° C) and 165° F (74° C) and continue cooking. Check the loss of weight every hour or so. When 15 percent of the weight has been lost, proceed to step 9.
9. When the sausage has lost at least 15 percent of the green weight, remove the links from the smoker, and cool the sausage in front of an electric fan for one hour.
10. Refrigerate the sausages, uncovered, overnight. The next morning, wrap them in plastic food wrap. Sausages that will not be eaten within a few days should be individually wrapped in plastic food wrap, placed in a plastic bag, and frozen.

Pepperoni Sticks

Pepperoni sticks are a great tasting snack food, and they are surprisingly easy to make. The instructions given below will result in a sausage weight loss of about 15 percent; it is a semi-dried, fermented-style sausage. If the drying proceeds until 20 or 25 percent of the weight has been lost, they will be even less perishable, and the flavor will be more concentrated.

CASINGS

Any size of casing from a small-diameter sheep casing to a medium-diameter hog casing may be used. However, please keep in mind that the required drying time increases as the diameter of the casing increases. If you wish to use the small hog casing, rinse 7 feet (210 cm), and refrigerate it overnight in about a cup of water. If 24 to 26 mm (1 in. to 1$\frac{1}{16}$ in.) sheep casing is to be used, prepare about 14 feet (420 cm). Rinse the casing again, and soak it in warm water for a few minutes before using.

THE MEAT FOR 2½ LBS. (1,150 G) OF PEPPERONI STICKS

Traditionally, beef is used for pepperoni, but pork can be used. A mixture of about 50 percent pork and 50 percent beef is suggested. Some or all of the beef may be in the form of beef heart, or wild game can be used. The meat, no matter what kind is selected, should contain about 25 percent fat, and the total weight should be 2½ lbs. (1,150 g). Cut the meat into ¾-inch (2 cm) cubes and refrigerate. While this meat is being prepared, chill the grinder and sausage stuffer in the refrigerator.

SEASONINGS AND OTHER INGREDIENTS

Dry ingredients
1¾ tsp. (8.75 ml) salt
½ tsp. (2.5 ml) Cure #1
1 Tbsp. (15 ml) paprika
1½ tsp. (7.5 ml) cayenne
½ tsp. (2.5 ml) garlic granules
¼ tsp. (1.25 ml) allspice
¼ cup (60 ml) Fermento

Wet ingredients
2 Tbsp. (30 ml) light corn syrup
¼ cup (60 ml) red wine
3 Tbsp. (45 ml) cold water

MIXING AND STUFFING

1. Grind the meats together with a ³⁄₁₆-inch (4.8 mm) or smaller plate. Refrigerate the ground meat for about 30 minutes.

2. Mix all dry ingredients thoroughly in a large mixing bowl. Add the liquid ingredients, and mix well again. Refrigerate this mixture for about 15 minutes.

3. Add the chilled ground meat to the seasoning mixture, and knead until it is well mixed and uniform. This will require about three minutes. Chill this meat and seasoning mixture again while the sausage stuffer and casings are being prepared.

4. Stuff the sausage into the casings, and twist into long links. Weigh one of the links, record the weight, and mark it with a colored string, or the like. This weight is called the *green weight*. Refrigerate the links overnight to permit the seasoning to be absorbed by the meat. Use an uncovered container, but cover the sausage with a paper towel.

5. The next morning, dry the stuffed sausage for one or two hours in front of an electric fan. The drying is finished when the surface is dry to the touch and the fingertips slide smoothly on the casing. Alternatively, dry the surface of the casings in a 140° F (60° C) smoker with no smoke, and with the chimney vents fully open.

6. Smoke at the lowest possible temperature for 2 to 4 hours. The temperature should be held below 120° F (50° C), if possible. From this point, until the smoking, cooking, and drying are finished, the chimney vents should remain fully open to encourage maximum drying of the sausage.

7. Raise the smoker temperature to between 170° F (77° C) and 175° F (79° C) slowly—over the period of one hour or so—and continue cooking, with or without smoke, until the internal temperature of the thickest link reaches 160° F (71° C). Weigh the link marked with the colored string to determine if this link has lost at least 15 percent of its green weight. If it has, the smoking and cooking are finished. Proceed to step 9. If not, go to step 8.

8. If the link marked with colored string has not lost at least 15 percent of its green weight, reduce the smoker temperature to between 160° F (71° C) and 165° F (74° C) and continue cooking. Check the loss of weight every hour or so. When 15 percent of the weight has been lost, proceed to step 9.

9. When the sausage has lost at least 15 percent of the green weight, remove the links from the smoker, and cool the sausage in front of an electric fan for one hour.

10. Refrigerate the sausages, uncovered, overnight. The next morning, cut them to single-portion lengths, and then wrap them in plastic food wrap. Sausages that will not be eaten within a few days should be individually wrapped in plastic food wrap, placed in a plastic bag, and frozen.

Spanish-Style Chorizo

True Spanish chorizo is dry cured and fermented under carefully controlled humidity and temperature conditions for about 20 days. Needless to say, if it is made in the traditional way, it is very difficult to make.

The Spanish-style chorizo described below will be semi-dry cured, but this will be done rapidly in a smoker. The tangy, fermented taste will be accomplished by using Fermento. This is a semi-dried sausage, but you can decide the extent to which it is dried. Traditionally, it is dried until it loses 25 percent of its moisture, but you might like it dried until only 15 percent of the moisture is lost. You decide. Try this sausage in soups, stews, or egg dishes.

Ancho chile powder is an important ingredient that you may not have on hand. Please see Appendix 1 for more information on this special chile powder.

CASINGS

If small-diameter hog casings are used, the processing time will be shortened. Rinse 7 feet (210 cm) of small hog casing, and refrigerate it overnight in water. Rinse again before using.

THE MEAT FOR 2½ LBS. (1,150 G) OF SPANISH CHORIZO

Prepare 2 lbs. (910 g) of lean pork and ½ lb. (225 g) of back fat—or 2½ lbs. (1,150 g) of fatty pork shoulder. Cut into ¾-inch (2 cm) cubes and refrigerate. While this meat is being prepared, chill the grinder and sausage stuffer in the refrigerator.

SEASONINGS AND OTHER INGREDIENTS

Dry ingredients
2 tsp. (10 ml) salt
½ tsp. (2.5 ml) Cure #1
¼ cup (60 ml) Fermento
1 Tbsp. (15 ml) paprika
1 Tbsp. (15 ml) *ancho* chile powder

1 tsp. (5 ml) cayenne
¾ tsp. (3.75 ml) garlic granules

Wet ingredients
2 tsp. (10 ml) light corn syrup
2 Tbsp. (30 ml) cold water

MIXING AND STUFFING

1. Grind the meat with a ³⁄₁₆-inch (4.8 mm) or smaller plate. Refrigerate the ground meat for about 30 minutes.
2. Mix all dry ingredients thoroughly in a large mixing bowl. Add the liquid ingredients, and mix well again. Refrigerate this mixture for about 15 minutes.
3. Add the chilled ground meat to the seasoning mixture, and knead until it is well mixed and uniform. This will require about three minutes. Chill the meat and seasoning mixture again while the sausage stuffer and hog casing are being prepared.
4. Stuff the sausage into the hog casing and twist the sausage rope into four long links. Use string to close the end of each link securely, and then cut between the ends to separate the four links. Tie the ends of each link together to form four rings. Weigh one of the rings, record the weight, and mark it with a colored string, or the like. This weight is called the *green weight*. Refrigerate the rings overnight to permit the seasoning to be absorbed by the meat. Use an uncovered container, but cover the rings with a paper towel.
5. The next morning, dry the stuffed sausage in front of an electric fan until the surface is dry to the touch. Alternatively, dry the surface of the casings in a 140° F (60° C) smoker with no smoke.
6. Smoke at the lowest possible temperature for at least two hours. Make sure that the smoke vents are fully open; this will facilitate the required drying of the sausage.
7. Raise the smoker temperature to between 170° F (77° C) and 175° F (79° C) slowly—over the period of one hour or so—and continue cooking, with or without smoke, until the internal temperature of the thickest link reaches 160° F (71° C). Weigh the sausage ring marked with the colored string to determine if it has lost between 15 percent and 25 percent of its green weight. If it has, the smoking and cooking are finished. Proceed to step 9. If not, go to step 8.
8. If the sausage ring marked with colored string has not lost the desired percent of its green weight, reduce the smoker temperature to between 160° F

(71° C) and 165° F (74° C) and continue cooking. Check the loss of weight every hour or so. When the desired weight has been lost, proceed to step 9.

9. When the marked sausage ring has lost the desired percent of weight, remove the rings from the smoker and cool the sausage in front of an electric fan for one hour.

10. Refrigerate the rings, uncovered, overnight. The next morning, wrap them in plastic food wrap. Sausages that will not be consumed within a few days should be individually wrapped in plastic food wrap, placed in a plastic bag, and frozen.

Summer Sausage

The tart taste of lactic acid in summer sausage makes it very popular. We produce this taste by using Fermento, a product made entirely from dairy products; we need not subject the sausage to a lengthy and difficult fermenting process.

Summer sausage got its name because it was made in the fall or winter, but it was intended to be eaten during the summer.

CASINGS

If 2½-inch (6.4 cm) diameter fibrous casing are used, two 12-inch (30 cm) casings will be required. Fibrous casing must be soaked for 30 minutes in warm water before stuffing. Be sure to put some warm water inside the casings.

THE MEAT FOR 2½ LBS. (1,150 G) OF SUMMER SAUSAGE

Prepare 1½ lbs. (680 g) of lean beef, ½ lb. (225 g) of lean pork, and ½ lb. (225 g) of pork fat. Cut into ¾-inch (2 cm) cubes and refrigerate. While this meat is being prepared, chill the grinder and sausage stuffer in the refrigerator.

SEASONINGS AND OTHER INGREDIENTS

Dry ingredients
2 tsp. (10 ml) salt
½ tsp. (2.5 ml) Cure #1
2 tsp. (10 ml) dry mustard—packed in the spoon
1 tsp. (5 ml) paprika
1 tsp. (5 ml) garlic granules
¾ tsp. (3.75 ml) ground coriander—packed in the spoon
½ cup (120 ml) finely powdered skim milk
¼ cup (60 ml) Fermento

Wet ingredients
1 Tbsp. (15 ml) light corn syrup
¼ cup (60 ml) cold water

MIXING AND STUFFING

1. Grind the meat with a ³⁄₁₆-inch (4.8 mm) or smaller plate. Refrigerate the ground meat for about 30 minutes.
2. Mix all dry ingredients thoroughly in a large mixing bowl. Add the liquid ingredients, and mix well again. Refrigerate this mixture for about 15 minutes.
3. Add the chilled ground meat to the seasoning mixture, and knead until it is well mixed. This will require about three minutes. Chill this meat and seasoning mixture again while the sausage stuffer and fibrous casings are being prepared.
4. Stuff the sausage into the fibrous casings. Insert an electronic cable probe in one of the chubs. Close the ends of the chubs with twine. Refrigerate the stuffed casings overnight to permit the seasoning to be absorbed by the meat. Use an uncovered container.
5. The next morning, dry the stuffed chubs in front of an electric fan until the surface is dry to the touch. Alternatively, dry the surface of the casings in a 140° F (60° C) smoker with no smoke.
6. Smoke at the lowest possible temperature for two hours or more.
7. Over a period of one hour, raise the temperature to 170° F (77° C) and continue cooking, with or without smoke, until the sausage reaches an internal temperature of 140° F (60° C).
8. Remove the summer sausage from the smoke chamber and finish cooking by steaming or poaching. Please see Chapter 6 for these cooking instructions.

Thuringer

Thuringer used to be a very popular lunchmeat, and it could be found in almost every grocery store. It is more difficult to find now, probably because fewer people prepare sandwiches for lunch at work or school.

Thuringer originated in Germany. It is much like summer sausage in taste and appearance.

CASINGS

If 2½-inch (6.4 cm) diameter fibrous casing are used, two 12-inch (30 cm) casings will be required. Fibrous casing must be soaked for 30 minutes in warm water before stuffing. Be sure to put some warm water inside the casing.

THE MEAT FOR 2½ LBS. (1,150 G) OF THURINGER

Prepare 2 lbs. (910 g) of lean pork and ½ lb. (225 g) of back fat—or 2½ lbs. (1,150 g) of pork shoulder. Cut into ¾-inch (2 cm) cubes and refrigerate. While this meat is being prepared, chill the grinder and sausage stuffer in the refrigerator.

SEASONINGS AND OTHER INGREDIENTS

Dry ingredients
2 tsp. (10 ml) salt
½ tsp. (2.5 ml) Cure #1
1 tsp. (5 ml) ground coriander—packed in the spoon
1 tsp. (5 ml) black peppercorns, cracked
1 tsp. (5 ml) paprika
¼ tsp. (1.25 ml) dry mustard powder—packed in the spoon
¼ tsp. (1.25 ml) ground nutmeg
½ cup (120 ml) finely powdered skim milk
¼ cup (60 ml) Fermento

Wet ingredients
1 Tbsp. (15 ml) light corn syrup
¼ cup (60 ml) cold water

MIXING AND STUFFING

1. Grind the meat with a ³⁄₁₆-inch (4.8 mm) or smaller plate. Refrigerate the ground meat for about 30 minutes.
2. Mix all dry ingredients thoroughly in a large mixing bowl. Add the liquid ingredients, and mix well again. Refrigerate this mixture for about 15 minutes.
3. Add the chilled ground meat to the seasoning mixture, and knead until it is well mixed and uniform. This will require about three minutes. Chill this meat and seasoning mixture again while the sausage stuffer and fibrous casings are being prepared.

4. Stuff the sausage into the fibrous casings. Insert an electronic cable probe in one of the chubs. Close the ends of the chubs with twine. Refrigerate the stuffed casings overnight to permit the seasoning to be absorbed by the meat. Use an uncovered container.

5. The next morning, dry the stuffed casings in front of an electric fan until the surface is dry to the touch. Alternatively, dry the surface of the casings in a 140° F (60° C) smoker with no smoke.

6. Smoke at the lowest possible temperature for two hours or more.

7. Over a period of one hour, raise the temperature to 170° F (77° C) and continue cooking, with or without smoke, until the sausage reaches an internal temperature of 140° F (60° C).

8. Remove the Thuringer from the smoke chamber and finish cooking by steaming or poaching. Please see Chapter 6 for these cooking instructions.

Turkey Salami

Salami made of domesticated birds or wildfowl is good if it is made of dark meat. The thighs of turkeys or chickens are the easiest to bone and use. Duck and geese, both wild and domesticated, are all dark meat, so any part of these birds may be used. Goose has a beefy flavor, so it makes particularly interesting salami.

No matter what kind of fowl is used, make sure to remove all tendons, cartilage, and the like, before grinding it.

CASINGS

If 2½-inch (6.4 cm) diameter fibrous casing are used, two 12-inch (30 cm) casings will be required. Fibrous casing must be soaked for 30 minutes in warm water before stuffing. Be sure to put some warm water inside the casings. (Note: A kosher and very traditional casing would be the skin from the neck of a turkey, goose, duck, or chicken. The ancient Romans are known to have used the skin from chicken necks to stuff sausage.)

THE MEAT FOR 2½ LBS. (1,150 G) OF BIRD SALAMI

Prepare 2½ lbs. (1,150 g) of dark meat, including the skin and a reasonable amount of fat. Cut into ¾-inch (2 cm) cubes and refrigerate. While this meat is being prepared, chill the grinder and sausage stuffer in the refrigerator.

SEASONINGS AND OTHER INGREDIENTS

Dry ingredients
2 tsp. (10 ml) salt
½ tsp. (2.5 ml) Cure #1
1 tsp. (5 ml) pepper, ground
1 tsp. (5 ml) black peppercorns, cracked
½ tsp. (2.5 ml) garlic granules
½ tsp. (2.5 ml) ground coriander—packed in the spoon
¼ tsp. (1.25 ml) allspice
⅛ tsp. (0.625 ml) cloves, ground
¼ cup (60 ml) Fermento

Wet ingredients
1 Tbsp. (15 ml) light corn syrup
1 Tbsp. (15 ml) sherry
2 Tbsp. (30 ml) cold water

MIXING AND STUFFING

1. Grind the meat with a ³⁄₁₆-inch (4.8 mm) or smaller plate, and refrigerate it for about 30 minutes.
2. Mix all dry ingredients thoroughly in a large mixing bowl. Add the liquid ingredients, and mix well again. Refrigerate this mixture for about 15 minutes.
3. Add the chilled ground meat to the seasoning mixture, and knead until it is well mixed. This will require about three minutes. Chill this meat and seasoning mixture again while the sausage stuffer and fibrous casings are being prepared.
4. Stuff the sausage into the fibrous casings. Insert an electronic cable probe in one of the chubs. Close the ends of the chubs with twine. Refrigerate the stuffed casings overnight to permit the seasoning to be absorbed by the meat. Use an uncovered container.
5. The next morning, dry the stuffed chubs in front of an electric fan until the surface is dry to the touch. Alternatively, dry the surface of the casings in a 140° F (60° C) smoker with no smoke.
6. Smoke at the lowest possible temperature for two hours or more.
7. Over a period of about one hour, raise the temperature to 170° F (77° C) and continue cooking, with or without smoke, until the sausage reaches an internal temperature of 140° F (60° C).
8. Remove the turkey salami from the smoke chamber and finish cooking by steaming or poaching. Please see Chapter 6 for these cooking instructions.

Appendix 1

Spices, Herbs, and Seasonings

Comments on the applications for the various spices, herbs, and seasonings that are listed below are generally limited to their use for sausage. Culinary specialists, among others, distinguish between a spice and an herb. The distinction is not necessarily maintained in the descriptions that follow.

ALLSPICE: The name of this spice comes from the fact that it has a flavor similar to a blend of three spices: cinnamon, cloves, and nutmeg. It is most commonly used with red meats such as beef, pork, and lamb.

***ANCHO* CHILE POWDER:** *Ancho* chile powder is moderately spicy, but it has a hint of sweetness. It can be bought on the Internet, but you may also find it in Latino grocery stores. Whole *ancho* chiles (dried *poblanos*) seem to be easier to find than the powder. I buy the whole, dried *ancho* chiles, remove the seeds, and grind them into a powder with a spice mill. This may be the fastest, easiest, and least expensive way to get the powder. If everything else fails, substitute regular chili powder for the *ancho* chile powder.

ANISE SEEDS: These small seeds have a mild licorice flavor, and they are sometimes used in sausage. Some varieties of Italian sausage, for example, use whole or powdered anise seeds as an essential ingredient.

BASIL: This essential herb for Italian cooking is also used to season lamb, poultry, fish, and shellfish. It is used occasionally for other meats such as beef, pork, and game. Basil is a member of the mint family.

BAY LEAF: Bay leaf is very pungent. Use sparingly. Bay leaf goes well with all red meats, variety meats (tongue, heart, etc.), and especially with game meats. If used in powdered form, consider a pinch (less than ⅛ teaspoon) to be equal to one bay leaf. When bay leaf is used in sausage, it is always used in powdered form.

BLACK PEPPER: See *Pepper.*

CARDAMOM: Some curry mixtures contain this aromatic, expensive, and pungent spice. Germans and members of other European cultures use cardamom to season sausage. Guatemala is now the largest producer. It imparts a complex flowery, fruity, piney, and eucalyptus-like flavor. Use sparingly.

CAYENNE: True cayenne is extremely hot; it is hotter than red pepper. Quite often, unfortunately, the names and labeling of these two spices are confused. Nevertheless, both products produce lots of heat, and they are used most often to flavor highly spiced meats and sausage. Neither cayenne nor red pepper is related to common black pepper.

CELERY SEED: The seeds come from a plant that is related to the celery that is grown as a vegetable. Use this spice sparingly in sausages and marinades. It has a bitter, celery-like flavor.

CINNAMON: The use of cinnamon to flavor pork, lamb, and other meats is not unheard of, but you should try it cautiously. Many palates rebel at the combination of cinnamon and meat. Nevertheless, cinnamon is required in small amounts to make certain kinds of ethnic sausage—the Italian mortadella, for example.

CLOVES: Use judiciously in sausage and with pork, beef, or fish. Cloves are very pungent. Used in excess, cloves can be mouth numbing and overpowering. When cloves are used in sausage, they are always used in powdered form.

CORIANDER SEEDS: The ground seeds have a mild flavor that is between the flavor of nuts and citrus fruit. Taste a pinch of it. If you like it, use it in sausage and on any kind of meat, poultry, or fish.

CUMIN SEEDS: Cumin is an essential ingredient in chili powder and curry powder. It has a strong and spicy-sweet taste, and it is commonly used to season meats. The Germans and other ethnic groups use it to flavor some varieties of sausage.

CURE #1: *Cure #1* (also called *pink salt* or *pink powder*) is nothing more than common salt with the addition of a very small amount of sodium nitrite (6.25 percent). A special process is used to bond these two ingredients so that the mixture will always be uniform. Pink food color is added so that this product will not be mistaken for common salt. Cure #1 is used as a curing agent and color fixer in many cured sausage formulas in this book. When processing smoked sausage, it is used to prevent botulism. The word *Cure #1* is neither a brand name nor a trade name; *Cure #1* is sausage makers' jargon for any brand of curing powder that consists of 6.25 percent sodium nitrite and 93.75 percent common salt. Cure #1 is sold under several brand names. The most common brands are the following: Prague Powder #1, Instacure #1, and Modern Cure.

DILL: Both dill seeds and dried dill leaves are used (the plant and leaves are sometimes called dillweed). Both dill seeds and dill leaves have a mild, caraway-like taste. Of course, the same herb is used to flavor dill pickles. Dill is often used on fish, lamb, and fowl. The use of dill in sausage is rare, and it is generally limited to fish sausage.

FENNEL SEEDS: These seeds have a mild licorice flavor, and they are sometimes used on oily fish and in sausages. Fennel seeds are essential in many Italian sausage formulas. Depending on the sausage formula and personal preference, they may be used whole, cracked, or powdered.

FERMENTO: Fermento is a manufactured seasoning made entirely from dairy products. It contains lactic acid—the same acid that is produced by bacteria when fermented, dry-cured sausage is made. The use of Fermento allows us to make products like pepperoni, summer sausage, and Thuringer without the lengthy and difficult dry-curing process. Please see Appendix 5 for sources of this product if you wish to make fermented-style sausage.

FIVE-SPICE POWDER: Five-spice powder is a classical Chinese seasoning blend. The blend usually contains five spices, but it sometimes contains six or seven. It invariably contains cinnamon, anise, fennel, and cloves, and it usually contains Szechuan pepper. (*Szechuan* is also spelled *Szechwan.*) Sometimes common black pepper is substituted for the Szechuan pepper, and sometimes ginger and licorice root is added. East Asian grocery stores stock this season-ing, and sometimes the United States-manufactured Sun Luck brand is avail-able at common grocery stores. Several recipes for this seasoning blend can be found on the Internet; use a good search engine and search for *five-spice powder recipe*.

FRENCH FOUR SPICES: See *Quatre Épices*.

GARLIC: Garlic granules or garlic powder is usually specified in this book, but garlic in other forms can be used in most cases. Substitute minced garlic or garlic juice.

GINGER: The root of this plant is used worldwide to season all varieties of meat, fish, and fowl. It has a distinctive bite and aroma. Individual tolerance for the aroma of this spice varies enormously. Start with a small amount and, if you like it, add a little more the next time. Fresh ginger (root)—grated, minced, or sliced thinly—can replace ginger powder in cures and marinades.

IMITATION MAPLE FLAVOR: Imitation maple flavor is a liquid prod-uct made of natural ingredients. It is used to impart an aroma similar to that of maple syrup. The most common brand is *Mapleine*, and it is manufactured under the *Crescent* trademark.

JUNIPER BERRIES: Most of the berries harvested from the juniper ev-ergreen tree are used to flavor gin. They are used occasionally in fish and meat marinades. Their use in sausage is rare, but not unheard of. Just a few berries will impart a piney, gin-like taste.

MACE: Mace is the outer covering of nutmeg. This spice can be obtained eas-ily at a reasonable price from ethnic grocery shops that sell products used in Indian cuisine. Both mace and nutmeg have a similar taste, and both are used in some sausage varieties. The sweet, nut-like taste can be imparted with very little mace or nutmeg. Use sparingly.

MAPLE FLAVOR: See *IMITATION MAPLE FLAVOR*.

MAPLEINE: See *IMITATION MAPLE FLAVOR*.

MARJORAM: This herb is closely related to oregano, and it has a similar, but milder, taste. These herbs are in the mint family. Both are widely used to season any kind of fish, meat, or fowl.

MINT: Lamb is sometimes seasoned with fragrant mint leaves before it is processed. There are many varieties of mint, and each variety has a distinctive aroma. The use of mint in sausage making is uncommon.

MSG: Monosodium glutamate is not a true seasoning; it is a flavor enhancer. It works to intensify other flavors. MSG is made from natural products, but it is considered a chemical food additive. Used in excess, it tends to produce a distinctive "MSG-intensified-flavor." Many people like it; many people don't. It is quite rare, but some people have an allergic reaction to this product if it is used in excess. The symptoms are dizziness, sweating, and chest pains; while the symptoms are unpleasant, to be sure, no fatalities have been reported. MSG is used occasionally in modern sausage formulations, but it is certainly not a traditional ingredient. However, if you like it, it can be added to almost any sausage recipe.

MUSTARD: Both powdered and whole mustard seeds are used in many varieties of highly seasoned sausages. The flavor is similar to, but sharper than, the prepared mustard we eat on hot dogs. Yellow seeds are milder than smaller brown ones.

NUTMEG: See *MACE*.

ONION: Granulated onion is often specified in this book, but powdered onion, minced onion, or onion juice can be substituted in most cases.

OREGANO: See *Marjoram*.

PAPRIKA: This bright red powder is made from certain kinds of ripened red peppers. The sweet paprika widely available in the U. S. has a very mild taste, and it is used for red coloration as well as for its mild flavoring. Hungarian paprika is considered the most flavorful, and there are several varieties.

PEPPER: Black pepper is the most widely used spice in the world, and it needs no introduction. White pepper is a little more aromatic than black pepper, but black pepper is more pungent than white pepper. However, the flavors of the two are essentially the same. Use powdered white pepper when the black specks are not desired. Alternatively, use black pepper *powder*—rather than granulated pepper—whenever large black specks would distract from the appearance of the product. Black pepper powder can usually be found in Asian food markets, and it will probably be cheaper than the white pepper powder sold in a common supermarket. White pepper is made from the husked berries of the pepper plant, but black pepper is made from the un-husked berries. The husk, of course, is black.

PINK POWDER: See *Cure #1.*

PINK SALT: See *Cure #1.*

POULTRY SEASONING: This blend of spices and herbs contains sage, thyme, black pepper, and—depending on the processor—may contain coriander, rosemary, allspice, onion powder, marjoram, celery seed, and cayenne. It is, as the name implies, excellent on poultry, but it is also appreciated for seasoning pork. In this book, it is used in *Warren's Country-style Bulk Breakfast Sausage* and some sausages that contain poultry.

QUATRE ÉPICES: This is a blend of four spices often used in French cuisine and sausage making. In the United States, this blend is often marketed under the translated name, "*French Four Spices.*" The formula varies, but probably the four spices most commonly used are the following: pepper, nutmeg, ginger, and cloves. It seems that pepper is always the predominant spice, but sometimes black pepper is specified and sometimes white pepper is called for. In some formulas, cinnamon or allspice replaces the nutmeg, ginger, or cloves. I make my own *quatre épices*, and I use the following formula:

1 Tbsp. (15 ml) ground white pepper
1 tsp. (5 ml) ground nutmeg
1 tsp. (5 ml) ground ginger
½ tsp. (2.5 ml) ground cloves

RED PEPPER: See *Cayenne.*

ROSEMARY: The needle-like leaves of this evergreen shrub have a strong, piney scent, and they are used sparingly to flavor game, poultry, fish, and other meats. It is occasionally used in sausage.

SAGE: This very aromatic herb is an essential ingredient in American country-style fresh sausage. It can be used to flavor all varieties of domesticated poultry and wildfowl, in addition to pork. Overuse can impart a musty taste. Avoid using sage with fish.

SAVORY: This herb has a peppery taste, and it is used with sausages and fowl. Summer savory is milder than winter savory, and it is the more popular of the two.

SEASONED SALT: A blend of salt and usually one other seasoning is known as seasoned salt. Examples are celery salt, garlic salt, lemon salt, and onion salt.

SEASONING SALT: This blend of salt, spices, herbs, and sometimes MSG, will improve the flavor of almost anything that is smoked. Excellent quality commercially produced blends are available, but it is a simple task to make seasoning salt.

THYME: (The pronunciation is *time*.) Thyme is an herb that has very small leaves, and the leaves have the aroma of mint. It is widely used with fish and fowl, and it is occasionally used with pork, veal, and mutton. It is a pungent, but pleasant, herb, and it is often used in sausage making.

TURMERIC: Turmeric originated in India, and is it probably best known as a curry powder ingredient. This golden powder is bitter and has a harsh aroma. Because of this, it is used as a food-coloring agent more often than as a seasoning. A small amount will impart a golden color to curry powder, and the gold color will make pale chicken broth appear to be rich and flavorful. It is almost never used in sausage formulations, but the recipe for *Curry Flavored Sausage* in this book calls for a small amount.

WHITE PEPPER: See *Pepper*.

Appendix 2

Fahrenheit < > Celsius Conversion Table

F	to	C	F	to	C	F	to	C
-35	=	-37.2	145	=	62.8	325	=	162.8
-30	=	-34.4	150	=	65.6	330	=	165.6
-25	=	-31.7	155	=	68.3	335	=	168.3
-20	=	-28.9	160	=	71.1	340	=	171.1
-15	=	-26.1	165	=	73.9	345	=	173.9
-10	=	-23.3	170	=	76.7	350	=	176.7
-5	=	-20.6	175	=	79.4	355	=	179.4
0	=	-17.8	180	=	82.2	360	=	182.2
5	=	-15.0	185	=	85.0	365	=	185.0
10	=	-12.2	190	=	87.8	370	=	187.8
15	=	-9.4	195	=	90.6	375	=	190.6
20	=	-6.7	200	=	93.3	380	=	193.3
25	=	-3.9	205	=	96.1	385	=	196.1
30	=	-1.1	210	=	98.9	390	=	198.9
35	=	1.7	215	=	101.7	395	=	201.7
40	=	4.4	220	=	104.4	400	=	204.4
45	=	7.2	225	=	107.2	405	=	207.2
50	=	10.0	230	=	110.0	410	=	210.0
55	=	12.8	235	=	112.8	415	=	212.8
60	=	15.6	240	=	115.6	420	=	215.6
65	=	18.3	245	=	118.3	425	=	218.3
70	=	21.1	250	=	121.1	430	=	221.1
75	=	23.9	255	=	123.9	435	=	223.9
80	=	26.7	260	=	126.7	440	=	226.7
85	=	29.4	265	=	129.4	445	=	229.4
90	=	32.2	270	=	132.2	450	=	232.2
95	=	35.0	275	=	135.0	455	=	235.0
100	=	37.8	280	=	137.8	460	=	237.8
105	=	40.6	285	=	140.6	465	=	240.6
110	=	43.3	290	=	143.3	470	=	243.3
115	=	46.1	295	=	146.1	475	=	246.1
120	=	48.9	300	=	148.9	480	=	248.9
125	=	51.7	305	=	151.7	485	=	251.7
130	=	54.4	310	=	154.4	490	=	254.4
135	=	57.2	315	=	157.2	495	=	257.2
140	=	60.0	320	=	160.0	500	=	260.0

$F=((9/5)C)+32$ $\qquad$ $C=(5/9)(F-32)$

Appendix 3

NOTE: When measuring salt by volume, the measurements will be accurate and consistent if fine-grain salt is used. An example of fine-grain salt is common table salt. Kosher salt, on the other hand, is a flaked salt rather than a fine-grain crystal salt. Because flaked salt is not as compact as fine-grain salt, one cup of kosher salt will weigh less than one cup of common salt.

Approximate Equivalents
(Volume to Weight Ounces of Salt)

1 cup salt = 10 oz.	½ cup salt = 5 oz.	¼ cup salt = 2.5 oz.
2 Tbsp. salt = 1.25 oz.	1 Tbsp. salt = 0.625 oz.	
1 tsp. salt = 0.208 oz	½ tsp. salt = 0.104 oz.	

Approximate Volume Equivalents
(Volume to Grams of Salt)

200 ml salt = 233 g	100 ml salt = 117 g	50 ml salt = 58 g
10 ml salt = 11.7 g	5 ml salt = 5.8 g	

Appendix 4

Weight and Volume Conversion Tables

Metric equivalents for U. S. weight and volume measurements are indicated throughout the body of this book. The measurements are not always precisely converted, but the conversion accuracy is sufficient, I believe, to produce essentially the same product. Precise conversion would result in very awkward measurements, and it might require brain-numbing calculations. Such precision is not needed.

The imperial (UK) units of measurement are not mentioned in the body of this book for two reasons. The first reason is that metric units are replacing the imperial units rapidly. The second reason is that great confusion could result because the words used for the imperial units of measurement are often the same words used for the U. S. units, even though the actual quantity may be different. You may assume the *weight* measurements in the British system to be the same as those in the U. S. system: An imperial pound is the same as a U. S. pound. If it is a *volume* measurement, you should assume that it is different from the U. S. system: An imperial gallon, for example is not the same as a U. S. gallon. The last table in this appendix will help with conversions of the imperial system to the metric system. Conversion to the metric system will allow conversion to the U. S. system, should that be necessary.

If you need additional help to covert one measurement to another system, try the Internet website *www.onlineconversion.com.*

Weight Conversion Table

	ounce(s)	pound(s)	gram(s)	kilogram(s)
1 ounce	1	$\frac{1}{16}$	28.35	0.028
1 pound	16	1	454	0.454
1 gram	0.032	0.002	1	0.001
1 kilogram	0.000032	2.2	1000	1

Volume and Fluid Conversions: U. S. < > Metric
This table does not represent precise conversions: 1 cup actually equals 236 ml, and 1 gallon equals 3785.4 ml, for example. However, such precision is meaningless for sausage making. The table presented below is quite easy to commit to memory, easy to calculate, and its accuracy is sufficient.

U. S. System	Metric (ml)	Metric (liters)
⅛ teaspoon	0.625 ml	
¼ teaspoon	1.25 ml	
½ teaspoon	2.5 ml	
¾ teaspoon	3.75 ml	
1 teaspoon	5 ml	
1 tablespoon (3 teaspoons)	15 ml	
1 fluid ounce (2 tablespoons)	30 ml	
¼ cup (4 tablespoons)	60 ml	
½ cup (8 tablespoons)	120 ml	
¾ cup (12 tablespoons)	180 ml	
1 cup (16 tablespoons)	240 ml	0.24 liter
1 pint (2 cups) (16 fl. oz.)	480 ml	0.48 liter
1 quart (4 cups) (32 fl. oz.)	960 ml	0.96 liters
1 gallon (4 quarts)	3840 ml	3.840 ml

British Volume Measuring System—Metric Conversion Table
If you compare the metric conversions for the British system of volume measurement to that of the American system, you will note that there are significant differences—in spite of the fact that the same words are used. For example, 1 US quart is about 944 ml, but 1 UK quart is 1,136 ml. Another interesting feature is that 4 UK teaspoons are equal to 1 UK tablespoon, whereas 3 US teaspoons are equal to 1 US tablespoon.

For food processing, the conversions indicated below are unnecessarily precise; they should be rounded off to a unit that is convenient to measure. One tablespoon, for example should be rounded off from 14.2 ml to 15 ml.

British volume-measuring system	milliliters	liter(s)
1 teaspoon	3.55 ml	
1 tablespoon	14.2 ml	
1 fluid ounce	28.4 ml	0.028 l
¼ cup	71 ml	0.071 l
½ cup (1 gill)	142 ml	0.142 l
1 cup (1 breakfast cup)	284 ml	0.284 l
1 fluid pint	568 ml	0.568 l
1 fluid quart	1136 ml	1.136 l
1 fluid gallon	4544 ml	4.544 l

Appendix 5

Equipment and Supply Resources

You should be able to obtain most of your equipment and supplies locally at places such as supermarkets, hardware stores, and home centers. For items that are difficult to find, consult the Yellow Pages under the headings of Butcher's Supplies, Culinary Equipment and Supplies, Restaurant Equipment and Supplies, Sausage-Making Supplies, etc. In some large cities, the local industrial suppliers are not listed in the common telephone directory, and you will have to consult a commercial or an industrial telephone directory. For example, companies that sell restaurant equipment do not normally sell to the public, so they might be listed in a special telephone directory. If your telephone company publishes such a directory, a nearby library may have a copy of it. Another option would be to request a copy from the telephone company.

Some equipment and supplies are most easily obtained by mail order, or by searching the Internet. If you are connected to the Internet, or if you have a friend who is, you will be able to find many suppliers who are eager for your business. The larger, well-established firms will send a free catalogue. A few suppliers are listed below, but you will find many more on the Internet.

THE SAUSAGE MAKER, INC.

The Sausage Maker, Inc. is one of the largest and one of the best-stocked suppliers of everything required for sausage making and smoking. They have a very comprehensive catalogue that they will send to you free of charge.

The Sausage Maker, Inc.   Tel: 1-888-490-8525
1500 Clinton St, Bldg 123   Fax: 1-716-824-6465
Buffalo, NY 14206-3099   www.sausagemaker.com

STUFFERS SUPPLY (CANADA)

Stuffers Supply Company is located in Canada. They offer a complete line of sausage-making equipment and supplies, and they provide friendly and personalized service. If you have any questions about sausage making, they will do their best to get an answer for you. In general, Stuffers does not ship to the United States because of the special paperwork involved, but they may be willing to ship to other countries.

Stuffers Supply Company
22958 Fraser Highway
Langley, British Columbia V2Z 2T9
Canada

Tel: 604-534-7374
Fax: 604-534-3089
bleathem@telus.net
http://www.stuffers.com

ALLIED KENCO SALES
This company has a very good free catalogue for anyone who butchers meat, smokes food, makes sausage, or cooks outdoors.

Allied Kenco Sales
26 Lyerly Street
Houston, TX 77022
Information: 713-691-2935
Order toll free: 1-800-356-5189

Fax: 713-691-350
Web site: www.alliedkenco.com
E-mail: aks@alliedkenco.com

PS SEASONING & SPICES
As the name implies, this company offers a great variety of seasoning and spices, but they also offer barbecuing, sausage-making, and cooking supplies. They would be delighted to send a free catalogue.

PS Seasoning & Spices
120 South Main Street
P.O. Box 69
Iron Ridge, WI 53035

Phone: 1-800-328-8313
Web site: www.psseasoning.com

BRADLEY SMOKERS
Bradley smokers, including the recommended Original Bradley Smoker, can be purchased in large stores selling sporting and outdoor goods. Barbecue supply shops usually stock them, too.

UNITED STATES
Bradley Smoker (USA), Inc.
644 Enterprise Ave.
Galesburg, IL 61401

Telephone: 1-309-343-1124 or 1-309-343-1125
Fax: 1-309-343-1126
www.bradleysmoker.com

CANADA
Bradley Technologies Canada, Inc.   1-800-665-4188
1609 Derwent Way   E-mail: info@bradleysmoker.com
Delta, B. C.   www.bradleysmoker.com
Canada V3M 6K8

UK and IRELAND
Grakka Limited   Telephone: 44 1803 712712
4 Halwell Business Park   E-mail: info@bradleysmoker.co.uk
Halwell, Totnes   www.bradleysmoker.co.uk
Devon, England 17 TQ9 7LQ

GRIZZLY INDUSTRIAL, INC.

Grizzly Industrial offers a 5-pound capacity vertical stuffer (also called *upright stuffer*), model H6252, for about $70. Cast-iron or stainless steel manual meat grinders may also be ordered from this company.

Grizzly Industrial, Inc.
www.grizzly.com
Order phone number: 1-800-523-4777

NORTHERN TOOL AND EQUIPMENT CO.

This company offers only a modest amount of food processing equipment, but the prices are very reasonable. Compare the prices for sausage stuffers and meat grinders, for example. They offer a lever-powered sausage stuffer for about $27 and a manual meat grinder for $15. Call the toll-free phone number to get a free catalogue. When you request a catalogue, be sure to mention that you need a catalogue that contains listings for *Food Preparation Equipment*. For international shipments, telephone or fax the International Sales Department: telephone 1-800-221-1589, fax 1-952-895-6889.

Northern Tool and Equipment Co.   Customer Service 1-800-222-5381
P.O. Box 1499   www.NorthernTool.com
Burnsville, MN 55337-0499

THE WOK SHOP—ALUMINUM CHINESE STEAMER

A good place to buy an aluminum Chinese steamer is at a large Asian food store. However, if you do not live near such a store, or if you can't find what you need for some reason, try The Wok Shop. It is located in the heart of San Francisco's Chinatown, but it sells a variety of Asian cookware on the Internet. They offer several sizes of aluminum steamers on their website. The 12-inch (30 cm) diameter size that I use sells for about $40.

If you want to search for other sites on the Internet, search for "wok steamer" (do not use quotation marks)—for some reason, these two words are effective in pulling up various sites, and some of these sites will have what you are looking for.

The Wok Shop   Tel: 1-415-989-3797
718 Grant Avenue   www.wokshop.com
San Francisco CA 94108

Appendix 6

Safe Cooking Temperatures

Product	°F and °C
Ground Meat & Meat Mixtures	
Turkey, chicken	165 (73.9° C)
Veal, beef, lamb, pork	160 (71.1° C)
Fresh Beef	
Medium Rare	145 (62.8° C)
Medium	160 (71.1° C)
Well Done	170 (76.7° C)
Fresh Veal	
Medium Rare	145 (62.8° C)
Medium	160 (71.1° C)
Well Done	170 (76.7° C)
Fresh Lamb	
Medium Rare	145 (62.8° C)
Medium	160 (71.1° C)
Well Done	170 (76.7° C)
Fresh Pork	
Medium	160 (71.1° C)
Well Done	170 (76.7° C)
Poultry	
Chicken, whole	180 (82.2° C)
Turkey, whole	180 (82.2° C)
Poultry breasts, roast	170 (76.7° C)
Poultry thighs, wings	180 (82.2° C)
Stuffing (cooked alone or in bird)	165 (73.9° C)
Duck & Goose	180 (82.2° C)
Ham	
Fresh (raw)	160 (71.1° C)
Pre-cooked (to reheat)	140 (60.0° C)

Appendix 7

Volume/Gram Conversion Chart

The following chart is for converting volume measurement of spices and other ingredients used in sausage formulations from United States standard volume measurements to metric weight measurement (grams)—and vice versa. Source: Len Poli's excellent website on sausage making. The easiest way to get to this helpful website is to use Google or any other search engine and search for "Len Poli's Sausage Making."

It is more accurate to weigh spices and ingredients than to measure their volumes. Consequently, many advanced amateur sausage makers and professional sausage makers weigh the spices with an electronic scale that has an accuracy of at least ¹⁄₁₀ gram. This is particularly true for European sausage makers; in Europe, weighing of spices and ingredients for any kind of culinary endeavor is common. Consequently, many sausage formulations measured with this system will be found on the Internet and in published literature on sausage making.

Of course, the easiest way to deal with these metric formulations is to purchase an accurate electronic spice scale and work in the metric system. The more difficult approach is to use the following chart and convert the grams to United States volume measurements. Careful calculation with basic algebra will be required to convert the metric weight measurements to American volume measurements, but the result will be sufficiently accurate to produce a reasonably close approximation of the original formulation. Occasionally, United States formulations expressed in ounces will be found; one ounce is equal to about 28 grams.

Some comments on using this chart: The most common United States unit of measure for spices and ingredients is the teaspoon (tsp.). If the unit of measure is *not* the teaspoon, that unit of measure will be in bold in order to help prevent mistakes. For example, *tablespoon* (**Tbsp.**) will appear in bold.

Amount	Ingredient	gram(s)
1 tsp.	allspice, ground	1.9
1 tsp.	Amesphos (phosphates)	3.8
1 tsp.	ancho chile	2.5
1 tsp.	anise seed, whole	2.1
1 Tbsp.	anise, star	2.0
1 tsp.	basil	1.0
1 tsp.	bay leaf, dried	0.6
1 cup	breadcrumbs	70.0
1 tsp.	caraway seeds	2.1
1 tsp.	cardamom seeds	2.0
1 tsp.	celery seeds	2.5
1 tsp.	chives, dry	0.3
1 Tbsp.	cilantro, dry	1.3
1 tsp.	cinnamon, ground	2.3
1 tsp.	citric acid	4.5
1 tsp.	clove, ground	2.1
1 tsp.	coriander, ground	1.8
1 Tbsp.	corn syrup, liquid	27.0
1 Tbsp.	corn syrup, solids	25.0
1 tsp.	cumin seed, ground	2.1
1 tsp.	Cure #1 (Prague Powder #1)	6.0
1 tsp.	Cure #2 (Prague Powder #2)	6.0
1 tsp.	curry powder	2.5
1 tsp.	egg white solids	2.25
1 tsp.	erythorbate	4.0
1 tsp.	fennel seed, whole	2.0
1 tsp.	fenugreek, ground	3.7
1 tsp.	file powder	2.0
1 tsp.	five-spice powder (Chinese)	1.6
1 clove	garlic	5.0
¼ cup	garlic cloves	35.0
1 tsp.	garlic granules	4.3
1 tsp.	garlic powder	2.8
1 Tbsp.	gelatin	8.5
1 tsp.	ginger, powder	1.8
1 tsp.	juniper berries	1.5
1 tsp.	mace, ground	1.7

Amount	Ingredient	gram(s)
1 tsp.	marjoram, ground	1.5
1 tsp.	MSG (monosodium glutamate)	4.5
1 tsp.	mustard, powdered	2.3
1 tsp.	mustard, yellow, seed	3.3
1 tsp.	nutmeg, ground	2.2
½ cup	nuts, hazelnuts, shelled	75.0
¼ cup	nuts, pine, shelled	30.0
½ cup	nuts, pistachio, shelled	60.0
½ cup	nuts, walnuts, halves	120.0
1 Tbsp.	onion flakes	5.0
1 Tbsp.	onion powder	8.0
1 tsp.	oregano, leaf	1.5
1 tsp.	paprika, ground	2.1
1 tsp.	parsley, dry	1.5
1 tsp.	pepper, red flakes	2.3
1 tsp.	pepper, black	2.1
1 tsp.	pepper, cayenne	1.8
1 tsp.	pepper, Szechwan	1.5
1 tsp.	pepper, white	2.4
1 tsp.	quatre épices	3.0
1 Tbsp.	raisins, whole	11.5
1 cup	rice, cooked	160.0
1 tsp.	rosemary, leaf	1.2
1 tsp.	sage, ground	0.7
1 Tbsp.	salt, kosher	12.0
1 Tbsp.	salt, table	22.0
1 tsp.	savory, summer	1.5
1 tsp.	savory, winter	1.5
1 cup	skim milk, powder	69.0
1 tsp.	soy powder	3.0
1 Tbsp.	sugar, brown	11.0
1 Tbsp.	sugar, dextrose (glucose)	9.0
1 Tbsp.	sugar, granulated	13.0
1 tsp.	tarragon, dry	3.0
1 tsp.	thyme, leaf	1.4
1 tsp.	turmeric, ground	3.0

About the Author

WARREN ANDERSON has worked as a chemical technician, an electronic technician, a carpenter's helper, a bilingual social worker, an Asian business specialist, and as an instructor of English as a foreign language. As an English instructor, Mr. Anderson taught at several Japanese universities for over twenty years. He also owned and operated a private English school in Kyushu, Japan. He speaks Japanese fluently.

Mr. Anderson is a graduate of the University of Oregon, where he studied the Japanese language and majored in East Asian Studies. He also earned a master's degree in International Business at Sophia University in Tokyo, Japan.

Photograph by Tom Anderson

While teaching and living in Japan, he took up the hobbies of food smoking and sausage making, and he has pursued these hobbies earnestly since 1985. At one point in time, he seriously considered launching a new career in Japan as a professional food smoker and sausage maker. He concluded, however, that it would be a better idea for him to use his teaching skills to write manuals about these subjects. Consequently, in 1995, he began to write two books so that he could share with others the knowledge that he had accumulated. The first book, *Mastering the Craft of Smoking Food*, was published in 2006.

Mr. Anderson returned to the United States in 1998, and is presently semi-retired; he lives with his wife in Aloha, Oregon, a suburb of Portland.

Index